HAWKS AND OWLS
OF EASTERN NORTH AMERICA

HAWKS AND OWLS
OF EASTERN NORTH AMERICA

DONALD S. HEINTZELMAN

RUTGERS UNIVERSITY PRESS —— NEW BRUNSWICK, NEW JERSEY, AND LONDON

LIBRARY OF CONGRESS CATALOGING-IN-PUBLICATION DATA

Heintzelman, Donald S.
   Hawks and owls of eastern North America / Donald S. Heintzelman.
     p. cm.
   Includes bibliographical references (p.   ) and index.
   ISBN 0-8135-3350-3 (hardcover : alk. paper)
   1. Hawks—East (U.S.) 2. Owls—East (U.S.) 3. Hawks—Canada, Eastern.
 4. Owls—Canada, Eastern. I. Title.
   QL696.F32H43 2004
   598.9'44'0974—dc21

                                 2003005741

British Cataloging-in-Publication data for this book are available
from the British Library.

The publication program of Rutgers University Press is supported by the
Board of Governors of Rutgers, The State University of New Jersey.

Manufactured in China

CONTENTS

PREFACE AND ACKNOWLEDGMENTS

Birds of prey, owls included, are among the most charismatic and fascinating birds found in eastern North America. Their regal appearance, superb powers of flight, seasonal appearances and disappearances, and especially mysterious owl activities capture the imagination of a growing group of enthusiasts, scientists, and the general public. It is at these people that this book is aimed.

By first providing basic information about ecology, conservation, hawk and owl migrations, citizen scientists, and recreational raptor watching, I hope readers will be drawn into the fascinating world of raptors and learn how they can be understood and appreciated. More detailed information then is provided for each of the species known to occur in eastern North America.

My original intent was to prepare a second edition of my *Hawks and Owls of North America* (1979). However, as I searched the ornithological literature after that date, it became clear an entirely new volume was needed reflecting some of the new information published about these birds. The only substantial reuse of text from the earlier volume is much of the chapter about raptor ecology (chapter 1). Otherwise, most of the text is new.

At the recommendation of my editors, I have restricted the geographic scope of this book to eastern North America—the area east of the Mississippi River, except for parts of Minnesota and Ontario. Other books already deal with western North America.

The following colleagues and friends graciously provided reprints of their ornithological publications which were extremely helpful as I wrote the text: Keith L. Bildstein, Reed Bowman, C. Ray Chandler, Allen Chartier, Kathleen E. Clark, Glen Coady, Bruce A. Colvin, Sheryl A. Dew, James R. Duncan, Mark R. Fuller, Laurie J. Goodrich, Charles J. Henny, Donald Hopkins, Eugene A. Jacobs, Richard Knight, Dan Kunkle, Randolph F. Lauff, Judith Louise, Frank Lyne, Mark Martell, Christian J. Martin, Karl E. Miller, Pierre Mineau, Joan L. Morrison, Ron Pittaway, John Pogacnik, Bill Pranty, Sandra L. Sherman, Philip Stoddard, and Eric Stolen.

Special thanks are extended to Anthony X. Hertzel, editor of *The Loon* (Minnesota Ornithologists' Union), for kindly searching that excellent ornithology journal for pertinent information and providing me with photocopies or originals of those articles. Similarly, John Swiderski, past president of the Georgia Ornithological Society, searched back issues of that organization's journal, *The Oriole,* and also provided copies of pertinent articles.

I am especially grateful to celebrated photographer G. Ronald Austing for generously allowing me to use his splendid black-and-white photographs. They add significantly to the overall beauty and educational value of this book. Other photographers who provided outstanding photographs include Allan D. Cruickshank, Helen G. Cruickshank, Wade L. Eakle, Harry Goldman, M. Alan Jenkins, Fred Tilly, Alan Wormington, and Dale A. Zimmerman. Rod Arbogast also permitted me to reuse his drawing of Short-tailed Hawks. My genuine thanks and appreciation is also extended to each of these colleagues.

A few additional illustrations are reprinted with the permission of the editors of *The Auk* and the *Journal of Wildlife Management.*

Special appreciation is extended to Dan Kunkle and the Wildlife Information Center, Inc., for allowing me to use that organization's superb research library and to make photocopies of pertinent articles.

Donald S. Heintzelman
Allentown, Pennsylvania

HAWKS AND OWLS
OF EASTERN NORTH AMERICA

AN INTRODUCTION TO RAPTOR ECOLOGY

Ecology is the study of the interrelationships of animals and plants and the environment in which they live. To employ ecology, it is necessary to discard older ideas which may suggest that hawks and owls are either good or bad. Sometimes it is difficult to consider hawks and owls objectively because they are carnivores, or flesh-eating animals. They kill to survive, and some people are shocked by such apparent brutality, in effect applying human moral judgments to wild animals. But when they stop to consider that most people in North America are meat eaters, they develop a better understanding of ecology generally, and predation in particular, as a vital and dynamic force in nature. Instead of making judgments about hawks and owls, the ecological approach tries to understand how birds of prey fit into the overall scheme of nature. All animals (and plants) have important roles in nature's great web of life, and each is important to the ecological welfare of animal and plant communities. Sometimes one animal may appear to be more important than another, but it's impossible to consider any living creature as "good" or "bad."

Several basic ecological processes function within all animal communities. For example, a plot of land contains limited quantities of food, water, protective cover, and breeding places useful to wildlife. They establish the land's carrying capacity. If too many animals

compete for the same food and shelter, or attempt to live on the same area, overcrowding results and the carrying capacity is exceeded. Perhaps all of the animals will survive, but some are forced to live on poorer parts of the land and to eat food that is less nourishing, palatable, or accessible. Some animals also may be more vulnerable to predators such as hawks and owls than are others living in spots with the best food and protective cover.

Generally, raptors kill and eat the smaller and more plentiful animals—at least insofar as predation in North America is concerned. Many animals killed by hawks and owls have themselves already eaten still smaller animals. Thus, from an ecological viewpoint, a step-by-step or chainlike series of events is created whereby larger and less numerous predators eat smaller and more plentiful animals. This is called a "predator food chain" or simply a "food chain." Each link in the chain serves as food for the animals that form the next higher link. Moreover, since all life must obtain energy to sustain itself, this needed energy is transferred from one link in the food chain to the next higher link via an ecological process known as "energy flow."

Armed with this background information, we should not find it difficult to understand why hawks and owls are essential members of the biotic communities in which they live. Keeping in mind the food habits of various

Sharp-shinned Hawks prey on small and medium-size birds and mammals.
Photo by Ron Austing.

raptors, it is interesting to examine in more detail several hypothetical food chains to see how they are formed and how they work.

The first is a food chain in an eastern northern forest, the second in a small wood-lot, and the third in an old field. Although different plants and animals form the chains, the same principles apply to each and, in fact, to all food chains regardless of their length.

In the first example, vegetation (flowers, vines, shrubs, and trees) forms the food chain's base because it manufactures food from carbon dioxide and water in combination with energy from the sun. Ecologists therefore consider plants as producers. Next plant-eating insects appear. They commonly are the first animals to eat food manufactured by plants. Insects, therefore, are called first-order consumers, or herbivores.

However, not all primary or first-order consumers are as tiny as insects. The white-tailed deer, with a biomass (size and weight) far in excess of an insect, also is a herbivore. All first-order consumers are essential members of food chains because they convert plant tissue into animal protein suitable for consumption by animals higher in the food chain. In our eastern northern forests, for example, wood warblers are common birds. But they cannot utilize plant foods directly. Instead, they eat insects which have eaten plants. Thus, wood warblers are second-order consumers. They indirectly obtain energy originally mobilized by plants. The next link in our forest food chain is a Sharp-shinned Hawk. Smaller than the powerful Northern Goshawk, to which it is related, the Sharp-shin occupies a third-order position in the chain of animal feeders: it is a third-order consumer. This hawk feeds upon small, forest-dwelling birds such as thrushes, vireos, and wood warblers. It receives its energy third-hand—by eating birds which have eaten insects which have eaten plants.

A second food-chain example deals with some of the plants and animals living in a woodlot. Similar ecological principles apply to these food chains. The producers are flowers, vines, shrubs, and trees. Ants and other insects form the first-order consumers. The Northern Flicker, a common woodpecker, is a second-order consumer, whereas the larger Cooper's Hawk is a third-order consumer and the final link in this particular food chain.

The third example is illustrated by the Barn Owls and American Kestrels that live in the agricultural regions of eastern Pennsylvania. Grasses and other plants of the old fields and meadows of this region are the producers. The prolific meadow vole, which feeds largely upon grasses, is the first-order consumer. The kestrels and Barn Owls then enter the food chain as second-order consumers. They frequently represent the end of the food chain. But if larger predators (such as Red-tailed Hawks) happen to be present and add another link to the chain, they become third-order consumers.

Those predators far removed from the plant producers receive only a tiny portion of the energy stored in plants. Much is lost while being transferred from consumer to consumer. Therefore, there must be larger numbers of producers but fewer consumers. Additionally, food chains are not endless in length. Some contain only one or two steps; others have five or more links. In general, long food chains are inefficient and rare because too much energy is lost while being transferred from animal to animal.

These three examples illustrate how hawks and owls fit into food chains. Still, this is only part of the story. Rarely do isolated food chains exist in biotic communities. Usually they are interconnected into food webs. Not uncommonly, an animal is a member of several food chains at once, depending upon its position in a food web. Almost all food webs are extremely complex, which is unfortunate because it makes them extremely difficult to study and understand. Indeed, only the most simple, such as those in polar regions, are relatively completely understood. Food webs operating in most eastern North American forests, woodlots, fields, and meadows still are incompletely investigated. Nevertheless, enough information exists to provide ecologists with a reasonably adequate understanding of their operation and environmental importance.

From the available information, one fact is clear: an adequate understanding of birds of prey can only be achieved by considering an area's entire raptor (hawk and owl) population in relation to the food and space used, the raptors' daily and seasonal movements, and many other critically related factors. Few such field studies have been made. One of the best, requiring four years of intensive investigation on a 36-square-mile area in Washtenaw County, Michigan, was completed by John J. Craighead and Frank C. Craighead, Jr. They published the results of their study in *Hawks, Owls and Wildlife*, which every raptor enthusiast should read.

The field studies which John and Frank Craighead conducted as the basis of their doctoral research give ecologists important insights into the complex roles that hawks and owls play in the balance of nature. For example, no single species of hawk or owl catches and kills members of all of the potential prey species in an area. But when the entire raptor population is considered collectively, all of the species of hawks and owls could do so. The predation pressure a population of breeding raptors exerts upon prey is applied in three important ways. First, this pressure is not constant, but is limited to certain critical periods. Second, predation pressure is highest when the prey density is at its greatest level. Usually this is during spring, immediately following the breeding season. And, third, collectively, birds of prey apply continuous, but proportionate, pressure upon a collective prey population.

The Craigheads' field studies also afforded some additional ecological insights into daily and seasonal activities of hawks and owls. They discovered, for example, that raptors (along with other predators) establish and maintain a balance or equilibrium among animal populations. Raptor predation operates according to definite patterns. The birds hunt where prey is most abundant and vulnerable, thus resulting in the most abundant prey being captured in proportion to their abundance. For example, if voles form 75 percent of the total available prey for a collective population of hawks and owls, white-footed mice 11 percent, game birds 8 percent, and small birds 6 percent, each of these animals more or less will be represented in similar percentages in the collective (combined) raptor kill for the area under study.

Another example illustrating raptor interactions with prey concerns the relationship of Northern Goshawks and Cooper's Hawks to other songbirds and rodents in northern Pennsylvania and New York.

During a 10-year period, an ornithologist closely studied the diet of adult and nestling Cooper's Hawks in the Ithaca, New York, region. For the twelve broods studied, birds made up nearly four-fifths of the diet and mammals the remaining fifth. The mammalian prey was almost entirely made up of chipmunks and red squirrels, while the birds included a more varied selection of European Starlings, Northern Flickers, Eastern Mea-dowlarks, American Robins, and Common Grackles. European Starlings were by far the most frequently captured and eaten of all avian prey. Interestingly, most of the Cooper's Hawks' prey consisted of young, inexperienced animals. Only occasionally were adult animals captured—presumably while protecting their young. At times even nestlings two-thirds grown were taken. This information gives us a fuller understanding of the ecological role that Cooper's Hawks play in helping to regulate some songbird populations. The hawks are vital participants in the food webs that exist within their nesting and hunting territories.

Comparative studies made at fourteen Northern Goshawk nests in New York and northern Pennsylvania also provided important insights into the ecology of these powerful hawks. These birds are the highest trophic (feeding) level raptors in the areas where they nest. Information gathered at the New York and Pennsylvania nests refuted many long-held ideas about the role that Northern Goshawks play in relation to Ruffed Grouse populations. Grouse were common in areas where Northern Goshawks nested. But only five grouse were taken as prey. In comparison, the raptors captured eighty-three crows, fifty-eight red squirrels, and a variety of other birds and mammals.

When the ecological roles and behavior of all of the Northern Goshawk prey were carefully considered, some remarkable insights into the ecological importance of these accipiters were obtained. For example, it was clear that Northern Goshawks in New York and Pennsylvania forests do not select a particular area for nesting because of high grouse populations. Indeed, they probably are instrumental in helping grouse populations to *increase* rather than to decrease. That's because red squirrels and crows destroy many Ruffed Grouse nests by feeding on grouse eggs or

An adult Northern Goshawk. These powerful hawks are top trophic-level predators in the forests in which they live. *Photo by Ron Austing.*

nestlings, or by chipmunks that push eggs out of the nest. Thus, by helping to control important predators on grouse, the hawks actually help to increase the numbers of these game birds.

Careful studies of other raptors in different habitats and areas also demonstrate the ecological value of these predators. My studies of nesting American Kestrels in eastern Pennsylvania provide a case in point. These raptors are the smallest and most colorful falcons in North America. They typically live in open areas such as fields, meadows, and farming districts. Some also have adapted to life in towns and cities and nest successfully close to human activity.

My studies were made in an agricultural area. During an eight-year period, twenty-one active kestrel nests were located on a Berks County farm several miles from Hawk Mountain Sanctuary. To avoid unnecessary disturbance, only fourteen nests were studied in varying degrees of completeness. All were in nest boxes placed in suitable locations. Of fifty-five eggs laid, forty-three (78 percent) hatched.

The food habits of the kestrels during spring and summer demonstrated that the falcons were important ecological members of their wildlife community. For example, during a four-year period, the prolific meadow vole was the single most important animal captured and consumed. But, at the same time, voles are also preyed upon by many species of hawks and owls. Clearly, these falcons played important roles in helping to control the numbers of some of the most prolific and abundant animals in the food chains and food webs of this farming district.

The kestrel's relationship with an explosive population of periodical cicadas illustrates some additional ecological concepts: the importance of habitat, and the concepts of availability and vulnerability of prey. Because the

A female American Kestrel. These small falcons prey on microtine and other small rodents, a few birds, and various insects. *Photo by Harry Goldman.*

cicadas are forest insects while the kestrels are birds of open fields and farmlands, the two species were essentially restricted to separate (but adjacent) habitats. A few cicadas spilled into the fields near the edge of the forest, however, and occasionally a kestrel entered the forest's edge. Ecologists refer to an area containing vegetation of two different, but adjacent, habitats as an "edge" or "ecotone." On the Berks County study site, the forest edge was poorly defined because there was an abrupt change from forest to field. But enough cicadas ventured into open fields, and enough kestrels entered the forest edge with sufficient frequency, to permit some cicadas to be captured by the falcons. Thus, in 1962, the only year during which the cicadas were present (they appear only once every seventeen years), these insects formed 16.5 percent of the kestrel's diet.

This interaction between falcons and cicadas illustrates several additional ecological principles. For example, in order for a predator to capture an animal, the animal must be available and vulnerable. It must not only live in an area in which a predator hunts, it also must occur in a situation that will allow it to be captured. In the case of the kestrels and cicadas, the insects were primarily potential prey species. Generally they were not vulnerable to the falcons in any significant degree because they lived in a habitat not very well suited for kestrel hunting techniques.

This example also illustrates another important ecological principle—all animals require specific habitats in which to live. Seldom does an animal leave that habitat for extended periods, except during migration or because of some unusual circumstances. In Berks County, Pennsylvania, the primary ecological role of the kestrels was to help to control the numbers of field rodents and insects. An occasional bird was captured only if it was available and vulnerable.

Many additional examples could be cited to illustrate the ecological importance of birds of prey. In Georgia, for example, Sharp-shinned Hawks and Cooper's Hawks preyed upon Northern Bobwhites, but other raptors were either beneficial or neutral. The Northern Harrier is a case in point. Harriers fed heavily upon cotton rats, a common rodent in the area. The rats were known to destroy many quail eggs. Thus it seemed that Northern Harriers helped to maintain, if not actually increase, local Northern Bobwhite populations by eliminating numbers of destructive rats. A delicate and effective ecological balance between predator and prey was at work—a balance that people could readily alter if they attempted to kill birds of prey.

Nocturnal birds of prey—the owls—play a similarly important role in eastern North American ecosystems. Many important field studies of owls have been reported by wildlife biologists, but two are particularly famous.

The first concerns the predation ecology of Great Horned Owls in Wisconsin and Iowa. This large-scale study, which lasted for 5 years, pioneered the use of examining the contents of pellets (compact masses of undigested fur, feathers, bone, and intact remains ejected by an owl through its mouth) as a tool for studying raptor diet. Over a 5-year period, the scientists collected data at eighty-four horned owl nests and examined the contents of 4,815 pellets and twenty-three food-containing owl stomachs. The pellet analysis was an especially valuable study technique.

The information that was gathered was particularly complete for the colder half of the year, but less so for the warmer half. For the most part, Great Horned Owls were opportunistic in their predatory activities. Whatever suitable prey happened to be most easily secured was captured. Some differences, however, occurred in the diets of the owls. These

Great Horned Owls are opportunistic predators.
Photo by Ron Austing.

prey species was extraordinarily fascinating. The meadow vole averaged almost 85 percent of all prey consumed during the three years the investigation continued. However, the percentage of voles consumed was not constant, but varied considerably between seasons and even years. At one point, for example, the voles dropped to only 57 percent of the diet whereas during another period it accounted for almost 97 percent of all food eaten by the Barn Owls. It is obvious that Barn Owls are very important ecological components of some Michigan ecosystems. Although many predators feed to a greater or lesser degree upon meadow voles, few predators feed upon the rodents as regularly, and in such large quantities, as do Barn Owls. Since these voles exhibit periodic population cycles, that is, "explosions" and "crashes" in numbers, it is likely that the different percentages of voles represented in the diets of the Barn Owls reflected cyclic phenomena of their staple food item. As with the kestrels and the cicadas, the diet of the Barn Owls

resulted primarily from variations in ecological conditions related to season and geographic location. Nevertheless, cottontails, hares, and other medium-sized mammals formed the greater part (up to almost 70 percent by volume) of the staple prey of the Great Horned Owls. Mice, other small mammals, and resident birds were somewhat less important as prey. Various other migratory birds, lower vertebrates, and invertebrates also were preyed upon occasionally. This study was the first, or one of the first, to try to understand the ecological role of the horned owl.

The second famous study dealt with Barn Owls living in the vicinity of East Lansing, Michigan. It lasted for three years and analyzed the skeletal and other prey remains preserved in 2,200 Barn Owl pellets from two sites. Although nearly seven thousand prey animals were represented in the pellets, the percentage of representation of the various

Barn Owls are distributed widely in North America and throughout the world. *Photo by Ron Austing.*

changes to meet the demands of an ever-changing food web.

———

Equipped with this ecological background, we can understand why hawks and owls, and predators in general, play extremely vital roles in biotic communities. We should also be able to understand why it is ecologically unwise to attempt to increase the populations of one species (usually game animals) by eliminating predators. Invariably, efforts of this type fail because they ignore basic ecological principles. They create unbalanced environments that frequently lead to extreme fluctuations in the populations of some animals such as rodents.

A Dutch ornithologist also pointed out that when considering wildlife communities living on an area, it is important to remember that birds of prey are excellent and inexpensive indicator species (biometers) reflecting an area's ecological diversity and environmental health. Birds of prey serve as good biometers for several reasons. First, they are large and easily observed. Second, when numerous *common* birds of prey live on an area, they demonstrate the presence of a healthy assortment of plants and animals living in various habitats. The raptors would not be common, or present at all, if the necessary plant and wildlife diversity upon which they depend for survival were not present.

Thus the ornithologist urges ecologists and conservationists to take special measures to protect areas with a rich assortment of common birds of prey because the raptors are common. If enough such efforts supporting common birds of prey are augmented, there is the probability that some future costly or controversial emergency actions (which are really last-minute efforts) in endangered species programs will not be needed. Ecology provides the foundation for a simple idea: save species when they are common.

HAWK MIGRATIONS

During spring and autumn, hawks migrate in large numbers between their wintering grounds in various parts of the Americas and their eastern North American breeding grounds. These seasonal migrations are fascinating, and complex, as more and more people discover when they become involved in studying the migratory travels of these impressive birds.

Frequently, particularly during autumn, raptors concentrate at certain locations be-cause of the natural topographic features existing there. Some notable bottlenecks are located along parts of the Atlantic coastline; the Kittatinny Ridge, extending relatively unbroken across parts of New York–New Jersey–Pennsylvania for more than 250 miles in a northeasterly to southwesterly direction; and the northern and western shorelines of the Great Lakes.

During spring, the southern shorelines of Lakes Erie, Michigan, and Ontario also tend to concentrate northward migrating raptors, but other concentration areas also occur at a few spots along the Atlantic coastline and elsewhere. When migrating hawks reach these places, thousands are sometimes counted in a single day, making hawk flights spectacular animal migrations.

To enjoy and appreciate hawk migrations, it is rewarding to visit watch sites during the migration seasons. Directions for visiting many sites are provided in *A Guide to Hawk Watching in North America,* and a general discussion of raptor watching is provided in chapter 6 (on raptor watching). Binoculars are necessary to see migrating birds better.

Seasonal migrations of raptors such as this Broad-winged Hawk are becoming increasingly popular wildlife attractions. *Photo by Donald S. Heintzelman.*

Spring Migrations

In many respects, spring hawk migrations are different from those that occur during autumn. In spring, in eastern North America,

A migrating Northern Harrier. These hawks are open terrain birds. *Photo by Fred Tilly.*

hawk flights generally are more widespread, at higher altitudes, and do not seem to concentrate at various geographic bottlenecks as readily as these birds do in autumn. Nevertheless, some excellent spring concentration points are known.

Apparently hawks migrating northward dislike crossing large bodies of water. Therefore, when they reach major geographic features, such as the Great Lakes, they divert their migration route eastward or westward along the southern shorelines of these lakes. The largest concentrations usually occur where bays or water inlets occur, and where land extends into the lakes just west of the sites used as watch sites. When hawks encounter the waters of inlets as they are moving eastward, they avoid crossing those waters and turn to follow the shoreline toward the southeast. However, at some of the western Great Lakes, the birds divert southwestward along the shorelines. Because other hawks migrating inland a mile or more from the main waters of the lakes also encounter waters from the inlets, flight lines at those locations tend to become narrower along the embayed areas. This results in concentrations of hawks. Large numbers of birds can sometimes be counted.

Other topographic features also influence migrating hawks as they pass along lake shorelines. For example, when open-country hawks such as harriers encounter woodlands, they sometimes divert their flight path to cross open fields. Similarly, at locations where open fields border lake shorelines, accipiters fly inland over woodlands or follow along the boundaries of woodlands and fields. Knowledge of the preferred habitats of various hawks sometimes can aid observers in locating the best spots to watch the birds during migration.

Weather conditions are important and influential factors affecting both spring and autumn hawk migrations. In spring, for example, hawk flights seem to occur most frequently when southerly winds prevail, there is a rise in air temperature, barometric pressure is falling, and a low-pressure area and cold front approach from a westerly direction. By looking for these conditions in newspapers or on television weather reports, hawk watchers sometimes can predict the occurrence of good spring hawk flights.

The bulk of spring hawk migrations occur during March, April, and May. Mid- to late April is particularly favorable for seeing substantial numbers of Sharp-shinned Hawks and Broad-winged Hawks along the southern shorelines of Lakes Erie, Michigan, and Ontario. For example, Braddock Bay near Rochester and Derby Hill near Mexico in upstate New York are major spring raptor migration watch sites along the southern shoreline of Lake Ontario. Whitefish Point in Michigan is another major spring raptor migration watch site.

Relatively limited spring hawk migration research has been done at most major autumn raptor migration watch sites. In recent years, however, some focus has turned to these raptor movements along the Kittatinny Ridge in eastern Pennsylvania. Although not as comprehensive or detailed as autumn raptor migration studies, they provide a snapshot and appraisal of the species composition, timing, and magnitude of these migratory movements.

In 1993, I summarized spring raptor migrations reported sporadically during the period 1967–1993 at Bake Oven Knob on the Kittatinny Ridge. Collectively, 4,052 raptors were counted. Broad-winged Hawks represented almost 60 percent of this total. Turkey Vultures, Ospreys, Sharp-shinned Hawks, Red-tailed Hawks, and American Kestrels appeared in much smaller numbers.

Although spring raptor migrations along the Kittatinny Ridge tend not to be as large as the ridge's famous autumn hawk flights, some excellent spring flights are recorded for Bake Oven Knob.

For example, during five hours of observation on the afternoon of March 31, 1993, from the parking lot at Bake Oven Knob, "a contin-uous movement of raptors headed upridge— many flying low overhead." Turkey Vultures were especially well represented with dozens appearing simultaneously and gliding rapidly toward the northeast. The day's count contained: "23 Black Vultures, 276 Turkey Vultures, 1 Northern Goshawk, 27 Sharp-shinned Hawk, 12 Cooper's Hawks, 23 Red-tailed Hawks, 9 Red-shouldered Hawks, 38 Broad-winged Hawks, 1 adult Bald Eagle, 5 Northern Harriers, 7 Ospreys, 1 Merlin, 56 American Kestrels, and 15 unidentified hawks."

On April 17, 1984, John Leskosky and I tallied 1,296 raptors migrating past Bake Oven Knob during only 2.5 hours of observation. Included were: "12 Turkey Vultures, 2 Northern Goshawks, 14 Sharp-shinned Hawks, 3 Cooper's Hawks, 22 Red-tailed Hawks, 1,198 Broad-winged Hawks, 3 Northern Harriers, 7 Ospreys, 14 American Kestrels, and 21 unidentified hawks."

Ornithologists at Hawk Mountain also published a summary in 1999 of sporadic spring raptor migration counts at that watch site for the period 1969–1998. They counted 7,433 migrating raptors. Six species—Osprey, Sharp-shinned Hawk, Broad-winged Hawk, Red-tailed Hawk, Northern Harrier, and American Kestrel—represent nearly all of their spring hawk flights. Broad-winged Hawks represented almost one-half of the birds counted, with the other species appearing in much smaller numbers.

Some notable spring raptor migrations are also reported from the southeastern United States. For example, a large raptor migration was reported on March 18, 1994, moving north past Cumberland Island, Georgia. During that morning, 25 Ospreys, 2 Swallow-tailed Kites, 1 Bald Eagle, 15 American Kestrels, and numerous Black Vultures and Turkey Vultures were counted. The Swallow-tailed Kites represented Georgia's earliest arrival date for the species. During the afternoon, an estimated 360 Ospreys, and a few other hawks, were also seen.

Autumn Migrations

Autumn is the most exciting season to observe large numbers of migrating hawks. Hundreds of thousands of birds then migrate southward. Although a trickle of hawks appear early in August and a few continue flying into mid-January, most flights occur during September, October, and November. It is then that visits to raptor migration watch sites are worthwhile.

Bald Eagles fly southward in small numbers during late August and September although their migrations continue in limited numbers during the entire season. Ospreys, too, usually reach peak numbers during mid- to late September, although on September 11, 1965, at Bake Oven Knob, Pennsylvania, I counted 102 of these splendid birds passing that watch site. This daily count record was surpassed on September 14, 2002, when 116 Ospreys were counted at Bake Oven Knob.

September is especially noted for spectacular migrations of Broad-winged Hawks. Not infrequently they appear in largest numbers (thousands in a single day) around mid-September at Bake Oven Knob and Hawk Mountain, Pennsylvania.

A large flight of migrating Broad-winged Hawks is spectacular. As many as 600 or more may mill around in a swirling "kettle" inside a thermal (an invisible bubble of warm air ris-

A large group or "kettle" of migrating Broad-winged Hawks inside a thermal.
Photo by Donald S. Heintzelman.

ing into the atmosphere). It is not unusual to count 2,000 or 3,000 Broad-wings on a peak flight day at some watch sites, and occasionally flights of 10,000 or more sometimes are reported from a few locations. These numbers are meager, however, compared with Broad-wing counts at the Holiday Beach Migration Observatory in southwestern Ontario. On September 15, 1984, an amazing 95,499 Broad-wings were counted there, as were 63,400 Broad-wings on September 18, 1993, at the same watch site.

October is equally exciting. At many watch sites, autumn foliage reaches its peak of color in mid- to late October, adding a spectacular backdrop to migrating hawks. Moreover, migrating waterfowl and songbirds also appear during October. Thus, birds ranging from kinglets, vireos, and wood warblers to Golden Eagles add zest to birding. Sharp-shinned Hawks pass southward in large numbers during early to mid-October. Sometimes hundreds, occasionally even several thousand, can be counted in a single day at some Great Lakes, Appalachian mountain, and Atlantic coastal watch sites. For example, 2,407 Sharp-shins were counted on October 17, 2001, at the Holiday Beach Migration Observatory in Ontario. Other raptors such as Cooper's Hawks, Merlins, and Peregrine Falcons also appear, increasing the excitement of hawk watching during October.

From late October into November, many larger and even more spectacular hawks pass migration watch sites in mounting numbers. Just about any cold and windy day in early November should produce many Red-tailed Hawks. Often some Red-shouldered Hawks, Northern Goshawks, Golden Eagles, and an occasional Rough-legged Hawk are also seen. Still other species migrating southward at this time include Cooper's Hawks, Northern Harriers (especially males), perhaps a late Osprey, or very rarely a Gyrfalcon. Sometimes a

October is a key autumn migration month for this immature Cooper's Hawk. *Photo by Fred Tilly.*

late seasonal movement of Bald Eagles is also reported at Pennsylvania watch sites—adding even more interest to hawk watching.

Some hawks passing raptor migration watch sites travel very long distances to their wintering grounds. For example, Ospreys and Broad-winged Hawks winter in Central and South America. Bald Eagles and Golden Eagles winter in the southern Appalachians, insofar as eastern eagles are concerned. Bald Eagles migrating down the Mississippi River, or wintering along various sections of that great river, return in spring to nest in the Great Lakes states and Canada.

Most Bald Eagles observed passing Bake Oven Knob and Hawk Mountain are Florida breeders returning there to nest, but comparative studies show that many eagles seen at Bake Oven Knob are not the same individuals seen downridge at Hawk Mountain, and vice versa. Moreover, not all Bald Eagles migrating across Pennsylvania are seen along the Kittatinny Ridge. Some are reported at the Militia Hill Hawk Watch and Rose Tree Park Hawk Watch near Philadelphia, Pennsylvania. This is south of the traditional ridge flight line in Pennsylvania. Bald Eagles are also seen at Cape May Point, New Jersey.

An immature Red-tailed Hawk hunting over the Kittatinny Ridge in New Jersey. During late October and early November many such hawks are seen migrating along the ridge after the recent passage of a cold front. *Photo by Fred Tilly.*

Some Bald Eagles seen along the Kittatinny Ridge are produced by reintroduction programs as opposed to Florida eagles returning south. A third group, seen from late November to mid-January, are Northern Bald Eagles moving south from their northeastern Canadian breeding grounds. During November, Bald Eagles also migrate south along the upper Mississippi River. One 2-day period in mid-November 1972 produced a count of 147 Bald Eagles.

One of the largest autumn migration counts of Bald Eagles in eastern North America was logged in 1994 at the Hawk Ridge Nature Reserve in Duluth, Minnesota, when 4,368 Bald Eagles were reported. On 31 October, 410 eagles were counted, followed by 578 on 19 November and a whopping 743 on 22 November. The November 1994 Bald Eagle count at Hawk Ridge amounted to 2,600 birds.

Hawk Migrations and Weather Conditions

The relationship between spring and autumn weather conditions and hawk migrations is reasonably well known. During spring, the largest numbers of migrating raptors seem to occur a day or two after the passage of a warm front—at least in eastern North America.

During autumn, the presence of a low-pressure area in upstate New York and southern New England, followed by the passage of a cold front across eastern Pennsylvania, results in strong northwest winds striking the north side of the Kittatinny Ridge that are deflected upward creating favorable raptor flight conditions.

Analysis of the Hawk Mountain migration database for 1934–1991 suggests the number of cold fronts crossing Hawk Mountain during autumn vary from year to year, with no long-term trend demonstrating specific numbers of fronts occurring. Within a particular autumn, the number of cold fronts passing Hawk Mountain do not affect the number of hawks counted during that autumn.

Nevertheless, the recent passage of cold fronts tends to increase the numbers of migrating raptors at Hawk Mountain on the day of the frontal passage, or within a few days. Moreover, different raptors (accipiters, buteos, and falcons) respond differently to

An adult Peregrine Falcon. The Florida Keys are part of an important autumn Atlantic coastal migration route and stopover area for these falcons. *Photo by Donald S. Heintzelman.*

changing wind and weather conditions in terms of numbers of individuals counted. Hence, cold fronts and strong northwest winds make hawks more visible because they are pushed closer to Kittatinny Ridge watch sites.

Stopover Habitats

Within recent years, ornithologists have come to realize it is not enough to protect and preserve only raptor nesting and wintering habitats. Because migration is a strenuous activity for raptors (and other birds) in unfamiliar terrain along migration routes, birds of prey need many suitable habitats—called stopover habitats—in which to rest and feed. In eastern North America, important stopover habitats are located along the Atlantic coastline from Atlantic Canada southward to the Florida Keys, along the Gulf Coast, and along inland migration flight lines and corridors such as the Kittatinny Ridge. Other important stopover habitats occur along the shorelines of the Great Lakes and the Mississippi River.

Much stopover habitat is being lost, however, along the Atlantic and Gulf coasts. That's why raptor conservationists encourage the general public and conservation organizations to protect, preserve, and even restore as much stopover habitat as possible. Raptors and other migratory birds need these places to rest and feed before continuing on their spring and autumn migrations.

We know very little about which specific stopover habitats are the most important for raptors, however, or how they are selected and used. Nor do we know much about how large stopover habitats should be to meet the needs of raptors. Nevertheless, some reasonable suggestions can identify some seemingly obvious stopover sites.

In New York, Fire Island National Seashore is important stopover habitat along that state's Atlantic coastline for falcons and some other raptors. Along the Atlantic Coast in New Jersey, however, so much coastal development has occurred that only a few natural areas of significant size remain as useful stopover habitat. These include Island Beach State Park, Edwin B. Forsythe National Wildlife Refuge, and the salt marshes in the vicinity of Cape May Point. Migrating raptors such as Merlins and Peregrine Falcons use each of these for feeding and resting.

South of New Jersey, Assateague Island National Seashore in Maryland and Chincoteague National Wildlife Refuge in Virginia are national seashore areas, and important stopover habitats for migrating Peregrine Falcons. The Virginia Coast Reserve's barrier beach islands, owned by The Nature Conservancy, is another autumn stopover area. Kiptopeke State Park similarly preserves important stopover habitat in coastal Virginia for raptors and other birds.

In Florida, the Keys are especially important stopover habitat for large numbers of migrant Peregrine Falcons. Farther south still, Dry Tortugas National Park provides stopover habitat—indeed, some raptors coming ashore on the Dry Tortugas are so weak and exhausted they are barely able to perch on a tree or shrub. On the Gulf Coast, Gulf Islands National Seashore also provides stopover habitat.

Based on the information in this chapter, it is clear that hawk migrations provide exceptionally favorable opportunities to see raptors. Do take advantage of these opportunities.

3

OWL MIGRATIONS
AND INVASIONS

Migrations

In contrast to spectacular diurnal migrations of hawks, owl migrations are little noticed and much more difficult to study. Because owls are nocturnal, we cannot establish watch sites in the same way we do for diurnal raptors. Instead, information is collected bit by bit, over long periods of time, after establishing owl banding stations (sometimes extensions of hawk banding stations). Indeed, without bird banding and, recently, radiotelemetry tracking, it is unlikely seasonal owl migrations could be studied.

Recoveries of banded Barn, Snowy, Long-eared, Short-eared, and Northern Saw-whet Owls indicate these birds are very migratory. Other owls also have some migratory movements, or at least they wander from time to time, especially during winter; these movements are correlated with changes in food supply. Other factors which may cause owls to migrate are not well understood.

BARN OWL

In the case of the Barn Owl, lows in vole populations are related to some migrations by these birds. Unusually cold winter weather also may cause some birds to migrate southward. It is believed that Barn Owl migrations occur among birds forming their northern population, living north of a line drawn through 35° North. Both young and adult individuals are involved in these migrations. Barn Owls then return north to within 200 miles of their hatching places by the first of April. Some individuals then continue northward within the 200-mile zone through April. Not until mid-April or early May do the last of the owls complete their migrations.

In eastern Pennsylvania, some owls are also migratory during winter and do not return until March. But other individuals are nonmigratory, even nesting in October and January.

An impressive difference between the average life span of northern and southern Barn Owls exists. The life span of 70 southern birds was 2 years, 2 months, and 26 days. That of 150 northern birds was 1 year, 1 month, and 4 days. Dangers encountered during migration, and perhaps geographic locations, may account for the shorter lives of the northern birds.

NORTHERN SAW-WHET OWL

Recent studies of Northern Saw-whet Owls demonstrate that these birds are far more common than was suspected previously. In part, that's because several dozen owl banding stations are now operating in eastern North America—and finding these birds just about everywhere they're searched for—including one eastern Pennsylvania backyard in an

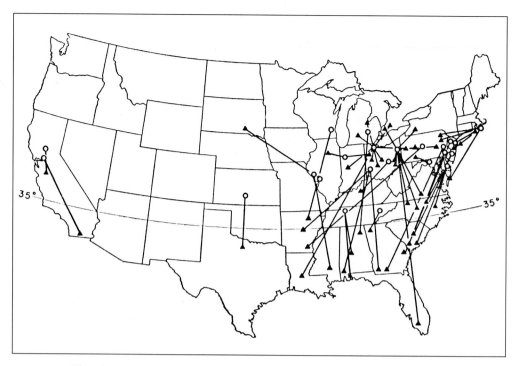

The migratory movements of Barn Owls banded as nestlings and recovered 100 miles or more from the location where they were hatched. Banding sites are indicated by circles, recovery sites by triangles. *From Stewart (1952) in* The Auk.

agricultural area surrounded by open farm fields.

Without the use of special techniques, however, these birds are very difficult to detect, even at close range, and are frequently overlooked. On several occasions, I saw these owls roosting in honeysuckle thickets but was unable to see them until someone pointed them out to me even though I was 3 feet from the birds. Their superb protective coloration and ability to remain motionless and blend into their surroundings are extraordinary. Nevertheless, in 2000, in Pennsylvania, a summer project called "Project Toot Route" discovered Northern Saw-whet Owls on 44 percent of the routes surveyed.

With the development and use of an "Audiolure" (recording of Northern Saw-whet Owl vocalizations) in combination with mist nets at bird-banding stations along the Great Lakes, Atlantic coastline, and along the Appalachian Mountains (such as the Kittatinny Ridge), it now is known that migrant Northern Saw-whet Owls are much more common during autumn than realized previously. Some owl enthusiasts believe these owls engage in broad-front migrations rather than following two distinct migration routes—one beginning in Ontario and extending southwestward through the Ohio River valley to Kentucky, the other along the Atlantic coastline from Maine southward to North Carolina. For example, one Northern Saw-whet Owl banded on the Kittatinny Ridge in Berks County, Pennsylvania, appeared two nights later at Assateague Island, Maryland. Other Northern Saw-whet Owls banded in Pennsylvania were recovered in western Ontario, southern coastal Maine, and in West Virginia, Maryland, and Virginia.

Some recoveries of Northern Saw-whet Owls banded in the eastern half of North

A Northern Saw-whet Owl. These are highly migratory owls. *Photo by Alan Wormington.*

Invasions and Irruptions

Ornithologists have long known that several North American owl species sometimes engage in impressive southward invasions and irruptions. Invasions pertain to Snowy Owls and Northern Hawk Owls breeding in Canada, whereas irruptions pertain to Great Gray Owls and Boreal Owls that are permanent breeding residents in Minnesota as well as Canada. Sometimes, such as in the winter of 1996–1997 in Minnesota, influxes of all four species provide exceptional opportunities to study these beautiful and fascinating birds.

Hence, when invasions occur, Snowy Owls and Northern Hawk Owls are the species to anticipate, whereas when irruptions occur ornithologists expect to see Great Gray Owls and Boreal Owls far south of their normal geographic ranges.

Unfortunately, there is a sad side, such as the 1995–1996 and 1996–1997 back-to-back owl invasions in Minnesota. During the first, a huge die-off of Boreal Owls occurred with 178 of 214 known birds found dead or dying. In 1996–1997, when an unexpected echo invasion occurred, 202 of 263 Boreal Owls were found dying or dead. Most starved to death by the time they reached Minnesota.

There is a fascinating ecological explanation why northern forest owls engage in periodic southward invasions. What is apparently *not* true is that northern owls are forced south from time to time because of deep snow and perhaps a crust of ice over the snow, preventing these predators from capturing voles. Rather, northern forest owl invasions are linked intimately with population crashes of voles in much the same way that population crashes of lemmings forces Snowy Owls to engage in periodic southward invasions.

Yet, there is still more to the explanation for northern forest owls. Deep snow and ice

America demonstrated specific migration patterns. Spring Northern Saw-whet Owl migrations, less well known than autumn migrations, occur from March through May, whereas autumn migrations begin in late September and continue into late November in New York, New Jersey, and Pennsylvania. Mid- to late October is the peak migration period.

In Minnesota, it is not unusual for above-average numbers of Northern Saw-whet Owls to appear along with irruptions of Boreal Owls—with many birds found dead, dying, or injured. A good many Saw-whets are found at bird feeders, in backyards, or even inside buildings. Because Northern Saw-whet Owls engage in seasonal migratory movements, however, it is not surprising that these birds appear during winter throughout Minnesota. Some are migrants from Canada, whereas others nested in northern Minnesota.

A Northern Hawk Owl. The occasional southward flights of these owls are called invasions. *Photo by Alan Wormington.*

crusts are not problems for these owls and do *not* prevent them from capturing voles, even though the mammals live beneath the top of the snow or ice crust. That's because a foot or so below the snow or ice surface, above-freezing temperatures prevail and dead leaves and other plants continue to break down via bacterial decomposition. That process releases carbon dioxide, increasing in concentration and annoys voles living in the places where gas concentration increases. Hence, the voles surface in holes in the snow or ice to escape the carbon dioxide gas build-up which makes them vulnerable to predation by Northern Hawk Owls, Great Gray Owls, and Boreal Owls.

SNOWY OWL

The Snowy Owl is a large, handsome bird that lives in the Arctic and sub-Arctic, where it feeds on lemmings and other small rodents. Its migrations are less regular than those of some other species, due primarily to its food habits, for the owls are forced southward in large numbers only about every 4 years. These migrations are called invasions. When lemmings are very abundant, there is no need for Snowy Owls to migrate. But when the rodents

become very scarce, as they do every few years, the owls are forced to seek other food and migrate southward.

The periodic cycles that characterize lemming populations do not necessarily occur at the same time over wide geographic areas. Therefore, a few Snowy Owls, representing geographic areas of limited size, migrate southward almost yearly and appear in the northern contiguous United States. But very large Snowy Owl invasions, which involve hundreds if not thousands of birds, only occur when lemmings are scarce over widespread sections of the Arctic.

Snowy Owl invasion records show that these birds invaded the eastern United States with regularity about every four years. Since 1882, the intervals between invasions stood at four of 3 years, nine of 4 years, and three of 5 years up to the 1945–1946 invasion.

In Minnesota, probably the best state to see northern owls during invasion years, ornithologists systematically began gathering Snowy Owl invasion data during the 1945–1946 invasion. Back-to-back Snowy Owl invasions occurred during the winter of 1995–1996, when 51 individuals were reported, and the winter of 1996–1997, with

153. Two additional back-to-back Snowy Owl invasions are reported for Minnesota: 92 in 1966–1967, followed by an echo invasion of some 41 in 1967–1968. Some 25 owls in 1990–1991 were followed by 121 in 1991–1992. In addition, the Snowy Owl invasion of 2000–2001 contained at least 111 birds, the fourth-largest studied invasion in Minnesota's history. The largest documented Snowy Owl invasion in Minnesota occurred in 1993–1994, when 351 individuals were reported.

Some other noteworthy Snowy Owl invasions in other states and Canadian provinces were documented in 1991–1992, when a minimum of 236 owls were seen in Ontario, plus others in Newfoundland, Nova Scotia, and Quebec, approximately 100 in New York, more than 70 in Massachusetts and other New England states, and still others in Illinois, Indiana, Michigan, New Jersey, Ohio, Pennsylvania, and Wisconsin.

When Snowy Owls migrate into the eastern United States, they are special Arctic visitors. More and more people appreciate and enjoy these birds.

NORTHERN HAWK OWL

During the winter of 2000–2001, an invasion of Northern Hawk Owls in northern Minnesota produced reports of 190 individuals. This was the third documented Northern Hawk Owl invasion containing 100 or more individuals in Minnesota's history. Most owls were healthy and able to find sufficient food to survive, but a few were killed by vehicles. Some other noteworthy Northern Hawk Owl invasions in Minnesota included 16 individuals in 1990–1991, and 159 in 1991–1992, as well as approximately 47 owls (but perhaps as many as 136) in 1962–1963, and an undetermined number in 1926–1927.

The 1991–1992 invasion produced large numbers of Northern Hawk Owls in other states and provinces, including approximately 102 owls in Ontario, 100 in Quebec, 27 in Michigan, 4 in Wisconsin, and others in Maine and New York.

GREAT GRAY OWL

Since 1960, ornithologists in Minnesota have carefully documented northern owl invasions and irruptions. The most spectacular Great Gray Owl irruption in the history of Minnesota, containing at least 394 individuals, was reported during the winter of 2000–2001. During the winter of 1995–1996, the second-highest number of Great Gray Owls was reported in Minnesota. In St. Louis County, for example, 123 individuals were documented, plus many others elsewhere in the state. Numerous Great Gray Owls commonly were seen along Minnesota's highways during the 2000–2001 irruption. Most

A Great Gray Owl photographed in southern Ontario, Canada, during an irruption year. *Photo by Alan Wormington.*

birds in this irruption seemed to be in good health, with only 26 found dead.

In 1990–1992, a major irruption of Great Gray Owls into Minnesota produced 134 or more of these large owls, and in 1991–1992 another large irruption occurred with at least 218 Great Gray Owls reported for the state. This latter irruption also produced large numbers of these birds in Michigan (55), Ontario (234), and Quebec (60). In 1983–1984, 432 Great Gray Owls were documented in Ontario.

BOREAL OWL

Boreal Owls are among the rarest owls seen by birders and ornithologists. Generally, they are encountered only during years when irruptions occur, and small numbers appear in northern parts of eastern North America, such as southern Ontario, northern Minnesota, and northern New England.

Ten documented irruptions of Boreal Owls in Minnesota represent "a nomadic/migratory response to fluctuating prey populations" as is known to occur for some European populations of this species. Supporting this idea is the fact that most Boreal Owls reaching Minnesota during irruptions were found in locations outside of their normal breeding locations in Canada and Minnesota.

For example, Boreal Owl irruption in Minnesota during the winter of 2000–2001 produced 259 individuals statewide, but 171 (66 percent) of the birds were found dead or dying (a common situation during these irruptions). The first individual appeared on September 9, 2000, and the last bird was found during the second week in April 2001. Of the owls whose ages were known, 90 percent were adults, compared with 24 percent during the winter irruption of 1988–1989, and 62 percent during the 1997–1998 winter irruption. The peak of the 2000–2001 irruption occurred during February and March, as did three earlier winter irruptions in Minnesota. The 2000–2001 irruption was the state's second-largest for Boreal Owls.

During October 1996 to April 1997, in parts of Minnesota, 263 Boreal Owls were reported—the largest irruption on record for the species. Unfortunately, the irruption reflected significant stress on the birds, and deep snow and a major crash of their prey base, which, in turn, forced the birds southward to locations where more food might be available. At least 202 Boreal Owls were found dead or dying during the winter of 1996–1997, whereas the previous winter, when another irruption had occurred, 176 dead or dying owls were reported. A small number of these were saved by raptor rehabilitators. During the 1996–1997 irruption, adult Boreal Owls formed 62 percent of the dead birds. That means that successful breeders were especially hard hit, eliminating an undetermined segment of the breeding population.

Much remains to be learned about these factors and their interactions, which means that very careful documentation of future irruptions is necessary, as is increased ecological research regarding the habitats occupied by these owls and how they use them. One research project, in progress since 1987, is an example of this type of research. The largest number of Boreal Owls detected during this study occurred during 1989, when 88 individuals were located, followed by 44 in 1997, and 41 in 1988.

As the 1996–1997 Boreal Owl irruption occurred in parts of Minnesota, nocturnal auditory surveys of this species, and other owls, were conducted to detect these birds nesting in the state's northern forests. Boreal Owls were detected on forty-four occasions during surveys along 411 miles of northern forest habitat.

Of females found on eight territories, four nested. Hence, during the winter of 1996–1997, a small number of resident Boreal Owls nesting in Minnesota were joined by several hundred more individuals coming from Canada's northern forests. That makes demographic studies of the birds difficult. Boreal Owl research in 2000, however, has implicated habitat degradation or depletion as a cause of long-term population declines of this species. In 2002, for example, 16 Boreal Owls were documented—the third-lowest count of Boreal Owls since 1987. Other low counts were 2 in 1996, 13 in 1998, and 16 in 1987.

4

RAPTOR CONSERVATION

Throughout the centuries, many people have been both inspired and threatened by hawks and owls. The enactment by the Pennsylvania legislature of the Scalp Act of 1885 is a case in point. The probable origin of Western man's misunderstanding of predators was explained to me in a letter by the late Robert Cushman Murphy of the American Museum of Natural History:

> The whole erroneous idea about control (meaning extermination) of predators arose in western Europe after man had to take charge of game management, as in English private 'parks.' In parts of the world where land use is still less artificial, as in Pennsylvania, a healthy supply of game birds, etc., depends upon a normal population of hawks, owls, and other predatory animals. They supply the basis upon which the welfare of life as a whole depends.
>
> The Azores Islands were named for hawks. It is very interesting that even today these islands have an extraordinarily large population of hawks, chiefly *Buteo,* and that along with them quail, woodcock, and vast numbers of small birds abound. The situation represents nature in proper balance.

The purpose of the English game parks was to provide good hunting sport. Anything tending to eliminate game was considered undesirable. Since birds of prey kill some game animals, they were viewed as "vermin" that should be destroyed. Yet field studies have shown that predatory birds often are only about 7 or 8 percent successful in their hunting attempts. Nevertheless, hawks and owls were resented as intruders and competitors. To the game managers, the obvious answer was to eliminate predators, presumably producing more game and better hunting.

Some Recent Raptor-Killing Cases

Despite current, widespread public support for raptor protection, some notable illegal raptor killing episodes recently occurred in the United States. For example, in the 1980s, in Virginia, between three hundred and four hundred federally protected hawks and owls were killed illegally by several "game keepers" employed on the 6,000-acre private estate of billionaire John Werner Kluge and his wife. No evidence was found, however, to directly link the Kluges to the illegal raptor killings on their estate.

A federal jury convicted head gamekeeper Sir Richard Musgrave, however, and two other British gamekeepers working for the Kluges of killing hundreds of hawks and owls. A fine of $15,000 was imposed, and all three foreign nationals were held for deportation proceedings. The next day the three British gamekeepers left for the United Kingdom.

In August 2002, the U.S. Attorney's Office for the Eastern District, Pennsylvania, filed a

"Three-Count Information" (an accusation where the defendant is presumed innocent unless and until proven guilty) against seventy-one-year-old Gwynne G. McDevitt and her employee Artimus C. Jenkins, for trapping and shooting 171 federally protected hawks on McDevitt's Doubledee Farm and Kennels near Newtown Square, Pennsylvania. McDevitt, the multimillionaire granddaughter of automobile magnate Walter P. Chrysler, paid Jenkins twenty-five dollars for each hawk he illegally trapped and killed—essentially a private bounty on the head of each raptor. Three federal counts were filed against McDevitt, and lesser charges against Jenkins.

Both McDevitt and Jenkins agreed to a proposed plea bargain to stay out of jail—18 months plus house detention, community service for 200 hours, 5 years' probation, and almost $130,000 in fines and restitution for McDevitt and probation and a $2,500 fine for Jenkins. A federal judge must approve the plea bargain agreements, with $42,250 to be paid to each of two nearby nonprofit environmental organizations.

To raptor conservationists the incident is disheartening and demonstrates that conservation, public education, and effective law enforcement remain essential, ongoing activities at local, state, national, and even international levels.

In March 1999, the president of the Pennsylvania Game Commission at the time attempted to secure a limited hawk and owl hunting season in Pennsylvania in the mistaken belief that better pheasant hunting would result. The birding, raptor-study, and conservation community in Pennsylvania, and even the staff of the Game Commission, vigorously opposed the ill-advised plan, which was resoundingly defeated.

Despite these disappointing episodes, most hunters do not shoot protected raptors. Indeed, the Wildlife Information Center, Inc., published two public opinion surveys measuring the extent of public support in Pennsylvania for various wildlife-related activities including raptor protection and Great Horned Owl protection. The surveys showed between 96.9 and 98.8 percent public support for raptor protection in Pennsylvania. These results suggest that public education efforts regarding raptors are generally effective.

Protective Laws and Regulations

A number of laws and regulations provide legal and regulatory protection for birds of prey in the United States. In 1918, the Migratory Bird Treaty Act provided basic legal protection for many species of birds in the United States. At various times since then, amendments were made to the treaty. In 1972, one such treaty amendment added thirty-two additional taxa of birds, including diurnal birds of prey and owls.

The Bald Eagle Protection Act of 1940 also was enacted to stop widespread shooting, trapping, poisoning, electrocution or other killing of our national symbol, the Bald Eagle. In 1962, the Golden Eagle was included in the act because enforcement of the law was difficult because hunters and most other people had a hard time distinguishing immature Bald Eagles from Golden Eagles. Other federal laws, especially the Endangered Species Act, also play major roles in providing legal protection (and restoration in the case of the Endangered Species Act) for raptors.

Regrettably, in November 2002, Congress enacted unrelated legislation that included an amendment exempting the Defense Department from the protection provided to birds by the Migratory Bird Treaty Act. Vigorous legal challenges are expected to try to overturn or repeal this exemption.

Natural Causes
of Raptor Mortality

Sometimes raptor losses are caused by natural events. Some important examples are discussed in this section.

EXTREME WEATHER CONDITIONS

Strong winds can destroy some Osprey and Bald Eagle nests, eggs, and nestlings by blowing their large stick nests to the ground. Similarly, nest failures of Swallow-tailed Kites in southern Florida occur more frequently in Australian pines than in native pines and cypress because Australian pines move and break more easily in strong winds. Drought and starvation are other causes of Snail Kite mortality. There also is an episode in which eight thousand migrating Swainson's Hawks in Panama were forced to the ground by a severe storm front, during which birds crashed through trees resulting in injured or stunned hawks on the ground.

Sometimes heavy rain, snow, or hail can cause the loss of some raptors and their nests, eggs, and nestlings. For example, unfavorable weather conditions (such as snow) and resulting nest abandonment are thought to be a major cause of Gyrfalcon nestling mortality. Extremely cold winter weather also is lethal to Barn Owls and many freeze to death during those conditions, whereas blowing and drifting snow can kill Snowy Owls on their nests. Heavy spring rains in Florida cause some Burrowing Owl burrows to collapse, killing adult and young owls inside, sometimes a significant cause of mortality for these birds.

PREDATION

Predators including raptors, crows, ravens, raccoons, striped skunks, red foxes, coyotes, black bears, bobcats, and wolverines also kill some birds of prey—usually eggs or nestlings, but occasionally adults. Great Horned Owls and Barred Owls kill some adult Snail Kites, with predation also being a significant cause of nestling mortality. Predation by Great Horned Owls on Red-shouldered Hawk nests is sometimes locally substantial. During one year it was responsible for one-third of nest losses in one area of New York, but it was not implicated in nest losses during other years or in other areas. Raccoons are also important predators on Red-shoulder nests, as are Red-tailed Hawks, Peregrine Falcons, martens, and fishers in northern parts of eastern North America. A Bald Eagle was also reported killing a Broad-winged Hawk.

Great Horned Owls are major predators of reintroduced Peregrine Falcons at cliff nest sites and are directly responsible for many failed attempts to return these falcons to historic cliff nest sites along rivers in Pennsylvania and other states. However, progress is being made along rivers in New England, and it is hoped that Peregrines will overcome horned owl predation elsewhere and slowly return to their historic cliff homes.

Quills from porcupines are especially dangerous to inexperienced Golden Eagles, and some birds have been found with numerous quills embedded in their feet, legs, and bodies, causing them to be emaciated and in danger of starvation. Proper veterinary care and rehabilitation is necessary for such birds.

STARVATION

Starvation is a major cause of Boreal Owl mortality during winters with very deep snow cover and low prey populations, which is when these birds engage in southward irruptions from their remote Canadian breeding grounds. Evidence from Minnesota indicates that hundreds of Boreal Owls perish during severe irruptive years. Additional evidence from Minnesota suggests that Boreal Owls occasionally engage in cannibalism when food is extremely scarce during winter.

DISEASES

Diseases rarely cause a significant number of deaths in raptors (2 percent in one study of 1,428 Bald Eagle necropsies). However, in 2002, 5 Cooper's Hawks, 2 Red-shouldered Hawks, at least 16 Red-tailed Hawks, and at least 18 Great Horned Owls were killed by contracting West Nile virus in the midwestern United States. Raptor biologists and conservationists are concerned that this virus may quickly spread to more raptors and cause increasingly large mortality among birds of prey throughout North America.

Human-Related Threats to Raptors

In spite of laws and regulations protecting raptors, a range of human-related threats still affect them negatively. It is useful to examine the most important of them.

THREATS TO AGRICULTURE

Raptors have long been viewed with disdain by some farmers. Their lack of understanding of birds of prey has often cast these birds in an unfavorable light due to their belief that raptors kill poultry and other small livestock, causing economic loss for farmers. On modern farms, however, relatively few animal losses are due to raptor predation, and the services that hawks and owls provide in removing voles, mice, and other rodents more than compensate for an occasional loss of a chicken or other animal.

ILLEGAL SHOOTING

Illegal shooting of raptors, including Bald Eagles and Golden Eagles, is a continuing problem in some states. Several Bald Eagles and Ospreys were shot in Pennsylvania since 2000, and in October 2001 a duck hunter in New Jersey killed a Peregrine Falcon, for which he was fined and ordered to pay restitution to that state's Endangered and Nongame Species Program. Snowy Owls and Northern Hawk Owls are also occasional shooting victims. Continuing law enforcement is essential to prevent illegal raptor shooting.

POLE TRAPS

In years past, game managers, operators of game farms, and others often used pole traps (steel-jawed traps placed on top of tall poles) to capture and remove hawks and owls from

A permanently disabled adult Red-tailed Hawk that was shot many years ago near Hawk Mountain in eastern Pennsylvania. The bird was rescued and later used in Hawk Mountain's educational programs. A few Red-tails are still shot illegally in the eastern United States. *Photo by Donald S. Heintzelman.*

wildlife management areas, shooting preserves, and other areas. Because birds of prey tend to land on tall perches such as poles, the raptors were easily captured in the traps. They were either killed or suffered broken legs or other broken bones, producing painful, lingering deaths. Some birds were not removed from pole traps for days or weeks after being caught. These traps were inhumane and indiscriminate in their victims. Hence, concerned citizens demanded they be made illegal, and they are rarely used today.

Success in eliminating the use of pole traps was based on a 1988 campaign launched by the Wildlife Information Center, Inc. Acting in cooperation with the Humane Society of the United States and using the federal Freedom of Information Act, the Wildlife Center secured photocopies of hundreds of pages of pole trap permits, annual reports, and related information documenting a dozen or more raptor species captured in pole traps used in

seventeen states. For example, the Pennsylvania Game Commission used pole traps at its pheasant-rearing farms. Cooper's Hawks, Northern Goshawks, Red-shouldered Hawks, Red-tailed Hawks, Rough-legged Hawks, American Kestrels, Merlins, and so-called "Chicken" Hawks and "Swamp and Mouse" Hawks were included on some reports of trappings to the U.S. Fish and Wildlife Service. A total of 907 Great Horned Owls, 479 of which were captured in Pennsylvania, were also reported, as was one Snowy Owl. Overall, 1,061 diurnal raptors and owls were killed in pole traps nationwide. The Wildlife Center then secured a change in the Code of Federal Regulations that makes it nearly impossible to receive a pole trap permit.

In 1988, the Toronto Humane Society provided evidence to Friends of Animals that pole traps were used illegally at the Kortright Waterfowl Park near Guelph, Ontario, Canada. The Federation of Ontario Naturalists

A Great Horned Owl captured and killed in a pole trap. *Photo by Harry Goldman.*

strongly opposed using these traps, but Ontario did little to stop the use of the devices—mostly on hunting preserves and game farms. As the result of unfavorable publicity, however, Kortright Waterfowl Park modified its pole traps so captured birds slid to the ground rather than hang suspended in the air. Nevertheless, the Federation of Ontario Naturalists pointed out that the modification made little difference, and protected raptors including Red-tailed Hawks, American Kestrels, and Great Horned Owls were still captured and killed.

In December 1994, a man in Delaware was cited by the Delaware Department of Natural Resources and Environmental Control for attempting to kill protected birds with pole traps. He paid fines, but several years later he was convicted again in federal court for poisoning a Bald Eagle.

Hence, one can understand the dismay among raptor conservationists on May 22, 2002, when the U.S. Fish and Wildlife Service (FWS) announced that five men, and the operators of a pheasant-rearing facility in Minnesota, were charged with alleged illegal use of pole traps to capture and destroy more than a hundred federally protected owls and hawks. As this book is being written, the case is in federal district court awaiting resolution.

To reevaluate the effectiveness of the 1988 change in federal regulations pertaining to uses of pole traps, in 2002 Friends of Animals (FOA) filed a Freedom of Information Act (FOIA) request with the U.S. Fish and Wildlife Service asking for copies of all permits, annual reports, and related pole trap documents issued and received by the FWS nationwide during the past few years. The FOIA request revealed a small number of padded pole trap uses (mostly for removal of Red-tailed Hawks and Great Horned Owls) in three regions of the continental United States—a very significant decline in pole trap use compared with their widespread use in the latter part of the twentieth century. Nevertheless, most raptor biologists and conservationists are opposed to all uses of pole traps including so-called padded traps that can still cause damage to the soft tissues on the legs and toes of raptors.

STEEL-JAWED LEG-HOLD TRAPS

Occasionally, Eastern Screech-Owls are accidentally captured in steel-jawed leg-hold traps used by trappers to catch muskrats. These captures are illegal and subject to prosecution by wildlife law enforcement agents. Moreover, since increasing numbers of people are opposed to trapping wild mammals for use by the fur trade, the capture of owls or other raptors in steel-jawed leg hold traps must be viewed as unnecessary and preventable.

ROAD KILLS, OTHER COLLISIONS, AND INJURIES

Collisions with motor vehicles is a continuing problem responsible for the deaths of many hawks and owls, including Sharp-shinned Hawks and Burrowing Owls. In an urban nesting area used by Burrowing Owls in Florida, for example, vehicles hitting the owls were responsible for 70.3 percent of the deaths and predation by domestic dogs or cats and other predators for 22.2 percent. One bird (3.7 percent) died during house construction and another bird was lost to an unknown illness. Most road kills of juvenile and adult owls in a Florida urban site occurred on residential streets where reduced speed limits were in place.

Sharp-shinned Hawks will also fly into windows, often with lethal results, and some Peregrine Falcons fly into hard objects, also receiving lethal impact injuries.

Collisions with vehicles, trains, and utility lines also cause the deaths of some Northern Hawk Owls, and collisions with vehicles cause some deaths of Northern Saw-whet Owls.

Regrettably, few if any measures are available to prevent road kills, but injured raptors should receive prompt veterinary treatment and appropriate rehabilitation care.

ELECTROCUTION

Electrocution of raptors landing on or taking off from perches on electrical utility poles occurs when high-voltage power lines are installed too close together and the wings of a large raptor such as a Golden Eagle or Great Horned Owl touch both wires, close the circuit, and electrocute the bird. This problem occurs to a limited extent in the eastern United States, but immature Golden Eagles are especially susceptible to electrocution in the western United States. Although substantial efforts are being made to eliminate this problem, electrocution remains an important but unnecessary cause of raptor losses.

HABITAT DEGRADATION OR LOSS

Habitat degradation and/or loss, mostly due to land development, is the single most serious, ongoing human cause of raptor mortality in eastern North America. That's because essential raptor nesting areas, wintering areas, foraging areas, and stopover habitats along migration flight lines, corridors, and flyways are increasingly undergoing development. Some American Kestrels also suffer from loss of natural nest cavities.

In Minnesota, intensive agricultural cultivation of land, plowing of pastureland and native prairie, and declines of burrowing mammals (badgers and Richardson's ground squirrels) seem to be associated with drastic declines of Burrowing Owls. Lack of nesting burrows may be the limiting factor.

Because the impact on wildlife caused by land development lacks the visual impact of a shooting, many people fail to recognize the enormous, continuing damage resulting from habitat degradation and loss.

In Pennsylvania, however, the Wildlife Information Center, Inc., has underway an ambitious, long-term habitat restoration project, the Lehigh Gap Restoration Project. Its goal is to restore some 750 acres of the Kittatinny Ridge's woodland at Lehigh Gap, continuing westward along the north side of the mountain for a considerable distance. This area is currently a federal Superfund site because of a century of lead, zinc, and cadmium pollution caused by the former New Jersey Zinc Company at Palmerton, Pennsylvania.

Dealing with habitat degradation or loss in foreign nations (where some North American raptors spend their winters) is especially vexing, but The Peregrine Fund and the Raptor Research Foundation are addressing these international concerns.

HUMAN DISTURBANCE AT NESTS

Human disturbances at raptor nests also cause some raptor mortality. The problem is best addressed by continuing public education programs and wildlife law enforcement. In some places, signs informing (and warning) the public not to enter or approach some raptor nesting areas are also helpful.

PESTICIDES AND OTHER CHEMICAL CONTAMINANTS

Pollution of aquatic food chains of Ospreys, Bald Eagles, and Peregrine Falcons by DDT after World War II caused widespread reproductive failures of these birds. Several large Osprey colonies were destroyed along the Atlantic Coast from New Jersey northward into New England. Southern Bald Eagles and the eastern population of the Peregrine Falcon also became federally endangered and nearly extinct.

Pollution of some raptor habitats, and food chains and food webs, by lead (and other

An adult Bald Eagle, such as those that suffered major population declines after World War II because of DDT pollution of their food chain, which caused eagle eggs to break or not hatch. DDT was banned in the United States and Canada in the early 1970s, and populations of these eagles are now fully recovering. *Photo by Ron Austing.*

heavy metals) and PCBs also cause raptor mortality, but prohibited use of lead shot is reducing lead pollution.

In the case of Swainson's Hawks that were poisoned in Argentina—their wintering ground—eighteen incidents account for 5,093 dead hawks after they ate grasshoppers from alfalfa fields that had been sprayed with monocrotophos and dimethoate. But ornithologists suspect that as many as 20,000 may actually have been killed. Recent efforts by conservationists reduced some of this mortality, but the problem is not completely resolved. This situation also illustrates how some raptor conservation issues touch on international affairs.

Some notable recent changes in the breeding status of Sharp-shinned Hawks have also been reported. In Connecticut, for example, Sharp-shins were considered common breeding birds early in the twentieth century, but by the early 1980s their numbers were declining. Indeed, only three nests of that species were reported in the state. But in 1983 and 1986, hawk watchers discovered Sharp-shinned Hawks nesting in Tunxis State Forest in Hartland, Connecticut.

What caused these changes in Connecticut's breeding Sharp-shinned Hawks? Part of the answer comes from Ontario, Canada. Eggs taken from the nests of Sharp-shinned Hawks (and Cooper's Hawks and Northern Goshawks) in south-central Ontario, during the period 1986–1989, were analyzed for chlorinated hydrocarbons and shell thinning. Detectable quantities of DDT, DDE, PCBs, and numerous other chlorinated hydrocarbons were found in the eggs, with highest levels found in Sharp-shin eggs, somewhat lower quantities in Cooper's eggs, and much lower quantities in Northern Goshawk eggs.

Eggshell thinning was not serious enough, however, to cause reproductive failures in Sharp-shins, Cooper's, or Goshawks. But three Sharp-shin eggs had eggshell thickness reductions in excess of 17 percent compared with pre–1947 eggshell thickness, suggesting some populations may be suffering some declines due to reproductive failures caused by DDE.

Blood samples from Sharp-shins captured during autumn at Hawk Cliff, Ontario, determined that most juvenile hawks visiting wintering grounds in Latin America had significantly lower organochlorine pesticides in their blood during their first migration than did the same hawks returning north as second-year birds. Apparently juvenile hawks pick up pesticide contamination from songbird prey eaten during migration as well as

An immature Golden Eagle representative of twenty-four raptor species known to be poisoned and killed by organophosphorus and carbamate pesticides in North America. *Photo by Ron Austing.*

In addition to the long-term effects of organochlorine pesticides on some birds of prey, ornithologists report direct poisoning of raptors by organophosphorus and carbamate pesticides, anticholinesterase chemical compounds that are extremely toxic for limited time periods but do not become magnified in predator food chains and food webs or accumulate in the fatty tissues of raptors.

When viewed from a regional perspective, pesticide poisoning can be significant—particularly when rare species are involved. Raptors that have been reported to be most affected in the United States were Black Vultures (61), Bald Eagles (243), Red-tailed Hawks (133), and Golden Eagles (144). Other poisoned raptors involving a dozen or more individuals included Mississippi Kites (17), Northern Harriers (14), Cooper's Hawks (12), Swainson's Hawks (20), and Great Horned Owls (18), and unidentified owls (15). In Canada, the species most effected by pesticides were Bald Eagles (64), Northern Harriers (30), and Red-tailed Hawks (24).

A review of the ornithological and pesticide contamination literature suggests that owls suffer few serious effects from pesticides. Burrowing Owls, however, are experiencing population declines, and research in Canada indicates that exposure to anticholinesterase pesticides (especially carbofuran) are responsible for the declines.

prey from the wintering grounds. Hence, Sharp-shinned Hawks are useful indicators for monitoring chemical contaminants in the environment.

Another study looked at DDE concentrations in blood plasma for migrant Peregrine Falcons captured during spring at Padre Island along coastal Texas between the period 1978 to 1994. There was a substantial decline in DDE blood plasma concentrations for these falcons.

Nevertheless, dangerous levels of DDT and other organochlorine pesticides are still trapped in some river sediments and become suspended again when dredging occurs—as happened in the lower part of Delaware Bay in New Jersey. Bald Eagles and Ospreys nesting close to the bay, and feeding on fish from that source, have again shown the thin-eggshell syndrome—a warning that possible reproductive failures are about to occur.

OTHER POISONS

Other poisons have also been used to purposely kill raptors such as Golden Eagles and Bald Eagles. A study of Bald Eagles and Golden Eagles killed by steel-jawed leg-hold traps and poison showed that strychnine was used on the birds.

In April 1977, a U.S. District Court judge sentenced a Delaware man to six months of home detention, more than $25,000 in fines and restitution, 5 years of probation, and 400 hours of community service for poisoning a Bald Eagle with the pesticide Furadan. This same man was cited and fined several years earlier for attempting to capture protected wild birds with a pole trap.

DECLINES OF NEOTROPICAL MIGRATORY SONGBIRDS

Declines of some neotropical migratory forest songbirds, some of which are Sharp-shinned Hawk prey species, are responsible for the loss of some bird-eating hawks. Forest fragmentation in eastern North America is responsible for some of these losses as well.

WIND GENERATORS

Wind generators (high-tech windmills) are planned for use in some parts of the eastern United States, so careful planning is taken to prevent eagle (and other raptor) casualties through hitting the rotating blades of wind generators. Nevertheless, much remains to be learned about the dangers that wind farms pose to raptors (some raptor mortality has been reported at wind farms in the western United States) and methods of preventing raptor mortality.

UNUSUAL CAUSES OF MORTALITY

In New York, an unexpectedly high number of immature Bald Eagles are killed while feeding on carrion on high-speed passenger train right-of-ways. The eagles are hit by trains running at speeds of 124 miles per hour in the lower Hudson River valley rail corridor. Most of these deaths occur during autumn and the overwintering period, when the birds appear in increasing numbers. Immature eagles are most vulnerable because they are more dependent on carrion than adult Bald Eagles. Unfortunately, the high-speed rail corridor is close to one of New York's most important Bald Eagle concentration areas.

Habitat Protection and Management

Protection, and sometimes management, of habitat is a basic conservation requirement that applies to all raptors in eastern North America, along with the monitoring of habitat quality. For example, preservation of the Oke-fenokee Swamp in Georgia is part of that state's Osprey conservation strategy. Ospreys are sensitive biological indicators of habitat quality, so ornithologists and raptor biologists also use Osprey breeding success as an indicator of wetland quality in New Jersey.

Preservation of a dozen Swallow-tailed Kite habitats in Florida is desirable because that state provides suitable habitat for only approximately two hundred pairs. Retaining native pine trees that are much taller than nearby trees, forming an uneven canopy in open pine forest stands with some trails and small forest roads, and preserving wetland vegetation and small hardwood hammocks are related components of conservation strategies for these kites.

White-tailed Kites are very rare birds in Florida, but ornithologists believe land conversion for agricultural uses may produce useful habitat for these birds. In Mississippi, White-tailed Kite nests in fields containing 148 or more acres and broom sedge plus several trees, brush, and grasses indicated to ornithologists that these areas may be habitats desirable for inclusion in conservation efforts for these kites.

Federally and state-endangered Snail Kites should survive in small numbers in Florida because of the rigid protection afforded them and their essential wetlands habitat. Remaining *refugia* wetlands, ponds, and lakes adjacent to Lake Okeechobee, and lakes elsewhere in south-central Florida, are used in times of extreme or extended drought, which explains why ornithologists want to identify and preserve them. Maintaining adequate freshwater levels and controlling increasing nutrient enrichment in marshes and other wetlands where Snail Kites occur are other essential parts of coordinated conservation plans for these birds. Control of invasive water hyacinth is also recommended.

Ornithologists studying Mississippi Kites in eastern North America recommend identifying and preserving mature or old-growth "raised islands" of woodland at least 198 acres in size that rise above the surrounding woodland. They also recommend establishing buffer zones as well as old tree stands around areas used for nesting, and preparing and maintaining uncultivated fields near kite nesting areas.

Northern Goshawk conservation measures include strict protection of remaining patches or islands of old-growth trees, or even larger expanses of old-growth woodland, plus large trees in second-growth woodland.

Management of forests allowing for retention of trees older than 40 years is advocated to preserve Broad-winged Hawk breeding habitat, especially in southeastern forests. Preservation of more extensive woodland and stopover habitat islands, and even development of new stopover habitat patches, is also recommended along migration routes used by these hawks.

Regulating real estate development on prime Swainson's Hawk habitat and preserving nest trees and planting more trees for use as nest sites are conservation measures that ornithologists have proposed to assist this species.

Loss of quality Crested Caracara habitat is continuing, especially the conversion of cattle ranchland to citrus groves in Florida. Elimination of palms, or major land use changes such as growth of dense weed or shrub cover due to removal of cattle on ranches also prevent caracaras from nesting in those areas.

Publicly owned lands play a minor role in preserving Crested Caracara habitat. Privately owned cattle ranches, however, and the land management practices employed on ranches (intensive grazing, mowing, burning, fertilizing, and plowing), overwhelmingly provide the necessary habitat supporting caracara nest sites. Hence, conservation biologists and governmental wildlife agencies are forced to deal with private land owners to maintain stable Crested Caracara populations in Florida. Their recommended conservation measures include preventing unnecessary human disturbances near nests, especially early in the nesting season, and keeping details regarding the locations of nests private.

Identification and preservation of Short-eared Owl breeding, wintering, and roosting habitats—including reclaimed surface mines—are recognized as being vital to the long-term conservation of these birds.

Boreal Owl conservation and management in Minnesota include preservation of overly mature aspen trees approximately 85 to 90 years old that have fungal decay and abandoned woodpecker holes, and black spruce trees that form adjacent lowland stands in which the owls roost, when both habitat types are within the same landscape. Keeping large-diameter snags in clear-cuts is also important.

Additional Raptor Management and Conservation Methods

A range of additional management techniques are included in raptor conservation programs. Some examples are discussed here.

ARTIFICIAL PERCHES

Hawks, eagles, and falcons frequently perch on dead trees, utility poles and wires, and similar high structures. These perches are essential components of raptor habitats and environment. Nevertheless, limited attention is devoted to studying perches and their relationship to local raptor populations or how artificial perches can be used as raptor management techniques.

Red-tailed Hawks make extensive use of hunting perches. This suggests that installation of tall poles, or keeping dead trees standing, is a useful management technique to make habitats as attractive as possible to Red-tails.

During the autumns of 1989 and 1990, numerous American Kestrels perched on utility poles and wires along a rural road that crosses a hilltop I called "Hawk Hill" in Heidelberg Township, Lehigh County, Pennsylvania. Fascinated, I studied the frequency of usage the kestrels made of the poles and wires. I drove over Hawk Hill ninety times during those autumns and observed one or more raptors on the hill on fifty-nine trips (65.5 percent). American Kestrels made up 73.3 percent of my sightings of the six raptor types observed there.

I intended to study this hilltop for five seasons, then publish a research paper on the results. The plan ended prematurely, however, when a utility company removed all the poles and wires from the top of the hill and its north slope. As a result, my research project took a sudden and entirely new and different focus—to determine what impact the loss of perches has on raptor utilization of what was previously an excellent hilltop for viewing raptors.

American Kestrels almost immediately stopped using the summit and north slope of the hill despite the availability of some tree and limb perches along the edge of a nearby woodlot. In addition, fewer American Kestrels used the remaining utility poles and wires. Clearly, the availability of utility poles and wires as perches was the limiting factor regulating the use, or lack of use, of that site by

kestrels. This was confirmed informally during the following years when relatively few American Kestrels were seen at Hawk Hill.

The management implications of this unexpected experiment are that perches are a vital part of American Kestrel (and probably other raptor) habitats, especially so for open field species. Perches can make the difference between a good site being used regularly or not being used at all by these birds. Hence, I recommend that one or more perches 15 feet or higher be installed or retained when old field ecosystems are being managed for raptor abundance and diversity.

NEST BOXES
AND RELATED STRUCTURES

Raptor conservationists frequently aid some birds of prey by putting artificial nest structures in appropriate habitats.

For example, on Martha's Vineyard, Massachusetts, dozens of Osprey nests are on the

Installing tall poles with platforms in habitats suitable for Ospreys is helping them to reoccupy and nest in parts of the northeastern United States. *Photo by Donald S. Heintzelman.*

island because people had paid to have a pole and platform placed on their property. Similar poles and platforms are used in other Osprey reintroduction programs elsewhere in eastern North America.

When Snail Kite nests in Florida are in danger of falling apart and the nestlings are lost, raptor conservationists put the defective nests in special baskets that assure the nestlings' survival.

American Kestrels, Barn Owls, Eastern Screech-Owls, Barred Owls, Boreal Owls, and Northern Saw-whet Owls also use nest boxes as substitutes for natural tree cavities. Such use maintains or increases their local breeding populations. Some representative American Kestrel nest box projects are established in Florida, Georgia, Michigan, Pennsylvania,

Tennessee, and Wisconsin. These boxes are useful components of conservation and management strategies for these birds.

Details about Hawk Mountain's "Adopt-a-Kestrel-Nestbox Program for Pennsylvania School Children" can be obtained by writing to the Adopt-a-Kestrel Nestbox Program, c/o Director of Research, Hawk Mountain Sanctuary, 1700 Hawk Mountain Road, Kempton, PA 19529; (610) 756–6961.

Great Horned Owls accept artificial nests including baskets (chicken wire cones with sticks and leaves) and rubber tires placed in tree crotches as a foundation for their nest. Great Gray Owls also accept open-topped nest boxes, nest baskets, and hand-built stick nests. Burrowing Owls will accept artificial burrows prepared for them.

A family of Great Horned Owls nesting in an old tire placed in the crotch of a tree.
Photo by Ron Austing.

RELOCATING NESTS AND BIRDS

Occasionally an Osprey nest needs to be relocated, as in Mattituck, New York, when a nest was built on top of a third-base lamp pole on a Little League baseball field. The nest was successfully relocated twice to a replacement pole and platform at a nearby pond and sanctuary. Relocating Osprey nests, however, is done only when absolutely necessary.

Because Great Horned Owls kill some Peregrine Falcons in reintroduction projects in rural areas, live trapping and relocation of some owls is sometimes also necessary.

CAPTIVE BREEDING AND REINTRODUCTION PROGRAMS

Osprey, Bald Eagle, and Peregrine Falcon reintroduction programs using hacking techniques (a controlled introduction of wild or captive-bred nestlings into the wild) are progressing well in restoring these raptors to satisfactory population levels in many states. For eagles and falcons, their wild populations have reached the point where Peregrine Falcons were removed from the federal list of endangered species, and the Bald Eagles may soon follow. In large measure, The Peregrine Fund at the World Center for Birds of Prey in Boise, Idaho, is responsible for these major raptor conservation successes.

One Mississippi Kite management program began in 1983 in western Tennessee. By 1998, a total of 280 nestlings were obtained in Kansas, with 266 hacked into the wild at three locations. One site was less than 93 miles southeast of an endangered kite population in southern Illinois.

On the other hand, Minnesota provides a good example of difficulties involved with respect to Burrowing Owl conservation and restoration. When 105 wild, preflight juvenile owls were hacked into the wild, none were seen again after departing the hack sites. Hence, raptor biologists do not recommend

continued Burrowing Owl reintroduction in Minnesota.

MONITORING POPULATIONS

Ornithologists and raptor biologists strongly advocate long-term population monitoring of all raptor species. Ospreys, Bald Eagles, Golden Eagles, Sharp-shinned Hawks, Northern Goshawks, Red-shouldered Hawks, Swainson's Hawks, Crested Caracaras, Gyrfalcons, Peregrine Falcons, Barn Owls, Snowy Owls, and Barred Owls are species for which population monitoring is especially appropriate.

MANAGING LOGGING

Ornithologists and raptor biologists recommend that logging in Minnesota be managed to avoid disturbances at active Osprey nests. Similarly, managing logging in Northern Hawk Owl and Great Gray Owl habitats can create open areas that provide the birds with long views to look for and capture prey on the ground. A few tees left in clear-cuts provide perches for feeding, resting, and vocalizing.

AVOIDING DISTURBANCES AT ROOSTS

Ornithologists strongly advocate protecting hawk and owls roosts from all types of disturbances. Species especially sensitive to disturbances at roosts are Long-eared and Short-eared Owls.

LOW-FLYING AIRCRAFT

Low-flying aircraft disturb nesting Swallow-tailed Kites and many other raptor species. Therefore, ornithologists and raptor biologists recommend that controls be placed on such flights to avoid disturbances or failures of nesting raptors.

SAFE TRAPPING METHODS

Usually when an occasional troublesome hawk or owl visits an area and must be removed for one reason or another, the bird can

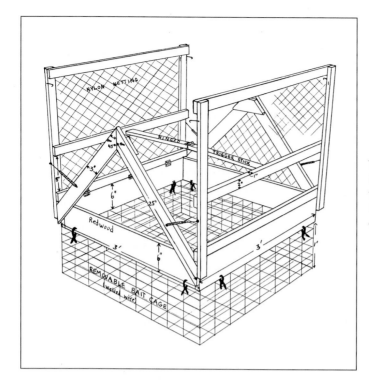

The redesigned, modified, and improved Swedish Goshawk trap developed by Heinz Meng. *From Meng (1971) in the* Journal of Wildlife Management.

be trapped alive in a safe and humane manner with a modified and improved version of the Swedish Goshawk trap. The new version is an important and humane advance in live-trap design.

VETERINARY CARE
AND REHABILITATION

During the past quarter century, much public interest has developed regarding veterinary care and rehabilitation of raptors that have gunshot wounds, broken bones, and other injuries. Currently, approximately 250 raptor rehabilitation centers are licensed in the United States, and similar facilities are in Canada. Most ornithologists advocate that wounded or injured hawks or owls be provided appropriate veterinary treatment and then taken to a nearby raptor rehabilitation facility for additional rehabilitation care. Birds that can't be fully rehabilitated and returned to the wild can remain useful in permanent captivity for educational purposes.

COMPENSATION FOR ECONOMIC LOSSES

In 1991, in Minnesota, a pair of Bald Eagles built and occupied a ground nest in an occupied agricultural field—a very unusual occurrence in the eastern United States. Two tenant farmers were required to stop farming the field, but they later received donations from two local conservation organizations and several Minnesota state agencies to compensate them for their economic losses.

PUBLIC OPINION POLLS

Public opinion in eastern Pennsylvania regarding protection for Great Horned Owls changed substantially during the twentieth century. By 1986 and 1988, most people approved of protection for these birds. Even among hunters, twenty-four (85.7 percent) wanted horned owls protected.

EDUCATIONAL PROGRAMS

Continuing public educational programs are a component of most raptor conservation efforts and can focus on all birds of prey and on their survival needs. These programs are usually both formal and informal and focus on all educational levels.

Bald Eagle Recovery from DDT Pollution

In New England, after DDT was banned, Bald Eagles established breeding territories in New Hampshire, at Quabbin Reservoir in Massachusetts, and along the Connecticut River at Northampton, Massachusetts. Between 1989 and 2001, a total of 115 Bald Eagles fledged in Massachusetts. Fifteen Bald Eagles also fledged in Connecticut since 1992.

New York has similar success in restoring Bald Eagles. From 1990 to 2001, an amazing 372 eaglets fledged. In Pennsylvania, eagle restoration produced 63 nests by 2002. The period with the largest population increases, 1997 to 1999, saw eagle nests all but double from 23 to 43 in that state.

Progress in Bald Eagle restoration also exists in New Jersey. More than 20 pairs were known in the state prior to the use of DDT. By 1970, however, only one active eagle nest remained—and its eggs failed to hatch. In 2002, however, 34 nesting eagle pairs were in New Jersey of which 28 pairs incubated eggs, producing 34 fledged eaglets. The state's overall Bald Eagle population is now secure despite two nest failures in 2002 (due to human disturbances), the inexperience of several breeding birds, and chemical contaminants in eggs in several nests.

In the Chesapeake Bay area, ornithologists celebrate a thriving Bald Eagle breeding population. By 2002, at least 600 nesting pairs were reported. Ornithologists now seek to protect undeveloped forested shorelines extending inland at least 4,593 feet, and for at least 4,462 feet of shoreline, as well as eagle roost trees, and to avoid indiscriminate log-

An immature Bald Eagle. These birds do not acquire their full adult plumage (white head and tail) until they are at least 5 years old. *Photo by Donald S. Heintzelman.*

ging or complete forest removal so Bald Eagle roost sites will not regulate Chesapeake Bay eagle populations.

Peregrine Falcon Recovery from DDT Pollution

Peregrine Falcon conservation and management efforts are focused on captive breeding, returning captive-bred young to natural habitats and nesting sites, and establishing self-perpetuating breeding in the wild. The Peregrine Fund (then based at Cornell University) and the Midwest Peregrine Falcon Restoration Project in Minnesota played essential roles in these efforts.

In Canada, releases of Peregrines south of the Arctic resulted in some 20 breeding pairs in Quebec and the Maritime Provinces, and some 30 pairs along the Labrador coast. The majority of Peregrines in the eastern United States, however, now breed in urban settings on ledges of tall buildings or bridges.

Reintroduced Peregrines also nest on Palisade Head, Minnesota, the state's largest cliff overlooking Lake Superior near Silver Bay. The cliff is extremely popular with climbers, but a sign informs visitors about nesting falcons, and no birds have been disturbed by rock climbers.

In northern New York and New England, however, some Peregrines now reoccupy some former nesting cliffs. These 42 cliff-nesting pairs represent 50 percent of the historical nesting population estimated for that part of eastern North America. Nevertheless, differences in habitats and the presence of Rock Doves and Mourning Doves in these habitats in parts of upstate New York and New England may become limiting factors regulating growth rates of future populations of cliff-nesting Peregrine Falcons in these areas.

In New Jersey, Peregrines were released into the wild from the Sedge Islands Wildlife Management Area in Barnegat Bay. By 2001, there were 17 nesting pairs. Five nested on bridges, and 12 on buildings and towers, with an overall production of 27 nestlings. One nest was discovered in an abandoned boat in a salt marsh. Nevertheless, New Jersey retains the Peregrine Falcon on its endangered species list.

In Pennsylvania, thirty-four historic Peregrine nest sites existed along the state's major rivers and tributaries (another ten sites did not produce young), but by the late 1950s the last nest was documented. In the 1970s, a Peregrine recovery program was begun along the Susquehanna River in Dauphin County. Additional Peregrine recovery involved eight major bridges in the Philadelphia area, some of which produced nestlings, and in 1999 a pair of Peregrine Falcons produced three young from the North Cross Valley Expressway bridge near Plains, Pennsylvania. During recent years, nest boxes or trays were also placed on selected tall buildings throughout the state—generally successfully. It is hoped the state's breeding Peregrines eventually will reoccupy their historic cliff nest sites.

Recovery of Peregrine Falcons in the southern Appalachians began with one hack site in Tennessee and another in North Carolina. Within 6 years, 34 young Peregrines were hacked in Great Smoky Mountains National Park and 21 in Cherokee National Forest. Two urban hack sites were also established in Chattanooga and Memphis. As of 1997, more than 350 Peregrines were hacked into the southern Appalachians. Additional hack sites were used in West Virginia, Virginia, North Carolina, South Carolina, and Georgia.

By 1997, two successful Peregrine Falcon nests were found in Tennessee—one cliff site in Great Smoky Mountains National Park (possibly the ledge last used by these falcons in 1942), and the second site on a bridge in Chattanooga. Peregrines also nested again in North Carolina, South Carolina, West Virginia, Virginia's mountains, Georgia, and Kentucky.

Peregrine Falcon recovery programs now have reached the point where this falcon was removed from the federal list of endangered species. Nevertheless, continued law enforcement and public education are needed to prevent illegal shooting of Peregrines.

Raptor Conservation and Ecotourism

Because raptors are large, charismatic birds, they have exceptional value in wildlife-friendly recreational activities such as raptor ecotourism—in other words, birders traveling to various places to see and photograph birds of prey. But as more and more wildlife habitat is lost because of badly regulated, or unregulated, land use in eastern North America, the future of raptor ecotourism cannot be di-

Birds of prey, such as this adult male Northern Harrier, are charismatic birds with exceptional ecotourism value. *Photo by Ron Austing.*

vorced from creative preservation methods of wildlife habitat and open space.

Fortunately, the linkage between hawk watching as a form of ecotourism and conservation is a growing component of land-use planning in some locations. Birders regularly visit Bake Oven Knob and Hawk Mountain, Pennsylvania, and Cape May Point, New Jersey, as well as many other autumn raptor migration watch sites to see and photograph raptors. The money people spend adds to some rural economies—several million dollars annually in the Hawk Mountain area alone. It is vital that local and other government and business officials understand this benefit thoroughly, and that they leverage ecotourism dollars that flow into local economies into improved land-use planning to assure permanent protection of important raptor breeding, migration, stopover, and wintering habitats.

Special Refuges and Natural Areas

In some instances, federal or state governments in the United States (federal or provincial governments in Canada) are responsible for the purchase of raptor migration, stopover, breeding, and wintering areas, but some private conservation organizations and/or private individuals also acquire these sites. Two examples are the Hawk Mountain Sanctuary and the Wildlife Information Center's Lehigh Gap Restoration Project in Pennsylvania.

In 2002, Friends of Animals established a National Registry and Network of Private Raptor Refuges that encourages private individuals in the United States and Canada to designate suitable land they own (usually 5 acres or more) as raptor refuges (all wildlife is protected on these areas), then register them with this nonprofit organization. Several refuges in Minnesota, Pennsylvania, and Oregon are now registered in this long-term project.

MIGRATION AREAS

Many important hawk migration watch sites in the United States and Canada are in private or public ownership. Hawk Mountain Sanctuary, a privately owned site in southeastern Pennsylvania, was the first refuge for birds of prey in the world. The Wildlife Information Center's Lehigh Gap Restoration Project near Slatington, Pennsylvania, established in 2002, is another example, as is Waggoner's Gap on the Kittatinny Ridge near Carlisle, Pennsylvania, which was recently obtained by Audubon PA.

Indeed, most former hawk shooting sites on the Kittatinny Ridge in Pennsylvania are popular hawk migration watch sites controlled by private, nonprofit, or governmental ownership. The Pennsylvania Game Commission also designated the entire length of the Kittatinny Ridge in southeastern Pennsylvania as the Kittatinny Ridge Birds of Prey Natural Area. The area runs from the Delaware Water Gap National Recreation Area southwest to Waggoner's Gap just north of Carlisle. Similarly, hawk migration watch sites on the Lehigh County section of the ridge were designated the Lehigh County Raptor Migration Area by a resolution issued by the first Lehigh County executive. Thus, the exceptional scientific and conservation-education significance of many of Pennsylvania's most important hawk-migration watch sites are recognized by state and county governments.

Some hawk migration watch sites in other states are also protected by private or governmental ownership. In Maine, the summit of Mount Cadillac in Acadia National Park is federally owned, and in Massachusetts Mount Tom State Reservation and Mount Wachusset State Reservation are in state ownership. In Connecticut, the National Audubon Society owns and operates the Audubon Center of Greenwich (an important autumn raptor migration site). In New York State the important watch site at Braddock Bay is in state ownership, while Derby Hill near Mexico, New York, is owned by a local Audubon Society. In New Jersey, the Montclair Hawk Lookout Sanctuary is owned by the New Jersey Audubon Society, while Cape May Point is a state park.

South of New Jersey, Washington Monument State Park in Maryland is in state ownership. In Virginia, a number of important watch sites are within the Blue Ridge Parkway (U.S. National Park Service). On the eastern shore of Virginia, Kiptopeke State Park is another government-protected autumn migration watch site. In the Florida Keys, a raptor research and education program in Curry Hammock State Park is located in the middle Keys.

Elsewhere, in Minnesota, the Hawk Ridge Nature Reserve is operated by the Duluth Audubon Society. It is one of the most important raptor migration watch sites in the Great Lakes region.

In Canada, the Holiday Beach Conservation Area, Ontario, is a government-owned raptor migration watch site. Formerly a provincial park, the site is now owned and managed by the Essex Region Conservation Authority (ERCA) and provides the nonprofit Holiday Beach Migration Observatory with a "hawk tower" from which autumn raptor migration observations and counts are made.

STOPOVER AREAS

A few raptor migration stopover areas are protected as migration watch sites, such as Cape May Point, New Jersey, and the Virginia Coast Reserve in Virginia owned by The Nature Conservancy. But little attention has been devoted to identification of other raptor stopover areas—or the features that make them important. Hence, there is still a need to identify, preserve, and protect these areas as important wildlife sites. This aspect of raptor conservation offers many opportunities to raptor biologists, conservationists, and land preservation organizations.

NESTING AREAS

Several important raptor nesting areas are also protected as refuges for birds of prey. In

New Jersey, for example, the Sedge Islands Wildlife Management Area near Island Beach State Park is a major Osprey nesting refuge. In Pennsylvania, the Middle Creek Wildlife Management Area owned by the Pennsylvania Game Commission protects a Bald Eagle nesting site. In the Great Lakes region, some federally protected Bald Eagle nesting areas are located in Superior National Forest and Boundary Waters Canoe Area Wilderness, Chippewa National Forest, and Tamarac National Wildlife Refuge.

WINTERING AREAS

A variety of wintering areas, many used by Bald Eagles, are established as special refuges for raptors. In Wisconsin, for instance, a group of individuals forming the Eagle Valley

Environmentalists, Inc., own several sites used by Bald Eagles during winter.

The Kittatinny Raptor Corridor Project

In 1992, a pioneering, long-term raptor conservation, education, recreation, and research program called The Kittatinny Raptor Corridor Project was launched by the Wildlife Information Center, Inc., in Slatington, Pennsylvania. It includes the famous Kittatinny Ridge raptor migration flight line, plus land extending outward for about 5 miles from the north and south bases of the ridge. Collectively, these components are called the Kittatinny Raptor Corridor, a 256 mile-long geographic feature that begins at Rosendale, New York, extends across part of northwestern

A rural section of the Kittatinny Raptor Corridor in Heidelberg Township, Lehigh County, Pennsylvania. The left side of the water gap on the Kittatinny Ridge in the distance is the wildlife sanctuary and headquarters of the Wildlife Information Center, Inc. *Photo by Donald S. Heintzelman.*

New Jersey, crosses into Pennsylvania at Delaware Water Gap, and continues nearly to the Maryland border. Land-use planning and open space preservation are major concerns of that project.

Among significant achievements of this project thus far are the purchase of 760 acres of the Kittatinny Ridge at Lehigh Gap and establishment of the long-term Lehigh Gap Restoration Project, continuation of the annual Bake Oven Knob Hawk Watch, publication and distribution of three installments of *The Kittatinny Raptor Corridor Educational Handbook,* establishment of numerous databases pertaining to Bake Oven Knob and other parts of the raptor corridor, preparation of a slide program about The Kittatinny Raptor Corridor Project for use at public events and meetings, production of an educational videotape titled "Middle School Hawk Watch-

ing" for use in local schools, hosting of an annual October "Hawk Fest," and creation of a landscape rephotography program for the raptor corridor.

In 2002, ten years after The Kittatinny Raptor Corridor Project was launched by the Wildlife Information Center, Inc., Audubon Pennsylvania unabashedly began promoting a similar version of The Kittatinny Raptor Corridor Project, claiming it was the first such effort and unique.

Selected Raptor Conservation Organizations

A large number of raptor conservation and rehabilitation organizations exist in eastern North America, each having its own unique focus and goals. The following are examples of some of these organizations. A more extensive

Another rural section of the Kittatinny Raptor Corridor in Heidelberg Township, Lehigh County, Pennsylvania. The Bake Oven Knob raptor migration watch site is the peak on the Kittatinny Ridge in the distance. *Photo by Donald S. Heintzelman.*

list is provided on the Website www.Riteinthe Rain.com/hawk.html.

BAKE OVEN KNOB /
WILDLIFE INFORMATION CENTER, INC.

The Wildlife Information Center, Inc., in Slatington, Pennsylvania, is a member-supported nonprofit organization involved in several major raptor conservation, education, and research programs. The oldest is the Bake Oven Knob hawk count in the autumn, begun in 1961 on a annual basis, and since 1998 continued by the center. In 1987, the center organized and hosted a national raptor conference organized around the theme of raptors and public education. Famous field-guide author Roger Tory Peterson was the keynote speaker. The center's long-term Kittatinny Raptor Corridor Project, launched in 1992, has already been discussed. In 2002, the center began its long-term Lehigh Gap Restoration Project. A major research library with more than 2,000 books, several hundred journals, and a vertical file containing more than 2,600 wildlife and conservation file folders is also part of the center. A number of other wildlife education and research programs take place at the Wildlife Information Center as well.

BRADDOCK BAY RAPTOR RESEARCH

This organization, established in 1985, was founded on the basis of earlier hawk migration research—especially by Laura and Neil Moon—and is a major spring raptor migration watch site. It is located near Rochester, New York, on the southern shoreline of Lake Ontario. In addition to counting migrating hawks and banding hawks and owls, it has educational programs that improve the public's knowledge and understanding of raptors. In late April, an annual Bird of Prey Week is held as part of the organization's educational program.

CAPE MAY BIRD OBSERVATORY

The Cape May Bird Observatory is a nonprofit organization associated with the New Jersey Aududon Society. One of its major responsibilities—since 1976, when annual hawk counting started at Cape May Point—is to coordinate the annual autumn raptor migration counts at the Point. The banding of migrant raptors and various educational activities, are also part of the programs at the observatory.

DERBY HILL BIRD OBSERVATORY

The Derby Hill Bird Observatory, located at the southeast corner of Lake Ontario 4 miles north of Mexico, New York, is owned by the Onondaga Audubon Society. Although the observatory is known primarily as one of the best spring raptor migration watch sites in eastern North America, all bird species are studied there. Since 1978, full-time counts of migrating hawks have been conducted at this location.

HAWK MIGRATION ASSOCIATION
OF NORTH AMERICA

Founded in 1974, the Hawk Migration Association of North America (HMANA) is a nonprofit organization whose primary goal is to study hawk migrations throughout North America. It also organizes occasional conferences and distributes several publications each year. In 2000, HMANA launched an ambitious three-part effort to use computers in data collection, analysis, and storage.

HAWK MOUNTAIN
SANCTUARY ASSOCIATION

Hawk Mountain Sanctuary near Kempton, Pennsylvania, was established in 1934 as a member-supported, nonprofit organization and the world's first refuge for birds of prey. Hawk Mountain's primary research efforts are its annual autumn raptor migration counts begun in 1934, now making up the world's oldest raptor migration database. The organization's primary conservation achievement is ownership and management of their land containing more than 2300 acres of central Appalachian forest, a small mountain wetland, a small section of the Little Schuylkill River, and 34 acres of upland fields and coniferous trees at its Acopian Center for Conservation Learning. The organization runs an international internship program and hosts visiting scientists at the Acopian Center. Hawk Mountain publishes a newsletter twice each year, and occasionally publishes books or booklets.

The story of the founding and formative years of Hawk Mountain is told vividly in Maurice Broun's classic *Hawks Aloft: The Story of Hawk Mountain,* one of the outstanding chapters in American wildlife conservation history.

HAWK WATCH INTERNATIONAL
(FLORIDA PROGRAM)

The primary focus of Hawk Watch International, a nonprofit organization, is mainly western North America, but it has one program operating in the Florida Keys. On Grassy Key in Curry Hammock State Park, hawk watchers have organized a long-term autumn raptor migration monitoring station with particular focus on Peregrine Falcons. The fact that this important watch site is located in a state park assures its long-term protection.

THE PEREGRINE FUND AND THE
WORLD CENTER FOR BIRDS OF PREY

The Peregrine Fund, currently based at the World Center for Birds of Prey in Boise, Idaho, is most famous for its pioneering captive breeding of Peregrine Falcons and release of these birds into their former eastern habitats. Various other rare raptors are also bred in captivity by this organization at its Idaho facility or elsewhere in the world. The Peregrine

Fund is involved with endangered raptor conservation activities worldwide. The organization maintains a major ornithological research library containing some seven thousand books, and thousands of reprints, at its Idaho facilities.

THE CANADIAN PEREGRINE FUND

Established in 1997, The Canadian Peregrine Fund is a charity in Canada whose primary purpose is the recovery of the Peregrine Falcon in Ontario and elsewhere in Canada and parts of the eastern United States. The organization operates "Falcon Watch Centres" from which tens of thousands of people can observe Peregrines from safe distances at various Ontario reintroduction sites. Research involving satellite tracking of Peregrines is used by ornithologists from this organization. The fund uses a variety of educational programs to inform students and the general public about Peregrine Falcons, their conservation status, and how reintroduction programs are restoring them into parts of Canada. A newsletter, *Talon Tales,* provides members with the latest progress in Peregrine Falcon conservation, education, and research programs.

THE RAPTOR CENTER
(UNIVERSITY OF MINNESOTA)

The Raptor Center is a pioneering raptor rehabilitation organization based at the College of Veterinary Medicine at the University of Minnesota. Because it is a teaching institution, both formal and informal educational programs are major efforts here. Research into raptor rehabilitation and, until recently, tracking migrating Ospreys and Swainson's Hawks by satellite have been included in its imaginative research programs.

RAPTOR RESEARCH FOUNDATION

The Raptor Research Foundation is a nonprofit organization dedicated to the scientific study of birds of prey. It annually organizes conferences that are attended by some of the world's leading raptor researchers as well as other raptor enthusiasts. It publishes the *Journal of Raptor Research,* a major scientific publication containing cutting edge raptor research papers and short notes.

THE RAPTOR TRUST

The Raptor Trust, founded in 1982, is located in Millington, New Jersey, and is one of the nation's oldest and largest raptor rehabilitation centers. It is "dedicated to the preservation and well-being of birds of prey." The Trust maintains a large, well-equipped facility, with seventy outdoor aviaries and cages providing permanent homes for some one hundred resident eagles, hawks, and owls representing more than twenty species.

During the period 1982 through 1999, some 40,000 injured and orphaned wild birds were received and treated at The Raptor Trust. Approximately one-half of these patients were later returned to the wild. Injured or sick birds are given appropriate medical and rehabilitative care with the goal of returning as many as possible back into the wild. Care is given so that the birds will not become dependent on people.

The Raptor Trust offers on-site and outreach educational programs pertaining to raptors for schools, scouts, and similar organizations. Experienced teachers present the programs, which include at least one live raptor (a nonreleasable bird held in permanent captivity at the Trust for educational purposes). The public is permitted to visit the Trust's facilities, which include an air-conditioned meeting room and library. A variety of raptor-related publications are also issued by the organization, including a book about New Jersey's owls.

WHITEFISH POINT BIRD OBSERVATORY

The Whitefish Point Bird Observatory is located in the Upper Peninsula at the northeastern tip of Michigan. It is a major site for counting spring raptor migrations. The American Bird Conservancy designated the site a Globally Important Bird Area. The observatory is affiliated with the Michigan Audubon Society, though its financial support comes from non-Audubon sources.

5

CITIZEN SCIENTISTS

"Citizen science" means using the skills and volunteer time of qualified amateur ornithologists to collect important, sometimes widespread, data, often by using the computer and Internet. This approach is increasingly important as raptor research programs are launched by nonprofit organizations and government agencies. However, citizen science is not new, and it has played an important part throughout the twentieth century.

Nevertheless, authentic citizen scientists are rare because few people, regardless of their interest in raptors, have the time necessary to study and achieve the level of competence required by the current professional standards of scientific methodology. Hence, it may be better to refer to volunteers as competent naturalists who provide data used by professional ornithologists and other scientists.

Life Histories of
North American Birds

One of the remarkable twentieth-century examples of a citizen scientist was a New England textile manufacturer and amateur ornithologist named Arthur Cleveland Bent (1866–1954). Bent is forever linked with his 23-volume *Life Histories of North American Birds* published by the Smithsonian Institution. Bent gathered an enormous amount of information from amateur and professional ornithologists throughout North America, combined the information with his data, then wrote the most comprehensive life history studies of North American birds available at the time. Adding substantial charm to his "life histories" was his very readable literary style.

Two volumes, published in 1937 and 1938, titled *Life Histories of North American Birds of Prey,* are of particular interest to hawk and owl watchers. Although somewhat dated, they remain worthwhile references and a starting point when seeking information about raptors.

Bald Eagle Banding

Canadian banker Charles L. Broley (?–1959) was another example of a citizen scientist who made major contributions to ornithology. Retired at age sixty, Broley traveled each winter to Florida's west coast, where he began the task of climbing to Bald Eagle nests in tall trees to band young eaglets. By the time he died in 1959, he banded more than 1,200 eaglets in Florida—a remarkable number that produced enough recoveries to define the annual northeastward postbreeding dispersal of Florida's eagles to northeastern North America, and their return to Florida during early autumn to begin their next breeding season.

In 1947, Broley published a landmark paper, "Migration and Nesting of Florida Bald Eagles." For the first time, ornithologists learned where Bald Eagles seen during autumn along Pennsylvania's famous Kittatinny Ridge were heading, where they were coming from, and where their breeding grounds are located. A new chapter in Bald Eagle biology and conservation had been written.

With so much experience gained while working with Florida's nesting eagles, Broley was the first person to fully realize that Bald Eagles were in trouble. He correctly suspected that the widespread, indiscriminate post–World War II use of DDT was responsible for the decline in the number of Bald Eagles being hatched. Charles Broley and others sounded the environmental alarm bell that Rachel Carson brilliantly amplified nationwide in 1962 in *Silent Spring*.

American Kestrel Nest Box Projects

Several examples of citizen science involve American Kestrel research and conservation in eastern North America, focusing on nest boxes. One is the American Kestrel nest box trail organized by Hawk Mountain Sanctuary, which is largely maintained by Hawk Mountain volunteers.

Hawk Migration Studies

Because most hawks are large and spectacular birds, it is not surprising that some citizen scientists find these birds irresistible and make them the subject of serious scientific studies— studies that enhance our understanding and knowledge of these birds. There are probably more volunteer citizen scientists involved in hawk migration studies than any other aspect of raptor biology.

An adult Broad-winged Hawk in overhead flight. Some eight hundred enthusiastic citizen scientists from the Hawk Migration Association of North America (HMANA) eagerly look forward to seeing thousands of these birds every year. *Photo by Donald S. Heintzelman.*

HAWK MIGRATION ASSOCIATION OF NORTH AMERICA

Another example of the role of citizen scientists working on raptor projects is the Hawk Migration Association of North America (HMANA), which recruits some eight hundred volunteer hawk watchers (mostly amateurs but also some professional ornithologists) each autumn (a lesser extent in spring) to make raptor migration observations and counts at hundreds of watch sites throughout the United States and Canada. Collectively, tens of thousands of hours of coverage are logged at these watch sites. Some of the data are posted on the Cornell Laboratory of Ornithology's Website, BirdSource, with the actual data sheets used at the watch sites deposited in an archive for long-term preservation. More recently, HMANA launched Raptors Online in the form of a project called HAWKCOUNT, linked to the http://hawkcount.org Website. The goal of this project is to have hawk watchers post their daily raptor counts gathered at migration watch sites directly into the HAWKCOUNT database, thereby eliminating paper records. HMANA also publishes a journal containing each season's data and articles pertaining to various aspects of hawk migration study.

RED-TAILED HAWK
MIGRATION STUDY

In 2000, the Wildlife Information Center, Inc., in association with the Little Gap Raptor Research Group, began a cooperative citizen science project involving Red-tailed Hawk migratory movements. Red-tails are captured by bird banders at Little Gap along the Kittatinny Ridge in eastern Pennsylvania. The hawks are then banded with leg bands, have certain secondary (wing) feathers marked (dyed) with pink, yellow, or green colors, then released. By the end of the 2002 autumn raptor migration season, hawk watchers and birders reported sightings of forty-three of the marked hawks distributed from Tennessee to Quebec, and from the Atlantic Coast to the inland raptor migration ridges.

Birders and hawk watchers spotting one of these color-marked hawks should secure the following information: name, address, and telephone number of the observer, date of sighting, time of day, location were the sighting was made (state, county, and specific location), age of bird (adult or immature), dye color, and behavior of the hawk when it was observed. Mail this information to the Wildlife Information Center, Inc., PO Box 198, Slatington, PA 18080 USA, or provide it via computer by accessing their Website at www.wildlifeinfo.org.

Roadside Raptor Surveys

MINNESOTA SURVEYS

During the spring of 2000, a pilot volunteer-based roadside raptor survey in three northern Minnesota counties (Carlton, Itasca, and St. Louis) was initiated by the Nongame Wildlife Program of the Minnesota Department of Natural Resources and the Natural Resources Research Institute of the University of Minnesota, Duluth. Its goal was to evaluate the feasibility and logistical complexity of engaging in a large-scale, volunteer (citizen science) roadside raptor survey program in Minnesota.

Diurnal raptors reported in one or more of the three counties included Bald Eagle, Northern Harrier, Sharp-shinned Hawk, Cooper's Hawks, Red-shouldered Hawk, Red-tailed Hawk, Rough-legged Hawk, and American Kestrel. Owls reported in one or more of the counties included Great Horned Owl, Barred Owl, Great Gray Owl, and Northern Saw-whet Owl.

In 2001 and 2002, similar roadside raptor surveys were again conducted in Minnesota. According to the Nongame Specialist, Minnesota Department of Natural Resources, an owl invasion occurred during the autumn and winter of 2001. Many starving Boreal Owls, numerous dead and living Great Gray Owls, and a few Northern Hawk Owls were reported or taken to the Minnesota Department of Natural Resources offices in Grand Rapids.

PENNSYLVANIA SURVEYS

In January and February 2001, a birder organized a series of experimental roadside raptor surveys throughout Pennsylvania. Similar surveys were done in 2002 and 2003, and a series of winter raptor survey guidelines were also published.

The first effort included more than sixty routes covered by citizen science birders in forty-five of the state's sixty-seven counties. Overall, more than 250 hours were expended by volunteers who covered 4,500 miles of roads looking for raptors.

Species typical of open-country habitats—Northern Harriers, Red-tailed Hawks, Rough-legged Hawks, and American Kestrels—were the birds seen in largest numbers. Future surveys will focus on determining midwinter Red-tailed Hawk and American Kestrel population trends, ages and/or sexes of Northern Harriers and American Kestrels, the magnitude of Rough-legged Hawk movements into Pennsylvania, and trends of numbers of vultures wintering within the state and their northern distribution. Shrike invasions will also be documented and miscellaneous owl reports will be issued.

Birds in Forested Landscapes

An important new cooperative research project utilizing citizen science resources, named Birds in Forested Landscapes (BFL), is in operation between the Cornell Laboratory of Ornithology and the U.S. Forest Service. This project studies the habitat requirements of Sharp-shinned Hawks, Cooper's Hawks, and several species of forest thrushes. Several hundred citizen scientist participants collected data on the number of thrushes breeding in forest patches of varying sizes—many sites in public forests owned by the U.S. Forest Service. To help coordinate this increasingly large citizen science project nationwide, a professional wildlife biologist was appointed as USFS Citizen Science Coordinator who works with many persons and birding organizations, universities, professional conservationists, and others.

Owl Monitoring Projects

Because most owls are nocturnal, they present vastly more difficult problems when ornithologists and raptor biologists attempt to monitor their presence and population status. Nevertheless, citizen science is involved with these birds, and efforts are being made in various locations in eastern North America.

CHRISTMAS BIRD COUNTS AND OWLS

Owls have long been reported on Christmas Bird Counts (CBCs)—a nationwide bird survey conducted at hundreds of sites ("count circles") for a one-day period, around the Christmas holidays, by birders, with the results published in *American Birds*.

OWL MONITORING PROTOCOL

A Nocturnal Owl Monitoring Protocol is now established by owl researchers to assure that data are comparable regardless of where they are collected in the United States and Canada. Technical details can be secured from Lisa Takats, 7th floor, O. S. Longman Building, 6909–115 Street, Edmonton, Alberta T6H 4P2, Canada. Her telephone number is (780) 422-9536, and her E-mail address is lisa.takats @env.gov.ab.ca.

Role of Volunteers in Raptor Conservation

The role of skilled volunteers in raptor and other wildlife conservation is one of increasing importance to professional ornithologists and raptor biologists, who routinely are unable to gather all the field data necessary for research and conservation efforts and programs. At Hawk Mountain Sanctuary, the use of skilled volunteers is essential to the effective operation of the sanctuary. Among tasks to which volunteers are assigned are assisting at the visitor reception center, entrance gate, parking lot, and on the raptor migration lookouts. They also present public education programs, gather field data and enter the information into computer databases, maintain the grounds and buildings, engage in clerical work, and assist with newsletter mailings. Collectively, volunteers log more than 12,000 hours per year, a service equal to six full-time paid employees.

Many other raptor and other wildlife conservation organizations make similar uses of volunteers with equal success—and a saving of limited operational funds. The key to these successes is appropriate supervision, screening, and selection of motivated volunteers, special training when necessary, and innovative ways of expressing appreciation for the hard work and valuable contributions.

6

RECREATIONAL
RAPTOR WATCHING

Why do people enjoy watching raptors? Certainly the beauty and power of these birds is the answer in many cases. One raptor enthusiast observed hundreds of elegant Swallow-tailed Kites swooping overhead and was held so spellbound he could recall no other comparable ornithological experience. Other hawk watchers recall similar enthralling experiences involving raptors to be equally formative in their lifelong interest in and passion for birds of prey. Much the same applies to owl watchers. Indeed, both hawks and owls truly are charismatic creatures!

This chapter provides an overview of many recreational raptor-watching activities in eastern North America.

Bald Eagle Watching

In addition to observing migrating Bald Eagles, it is also possible to watch eagles during winter and summer—especially the former—at selected locations in eastern North America.

WINTER BALD EAGLE WATCHING AREAS

There are some excellent winter areas where Bald Eagles concentrate, thereby providing eagle watchers with opportunities to see and sometimes photograph these birds. The following locations are representative of these areas.

- The mouth and lower reaches of the Connecticut River, via eagle watching boat trips departing from Essex, Connecticut, during the annual Connecticut River Eagle Festival organized each February by the Connecticut Audubon Society.

- The Hudson River from Kingston to Croton, New York, where Bald Eagles winter because of open water and availability of fish due to power plant discharges. Suitable eagle watching sites include Norrie Point State Park, Riverfront Park in Peekskill, and the Verplank waterfront.

- The upper Delaware River valley in Sullivan County, New York, including (1) Rondout Reservoir, Grahamsville, (2) the Rio Reservoir and Mongaup Falls Reservoir Observation Hut, Forestburgh, (3) along the Delaware River and Route 97 from Barryville and Minisink Ford to Callicoon, and (4) the Basha Kill Wildlife Management Area, Wurtsboro.

- The lower Susquehanna River valley in Pennsylvania and Maryland between Norman Wood Bridge to below the Conowingo Dam, where Bald Eagles and some Golden Eagles congregate.

- Many areas near locks along the upper Mississippi River, such as the National Eagle Center at Wabasha, Minnesota, and Cassville, Wisconsin.

- Along the Wisconsin River, where open water occurs below the Prairie du Sac Dam, such as the Ferry Bluff Eagle Council Overlook in Sauk City/Prairie du Sac, Wisconsin, during January at the annual Bald Eagle Watching Days.
- At the meeting of the Mississippi and Rock Rivers, where annual Bald Eagle Appreciation Days are held in Rock Island, Illinois.
- Along the Illinois River at Pere Marquette State Park near Grafton, Illinois.

SUMMER BALD EAGLE WATCHING AREAS

During summer, it is also possible to observe nesting Bald Eagles, although care must always be used not to cause disturbances near nests. Some suitable locations include the following:

- Lakes and shorelines of Superior National Forest and Boundary Waters Canoe Area Wilderness, Grand Marais, Minnesota.
- Larger lakes and shorelines in Chippewa National Forest near Cass Lake, Minnesota.
- Throughout the Tamarac National Wildlife Refuge near Rochert, Minnesota.
- The Taylor's Falls-to-Stillwater section of St. Croix National Scenic Riverway near St. Croix, Wisconsin.

Osprey Nesting Cruises

In Lake Barkley State Park, near Cadiz, Kentucky, Osprey nesting cruises offer the public opportunities to see these state-endangered birds as they feed nestlings in active nests in the Kentucky part of Lake Barkley. Each cruise lasts for one and one-half hours and includes views of the Lake Barkley shoreline. Cruises depart from the Barkley Lodge 7 miles west of Cadiz, Kentucky. The public can also participate in Osprey nesting surveys in early July. Binoculars are provided to persons needing them.

Hawk Watching from Migration Watch Sites

Recreational hawk watching in North America was born in 1934 at Hawk Mountain in Pennsylvania. By the end of the twentieth century, approximately two thousand raptor migration watch sites were cataloged in North and Central America and the West Indies.

Today, recreational hawk watching has never been more popular. Indeed, sometimes the hawk-watching rewards are very impressive. For example, at the Hawk Ridge Nature Reserve in Duluth, Minnesota, one hawk watcher saw 33,636 hawks one September 17th, including 29 Bald Eagles, 172 Northern Harriers, 1,597 Sharp-shinned Hawks, 31,324 Broad-winged Hawks, plus lesser numbers of several other species, including two Swainson's Hawks. It's those "red letter days" that keep hawk watchers confirmed addicts, and are magnets for attracting new enthusiasts.

Hawk watchers regularly use Goat Peak in Mount Tom State Reservation near Springfield, Massachusetts, for observations. Along coastal Connecticut, at New Haven, Lighthouse Point Park is another popular watch site. In New York State, an outstanding spring watch site, Derby Hill, is located along the southern shoreline of Lake Ontario near the town of Mexico. Another equally important spring watch site in New York along Lake Ontario is Braddock Bay near Rochester. Hook Mountain, another autumn New York site, is located just north of Nyack overlooking the Hudson River.

New Jersey has several excellent autumn hawk migration watch sites. The one with the largest flights is Cape May Point at the extreme southern tip of the state. Thousands of migrating birds, including songbirds and raptors, are seen there on favorable days (especially when northwest winds occur).

The North Lookout at Hawk Mountain Sanctuary in eastern Pennsylvania. This is the most famous raptor migration watch site in North America. *Photo by Donald S. Heintzelman.*

Pennsylvania has several major raptor migration watch sites. Some are on the famous Kittatinny Ridge. Hawk Mountain is the most famous, but Bake Oven Knob, upridge from Hawk Mountain, is another outstanding site.

Along the northern and western shorelines of the Great Lakes one finds additional excellent autumn hawk migration watch sites. One of the best, Hawk Ridge Nature Reserve, is located in Duluth, Minnesota. In southwestern Ontario, the Holiday Beach Migration Observatory is another excellent site, as are Hawk Cliff and Point Pelee in Ontario, and Lake Erie Metropark in Michigan near Detroit.

In Florida, Grassy Key in Curry Hammock State Park is another important autumn raptor migration watch site. Peregrine Falcons are especially notable attractions here.

Roadside Raptor Watching

Roadside raptor watching is also recreational hawk watching. Hawk watchers slowly drive along rural roads with little traffic looking for Northern Harriers, Red-tailed Hawks, American Kestrels, and other species perched on trees, utility poles, or wires, or flying. Raptor watching can also be done along Interstate or other high-speed highways, but *safe driving* must remain the primary concern. Sometimes Red-tailed Hawks and American Kestrels perch on light supports at exit ramps, trees, and other structures.

Raptor Watching at Public and Private Wildlife Refuges

National and private wildlife refuges, and state wildlife management areas such as Middle Creek in Pennsylvania, sometimes allow birders to see and occasionally photograph Bald Eagles and other raptors. I have also seen Ospreys, Bald Eagles, Northern Harriers, Golden Eagles, a Gyrfalcon, and Peregrine Falcons on the 40,000 acres forming the Brigantine Division of the Edwin B. Forsythe National Wildlife Refuge near Oceanville, New Jersey.

Owl Prowls

Owls are much less well known to birders, let alone other folks, than are hawks, eagles, and falcons. That's because owls are nocturnal animals. Hence, finding and seeing them differs significantly from watching raptors during daylight hours. The following owl-watching guidelines are based on recommendations from Canadian owl watchers and information provided in my *Guide to Owl Watching in North America.*

- The safety and welfare of owls MUST be the highest priority during owl prowls.
- Plan owl prowls for two hours after dark, or an hour before sunrise.
- Many owls are especially active on moonlit nights.
- *Never play owl vocalization recordings for extended periods of time* at any location to avoid destroying or disrupting owl nesting activities. Especially avoid using recordings in birding areas that are very heavily used.
- If possible, limit participants on an owl prowl to two or three people.
- Select owl prowl areas as far away as possible from houses and barking dogs.
- Keep written records of the dates, locations, owl species, and numbers of all owls that are encountered. This information is of value to ornithologists.
- If police stop and ask what you are doing, explain your seemingly strange activities. Have available a basic owl reference such as my *Guide to Owl Watching in North America* to verify your explanation. However, if police insist you move, do so—but contact the local chief of police the next day and clear the record regarding future owl prowls.

Other sources of assistance to help people learn how to locate, hear, and see owls may be available from local bird clubs or Audubon chapters. Sometimes they schedule their own owl-watching field trips.

WHAT SPECIES TO EXPECT ON AN OWL PROWL

The Eastern Screech-Owl is one of the owls most likely to be encountered on an owl

An Eastern Screech-Owl. These birds are among our most common owls. *Photo by Donald S. Heintzelman.*

prowl, and is often the first owl heard and observed by birders.

In December and January, Great Horned Owls are often heard calling from woodland. These large and powerful owls are usually the first to begin nesting each year, so an early winter owl prowl is likely to reveal their presence by listening for their vocalizations. Long-eared or Short-eared Owls may be seen on other owl prowls with a knowledgeable leader who knows about a roost site if the birds are not approached closely, loudly, or rapidly. Do *not* attempt to flush roosting owls to see them in flight!

During years when Snowy Owls, Northern Hawk Owls and Boreal Owls, and, rarely, huge Great Gray Owls engage in southward movements, they are seen in places like northern Minnesota and southern Ontario. Farther south, Snowy Owls appear on open spaces at some airports and along undeveloped Atlantic coastal areas.

RECORD OWL PROWLS

Several exceptionally successful owl prowls in eastern North America produced sightings of record numbers of birds. The one that produced sightings of the largest number of owl species—ten in a single day—occurred on December 30, 1995 in southern Ontario, Canada. Only the Barn Owl was missing from the list. Another outstanding owl prowl occurred on December 8, 1956, in the New York City area, when several birders observed during one 24-hour period the eight owl species that occur regularly in the northeastern United States.

Other Types
of Owl Watching

Other owl watching activities also occur in eastern North America. Two examples are discussed here.

BOREAL OWL WATCHING IN QUEBEC

One birder, age eighty, from California may be the North American champion when it comes to making an extraordinary effort to see a Boreal Owl. She flew from California in February to Baie-Comeau in southeastern Quebec on the north shore of the St. Lawrence River, then rode with a guide on a snowmobile into a dense forest in subfreezing temperatures at night to successfully see, and even *feed,* one of the owls with a live mouse held out in her hand! Check off number 703 on her life list!

WATCHING A BOREAL OWL
AT A MINNESOTA NATURE CENTER

On January 16, 1997, at Springbrook Nature Center in Fridley, Minnesota, a live Boreal Owl appeared unexpectedly and was the star attraction for birders across the United States.

The owl seemed indifferent, and undisturbed, even when people stood only 10 feet away. The bird remained for 66 days during which hundreds of thrilled birders individually, and in groups, arrived daily to observe the rare bird—a species most visitors had never seen. The nature center staff fed the owl one live mouse daily—conducting fifty-five public owl feeding programs attended by 1,240 fascinated people. They represented sixty Minnesota cities, twenty-five states, four foreign countries, and ranged in age from infants to people ninety-eight years old.

Keeping Written Records
of Raptor Observations

Enjoyable as it is to observe raptors, it is nearly as enjoyable to keep written records of raptor sightings because one can look back over years or decades of outstanding raptor sightings and recall wonderful past birding adventures. The *All-Weather Hawk Watcher's*

An immature Red-tailed Hawk breaking on its approach to a perch. Raptor photography is a fascinating and worthwhile activity. Ron Austing is one of the world's great bird photographers. He produces superb photographs—the kind every bird photography enthusiast also seeks to secure. *Photo by Ron Austing.*

Field Journal is ideal for this pastime because it includes a checklist of the diurnal raptors in North and Central America and the West Indies, is formatted for recording weather and travel data, and has space to write field notes. The publisher, J. L. Darling Corporation, Tacoma, Washington, also created a section on its Website at www.RiteintheRain.com /hawk.html for raptor enthusiasts, and provides a bibliography of diurnal raptor books as well as names and contact information for various raptor conservation organizations.

An example of a general bird checklist including raptors, *Ontario Bird Checklist 2002*, is published by Ontario Field Ornithologists, Toronto, Ontario, Canada. It is useful for all bird species reported in that province. The American Birding Association, and some Audubon organizations, have similar bird checklists available.

Raptor Photography

Some hawk watchers are also devoted raptor photographers who enjoy taking photographs of these birds. Generally, a 35mm single-lens reflex camera equipped with a 400mm telephoto lens is standard equipment for this type of photography, but some photographers use 500mm or longer (and more expensive) focal length telephoto lenses. Digital cameras should have the highest built-in *optical* magnification available, or with digital cameras permitting interchangeable lenses, one of the very long telephoto lenses should be used.

7

OSPREYS AND NORTHERN HARRIERS

Osprey *(Pandion haliaetus)*

The Osprey is a fish-eating cosmopolitan raptor. Its large size, striking coloration, and highly migratory habits make it visible to far more people than many other raptors.

HABITAT Ospreys are hawks of coastal areas, bays, lakes, rivers, large reservoirs, and other wetlands. During migration, they occur for brief time periods along inland mountains, even in cities, and on other landscapes not normally associated with these birds.

DISTRIBUTION In eastern North America, Ospreys occur as breeding birds from the Atlantic and Gulf coasts inland to the Great Lakes, but are absent from the Mississippi River area. Three of North America's five regional Osprey populations occur in eastern North America: (1) Atlantic coastal birds, (2) Florida and Gulf Coast birds, (3) and Great Lakes birds. Some formerly large and famous colonies declined catastrophically due to DDT pollution, but have now returned to reasonable population levels. Especially large numbers of breeding Ospreys occur in the Chesapeake Bay area.

Many Osprey reintroduction projects in the northeastern states allowed these hawks to reoccupy former breeding areas after becoming locally and regionally extinct due to DDT

pollution of food supplies and disruption of egg production. In Canada, Ospreys also breed widely throughout Ontario, the southern half of Quebec, southern and eastern parts of Labrador, and on the islands of Atlantic Canada.

Almost all eastern North American Ospreys migrate during autumn to Central and South America—in some cases via the West

An adult Osprey. These fish-eating hawks are distributed widely in eastern North America. *Photo by Ron Austing.*

Indies. Birds fledged in North America during a given breeding season remain on their Latin American wintering grounds for 18 to 20 months, but do not breed there, then return to North America to breed for the first time. Ospreys reported in winter in the eastern United States include an individual observed in Minnesota in late January 1976.

FOOD HABITS Ospreys feed on many species of fish, including catfish in Florida, bluegills and yellow perch in Minnesota, and salmon and trout in Labrador. There are important seasonal adjustments or changes in species of fish used by Ospreys in various parts of eastern North America.

Occasionally, they eat a few non-fish items including ducks, night-herons, and crows. An Osprey in Pennsylvania on November 9, 1990 (a late date), was seen carrying what was believed to be a muskrat. Frogs and small snakes are also captured and eaten.

New Jersey's 2001 Osprey nesting project report provided insights into Osprey food habits and their possible relationship to productivity. Low breeding productivity in an area such as Great Egg Harbor and Tuckerton may be due to prey availability and disturbance. Menhaden have traditionally been a favorite food of Ospreys because they swim near the surface of the water. This study found, however, that flounder represented four out of five nest deliveries. Since flounder are bottom dwellers and therefore a more difficult catch for Ospreys, the birds' reliance on them apparently reflects declining menhaden numbers. The study also found that nestlings died around 3 weeks of age, just at the point when their growth rate, and demand for food, is highest.

NESTING AND LIFE CYCLE Adjustment of timing of Osprey courtship depends on the geographic location where the birds are lo-

cated. In Minnesota, courtship occurs from late April to early May followed by nest repairs, then copulation.

Aerial pair formation (or re-formation) displays include the sky dance, high circling, and hover flight. Ospreys are typically monogamous for life. However, if there are many females in an area, polygamy sometimes occurs.

Osprey nest building or refurbishment begins soon after the birds return from their wintering grounds. In eastern North America, they are placed as single nests at the tops of trees, or fairly close to one another in loose colonies. They are constructed of large sticks, with new materials added year after year until the nests become very large. The hawks pull dead limbs from trees, and also pick them up from the ground, for use in their nests.

In Minnesota, Osprey nests are flat, round structures made from dead sticks, sedges, grass, and lichens compared with cone-shaped Bald Eagle nests. Nests are generally placed at the top of dead trees, on the dead upper part of living trees, on cross supports of steel and wood utility poles, and occasionally among branches of living trees. Elsewhere nests are also placed on cart wheels, windmills, old chimneys, large tanks, billboards, channel markers, duck-hunting blinds, tall poles with platforms on top, and so on. Strong winds sometimes blow nests down. In Minnesota this results in the destruction of as many as 10 percent of an area's nests.

Occasionally, Ospreys will take over and use a Great Blue Heron nest. Sometimes they also build alternative nests in nearby locations. Other birds (wrens, swallows, grackles, House Sparrows) sometimes build their nests on the sides of very large Osprey nests.

Eggs are deposited from January to mid-May, depending on the Ospreys' location in eastern North America. Three (rarely two or four) creamy white eggs, heavily blotched with browns, are deposited at 2- or 3-day in-

An Osprey nestling in New Jersey. *Photo by Donald S. Heintzelman.*

tervals. Incubation requires about 38 days and is done mostly by the female.

Eggs hatch by mid-June, and nestlings fledge during mid-August in the Middle Atlantic states. The female tends the nestlings and the male fishes (from pre-sunrise to post-sunset from perches or aloft) and provides food for the family. After leaving the nest at about 44 to 59 days old, and when first flight is achieved at 52 to 53, juvenile Ospreys remain close to the nest as they practice fishing.

In locations where several active Osprey nests are located relatively close together, such as along parts of the Atlantic Coast, newly fledged Ospreys sometimes visit the neighboring nests several times per day but return to their own nest by day's end. At this stage, the parents feed whatever juvenile Ospreys happen to be in their nest—perhaps because the adults can't recognize their own fledged young. By late September, juvenile Ospreys are engaged in southward migration.

Ornithologists recorded several large colonies of nesting Ospreys along the Atlantic Coast of the United States during the nineteenth, twentieth, and early twenty-first centuries. Unfortunately, most large concentrations of nesting Ospreys collapsed because DDT contaminated the Osprey food chains and food webs. Nevertheless, one inland concentration of more than eighty nesting Ospreys in southern Massachusetts disappeared toward the end of the nineteenth century long before pesticide contamination existed. Even so, some Ospreys in the Chesapeake Bay area bred successfully during the DDT era. Ospreys also nest in Georgia, especially in coastal areas. But in Florida, differences in breeding success were determined, with Florida Bay birds much less successful than birds foraging in the Atlantic Ocean. But Ospreys nesting in gulfside and the lower mainline Keys exhibited satisfactory breeding success.

The oldest known Osprey lived for 26 years and 2 months.

BEHAVIOR One of the charming traits of some nesting Ospreys is their lack of wariness of people and their willingness to nest close to human habitation and activities. Sometimes the hawks become so tame they almost become wildlife pets.

In Minnesota, however, a male Osprey, nesting in a colony of Great Blue Herons, was intolerant of herons nesting nearby and harassed them sufficiently to force them to abandon their nests. Nevertheless, this particular Osprey was not typical of fish hawks, and other examples exist of Ospreys nesting in close proximity with Great Blue Herons with no aggression exhibited by the hawks.

The long legs of an Osprey help it reach underwater, and its four toes with their long, sharp talons and a reversible outer toe enable the bird to place two toes in back and two in front when grasping a fish. Sharp little spines on the bottom of the feet also help an Osprey to grasp and hold onto a slippery fish.

An Osprey typically fishes alone, often flying slowly or hovering over the water searching for fish, then diving and hitting the water with a splash as a fish is captured. Occasionally several Ospreys fish together if an abundance of fish is available. Moreover, Ospreys nesting in loose colonies use them as information centers, similar to those used by Black Vultures, which help the hawks find food by watching where their neighbors locate fish.

Bald Eagles are famous for robbing Ospreys in flight of a fish they are carrying by forcing the hawk to drop its fish, after which the eagle quickly grasps the prey and claims it for itself. There is also a report of a Great Blue Heron in Minnesota robbing an Osprey of a fish it dropped, and which the heron recovered.

Ospreys are spectacular birds when in flight. They use various flying styles depending on the circumstances and time of year. When fishing, as already mentioned, an Osprey frequently hovers above water before gliding or plunging down and grasping the fish in its talons. At other times, such as during migration, thermal soaring is used occa-

sionally when winds are very light or calm. During autumn, many migrating Ospreys fly along inland mountains such as the Kittatinny Ridge in Pennsylvania and make full use of deflective updrafts to soar and glide—often with their long wings pulled back into a distinctive crooked position. Occasionally, however, when light winds occur, limited flapping flight is used by these big raptors. Sometimes, during migrations, Ospreys also vocalize loudly and can be heard from long distances.

The most impressive single-day Osprey flight I have observed occurred on September 11, 1965, at Bake Oven Knob in Pennsylvania. Throughout the day an excellent count of these birds developed, but the highlight of the day's flight took place late in the afternoon when forty Ospreys appeared. Once or twice, seven of them approached me head-on, gliding and soaring in a bomberlike formation while bathed in mellow late-afternoon light. An astonishing count of 102 Ospreys resulted by the end of the day.

These fish hawks make various vocalizations, typically a loud, ringing, staccato *cheep-cheep* whistle heard over long distances. During the mating sky dance and high-circling display, the male especially makes a prolonged, shrill *cree-cree-cree* sound.

MIGRATION Ospreys are participants in spectacular autumn migrations in eastern North America. At Bake Oven Knob and Hawk Mountain in eastern Pennsylvania, hawk watchers sometimes see dozens of migrating Osprey daily during mid- to late September. The largest Osprey flight at Bake Oven Knob was reported on September 14, 2002, when hawk watchers counted 116 fish hawks migrating past that watch site.

A large spring Osprey flight was also reported on April 14, 1990, at Smith Gap, Northampton County, Pennsylvania, when

108 Ospreys passed the watch site. Another spectacular spring flight of Ospreys along the Atlantic Coast occurred on March 18, 1994, at Cumberland Island, Georgia, when an estimated 360 Ospreys were flying north along the west side of the island.

The breeding grounds used by Ospreys migrating along the Kittatinny Ridge in Pennsylvania are not precisely known, but they probably include inland sites in Pennsylvania, New York, New England, and eastern Canada. Approximately 95 percent of Ospreys observed at Bake Oven Knob are adults, whereas the majority of Ospreys migrating along the Atlantic Coast in the Middle Atlantic and southeastern states are juveniles. This represents a marked differential migration pattern for these birds.

Much of what we know regarding the origins (natal locales) and migratory routes of eastern North American Ospreys is derived from recoveries of banded birds. Banding recovery information shows that most Ospreys nesting in the eastern United States winter in South America or, to a lesser extent, the West Indies. Moreover, field studies in Cuba indicate that many migrant Ospreys use parts of that island as stopover habitat before continuing farther southward.

Satellite tracking of adult Ospreys from their breeding grounds in north-central Minnesota, Shelter Island, New York, and southern New Jersey reveal that different populations of Ospreys use different migration routes. Females depart before males, travel farther, and winter farther south than males. Individual Ospreys also reuse the same migration routes.

East Coast birds followed the Atlantic Coast southward through Florida and across the Caribbean. However, Ospreys from eastern Long Island first flew westward along the island, then south across Delaware and Chesapeake bays; but they remained east of the Appalachian Mountains as they followed a broad front across the eastern half of Virginia and the Carolinas. Hence, adult Ospreys observed inland along the Kittatinny Ridge in Pennsylvania during autumn are not coming from eastern Long Island or southern New Jersey breeding locales—an important insight. By the time the birds arrived in Georgia, the migration route narrowed, and when they arrived in Florida some followed the Atlantic Coast southward, whereas others went across the peninsula to the Gulf Coast. The East Coast birds then moved south across the Florida Keys, arrived on Cuba's north coast, then moved southeast across Cuba before crossing over Hispaniola and the Caribbean to landfall in South America. From there the Ospreys continued southeast across Venezuela into Brazil. Doubtless some of these birds winter along the Amazon River, where I have seen Ospreys, and even south of that massive river complex.

Satellite tracking of Ospreys breeding in Minnesota indicate these birds use three southward migration routes. Some individuals fly south through the central United States and along Mexico's Gulf Coast, then south through Central America along the west coast of Honduras, El Salvador, and Nicaragua, then along the Caribbean coasts of Costa Rica and Panama into Colombia. Some individuals use the second route and follow the Mississippi River valley south across the Gulf of Mexico to Mexico's Yucatan peninsula. From there they continue southward through Central America into Colombia. Others use a third route south across southeastern Illinois, Kentucky, Tennessee, Alabama, and Georgia into Florida and from there south along the Gulf Coast, and the Keys to Cuba and beyond.

POPULATION During the DDT era in North America, when populations of Bald Eagles and Peregrine Falcons and some Ospreys were crashing, autumn Osprey counts at Hawk Mountain exhibited an increasing trend.

The explanation provided by Hawk Mountain's ornithologists, based on an earlier hypothesis by Roger Tory Peterson, was that Ospreys counted at Hawk Mountain originate from "unpolluted Canadian lakes" whose Osprey populations had limited or no exposure to DDT. There is some evidence that Ospreys nesting in the early 1970s in southeastern Canada were reasonably abundant, which might help to explain migrant Osprey counts at Hawk Mountain. In addition, most Ospreys observed migrating during autumn past Bake Oven Knob are adult birds with only 5 percent or less immatures. Since most immature Ospreys in northeastern North America migrate along the Atlantic coastline rather than inland mountains such as the Kittatinny Ridge, this differential migration conforms to the explanation provided by Hawk Mountain's ornithologists to explain increasing Osprey counts there during the DDT era.

In the 1980s, the world population of the Osprey was estimated between 25,000 and 30,000 pairs. During recent years in the northeastern United States, Osprey populations appear to be stable or increasing. Indeed,

the autumn 2002 migration count of 794 Ospreys at Bake Oven Knob in Pennsylvania was the highest in the four-decade history of that watch site.

Northern Harrier (*Circus cyaneus*)

Northern Harriers (especially adult males) are especially beautiful raptors. Striking differences in coloration among juveniles, adult females, and adult males offer varied opportunities to enjoy the full beauty of these birds.

HABITAT The breeding habitats of Northern Harriers in eastern North America are saltwater and freshwater marshes supporting dense emergent vegetation, and open upland fields suitable for foraging. The niches of Northern Harriers and Short-eared Owls overlap. During migration, harriers frequently are seen quartering low over fields or pastures seeking prey. Wintering habitats for Northern Harriers are open agricultural and old fields, coastal estuaries, and saltwater and freshwater marshes.

DISTRIBUTION Northern Harriers are distributed widely during their breeding season

An adult male Northern Harrier.
Photo by Ron Austing.

An adult female Northern Harrier at her nest with nestlings. *Photo by Allan D. Cruickshank.*

from the southern shore of Hudson Bay in Ontario, central Quebec, southern Newfoundland, and Atlantic Canada southward roughly throughout northern New England, New York, extreme northern Pennsylvania, and all or part of the Great Lakes states. In 1998, Northern Harriers nested at Churchill Falls, Labrador—the first documented nesting record for Labrador. Additional observations suggest Northern Harriers nest elsewhere in the province.

The wintering range of these harriers in the eastern United States extend southward through the southern half of the midwestern states, and southeastern states, to southern Florida and the Gulf Coast, with some individuals venturing into the Greater Antilles and Central America.

FOOD HABITS Northern Harriers are opportunistic predators. Their diet varies from season to season, location to location, and local availability and abundance of prey.

Spring and summer diets generally include small mammals (voles, ground squirrels, shrews), birds (waterfowl, Eastern Meadow-larks, Bobolinks, Red-winged Blackbirds, passerines, waterfowl), amphibians and reptiles (frogs and snakes), and insects (beetles, crickets, grasshoppers, locusts).

Winter diets include many mammals (shrews, voles, mice, house mice, harvest mice, cotton rats, rice rats, rabbits) and birds (passerines, Eastern Meadowlarks, Northern Cardinals, Song Sparrows).

NESTING AND LIFE CYCLE Northern Harriers are seasonally monogamous but will sometimes engage in bigamy and even polygamy with up to five females in a harem. Loose colonial nesting also occurs.

Pair bonds and nest territories are established by a male and female engaging in sky-dance displays at their breeding grounds. Copulation usually takes place on the ground, occasionally on fence posts, or as high as 10 feet in a tree.

Nest construction occurs between late April and early June, with either sex starting the process and both taking materials to the nest, which requires up to 2 weeks to complete. Nests are placed on the ground in various types of tall wetland vegetation, such as cattails, as well as in upland areas. Green grass or other vegetation is taken to the nest. Some nests are merely shallow depressions in the ground with grass added.

Four to six dull, smooth white eggs generally are deposited 2 days apart from mid-April to mid-July, with May and June representative, depending on geographic location. Incubation lasts for 30 to 32 days, and is done mostly by the female although the male participates slightly.

Nestlings hatch from May into July. The male does all the hunting and food delivery until the nestlings are at least 5 days old, after which the female will also do a limited amount of hunting. Sometimes aerial transfer of prey occurs between the parents, with the male dropping prey to the female who catches it in midair. When they are 15 to 20 days old, nestlings sometimes venture short distances from their nest—but return to be fed by their parents. Nestlings and adults eat similar prey. Nestlings fledge when about 6 weeks old, but juveniles remain relatively close to the nest for several weeks. Sometimes juveniles rob each other of prey provided by their parents.

The oldest known Northern Harrier lived for 16 years and 5 months.

BEHAVIOR Northern Harriers sometimes walk or hop when gathering nest materials, retrieving prey, or returning wayward nestlings to the nest. These harriers also engage in play behavior—especially juveniles, who pounce on objects.

A juvenile Northern Harrier on the Buena Vista Wildlife Refuge in Wisconsin stood on the ground among a flock of Greater Prairie Chickens without trying to capture one, nor did the chickens attempt to flee from the hawk. Sometimes fledged juveniles become pests to their parents. One young harrier was observed grabbing its mother's tail, and the parents of some juveniles sometimes almost have to drive their offspring away from their natal locales. When juvenile harriers finally do begin migrating, they pause at stopover habitats, establishing short-term home ranges there, before continuing on to their winter range.

Several types of flight are used by Northern Harriers. Many fly slowly, quartering low over upland fields or pastures, or wetlands, searching for prey. Often the birds buoyantly tip or tilt, glide, and flap several times as they move back and forth over these habitats. The distinctive dihedral or V position in which they hold their wings is a useful field mark. During migration they glide and soar with occasional wing beats, in rather unsteady flight, on deflective updrafts along the Kittatinny Ridge. When there is little or no wind, harriers use thermal soaring.

Roosting is on the ground during the nesting season, and during autumn and winter it is communal. Occasionally Short-eared Owls share the roosts. Some communal roosts are used for a decade. Sometimes play is used at roosts during winter. Northern Harriers also have very acute hearing.

A range of other birds, including swifts, swallows, crows, blackbirds, starlings, and sparrows, sometimes mob Northern Harriers. In one case in Wisconsin, a male, while engaged in its sky dance—a vital part of courtship—was mobbed by blackbirds, and in another equally badly timed episode a male harrier was mobbed by a Red-winged Blackbird as he transferred prey to his mate.

In Wisconsin, studies of Northern Harrier agonistic behavior demonstrate that a harrier usually initiates aggressive behavior against raptors larger than itself such as Red-tailed Hawks. Sometimes Northern Harriers will engage in interspecies interactions during migration. At Bake Oven Knob, Pennsylvania, for example, I observed a female Northern Harrier attempting to capture a flying male American Kestrel. The falcon, however, avoided capture by using twists and turns to outmaneuver the harrier.

A rapidly uttered, high-pitched *kek* alarm, distress, or threat vocalization is used commonly by Northern Harriers, in addition to various other calls.

MIGRATION Northern Harriers are medium- to long-distance migrants. Northward spring migrations occur from late February to late May, with most hawks arriving on their breeding grounds from late March to mid-May, depending on their geographic locations.

In Pennsylvania, autumn migrations occur at Bake Oven Knob and Hawk Mountain from early August through mid-December, with most appearing from early September through November. Typically, juveniles and females appear in September and October, whereas adult males are largely seen in November.

Northern Harriers migrate individually along the Atlantic coastline, inland ridges, and northern and western shorelines of the Great Lakes, stopping from time to time to quarter low over marshes and upland fields to search for food. These hawks also cross smaller bodies of open water such as the Bay of Fundy and Delaware Bay.

Record autumn migration counts of Northern Harriers include 1,636 at the Holiday Beach Migration Observatory in southeastern Ontario in 1989, 369 at Bake Oven Knob in 1970, and 475 at Hawk Mountain in 1980.

POPULATION In 1986, the winter population of the Northern Harrier in North America was estimated at 110,000 individuals. Population levels of Northern Harriers vary, however, depending on changes in local prey numbers. Moreover, long-term population numbers of these hawks vary considerably in various regions of eastern North America and among migration watch sites. From 1976 through 2001, at Bake Oven Knob in Pennsylvania, however, a long-term declining trend exists in autumn Northern Harrier migration counts.

Several states provide special conservation status to Northern Harriers. The species is "endangered" in Connecticut, Illinois, Indiana, Iowa, Missouri, New Jersey, and Rhode Island, "threatened" in Massachusetts, New Hampshire, New York, and Tennessee, a "species of special concern" in Michigan, Vermont, and Wisconsin, and "vulnerable" in Pennsylvania.

8

KITES

Kites are endowed with long, narrow wings and graceful flight. Four species occur in eastern North America. None is common, several are rare, and the Snail Kite is endangered in its very limited geographic range in south-central Florida.

Swallow-tailed Kite
(*Elanoides forficatus*)

The gregarious Swallow-tailed Kite is one of the most delicate and graceful birds in North America. Boldly contrasting dark and white plumage and a deeply forked tail make the birds unmistakable.

HABITAT The habitat of the Swallow-tailed Kite consists of prairielike open areas supporting small, easily secured prey, and containing tall trees or small islands of trees forming uneven canopy heights suitable for nest sites. Pine forest edges near riparian habitats, swamps, or lakes along coastal plains, and cypress or pine stands in standing water, are prime kite habitat, especially in locations free of human disturbance.

DISTRIBUTION Swallow-tailed Kites are now restricted as breeding birds to Florida and north along the Atlantic coastal plain into South Carolina, as well as parts of Alabama, Mississippi, and Louisiana.

Extralimital Swallow-tailed Kite records in eastern North America are reported from Massachusetts, Michigan, Minnesota, New Hampshire, New York, Pennsylvania, Vermont, Wisconsin, Ontario, and Nova Scotia.

FOOD HABITS Swallow-tailed Kites are opportunistic predators. Their small prey is varied. Insects (and even entire wasp nests carried to kite nests), frogs, lizards and snakes, young birds, eggs of birds, bats, and small fish

A Swallow-tailed Kite in flight. *Photo by Dale A. Zimmerman.*

are taken—with insects captured in flight being especially important food items. Food is eaten while the kites are aloft.

NESTING AND LIFE CYCLE Swallow-tailed Kites are monogamous. Pair formation is intact or soon forms after these birds arrive in Florida with courtship already underway, sometimes near old nest sites that are reused. Both sexes participate in nest refurbishment or construction. However, many refurbished nests are abandoned before eggs are deposited, and new nests are constructed nearby. Some evidence suggests nests tend to be slightly clumped together. Sometimes extra, non-breeding kites associate with nesting birds and even bring nest materials and food to breeding pairs, which reject the offerings. Territories around their nests extend approximately 164 to 328 feet.

Nest construction occurs from early March to early May. Twig nests are placed in the tops of tall pines or other very tall living trees along trails or other thinly wooded areas with uneven canopies. Small sticks form the nest, with Spanish moss used as a nest lining. In Florida, two or three whitish eggs with dark brown or reddish brown markings usually are deposited during a 2-day period at the end of March. Incubation by both sexes requires approximately 28 days.

The female broods her nestlings for a week, with limited assistance by the male, who confines his efforts to hunting during the first half of the nesting period. When the nestlings are 2 or 3 weeks old, some females also engage in some hunting. Feeding of nestlings occurs at various irregular times throughout the day.

At 34 days of age, nestlings in Florida stand on the edge of their nests spreading and exercising their wings. They are capable of flying from their nest after 35 days of age, but actual flights from the nest occur a bit later at 38 to 41 days.

BEHAVIOR In South Carolina, Swallow-tailed Kites usually make midday foraging forays to feed on insects living over marshes, rivers, agricultural fields, orchards, pine woodland, hardwood hammocks, and even suburban areas and may venture as far as 15 miles to visit these foraging areas. Sometimes, after the nesting season, up to forty Swallow-tailed Kites forage in groups when capturing insects in flight.

During the breeding season, night roosts containing up to about thirty kites are established within 3.1 miles of active nests. Swallow-tailed Kites (adults and juveniles) also gather in sizable postbreeding communal roosts or congregations in summer, then in smaller roosts for a few days in some southeastern states, followed by southwestern migratory movements. For example, from July 8 to at least August 19, 1997, at least fifty-two Swallow-tailed Kites were seen at a hay field in southern Georgia—the largest known congregation of individuals of this species reported to date in that state. Six juvenile birds (probably from a local breeding site) were being fed thousands of June beetles and dragonflies by adults.

Swallow-tailed Kites drink while in flight, not unlike a huge swallow, as the birds dip from the surface of quiet waters. However, they are also able to outclimb vultures and most soaring hawks when thermal soaring. Curiously, for birds that are so graceful when aloft, they are quite clumsy when landing at their nests.

Swallow-tailed Kites and Red-shouldered Hawks frequently engage in agonistic behavior in Florida, suggesting there may be conflicts between the two species while foraging. Kites in close proximity to their nests also attack vultures, Bald Eagles, Ospreys, buteos, and Peregrine Falcons. Sometimes twenty or more Swallow-tailed Kites near their nests also mob predators but do not actually strike them.

Vocalizations of Swallow-tailed Kites consist of *klee-klee-klee, tew-whee, eeep,* and *chitter* sounds. These kites tend to vocalize in the morning and late afternoon, and early in the breeding season.

MIGRATION Swallow-tailed Kites are migratory in North America. Spring arrivals appear in southwestern Florida the last two weeks in February, but somewhat later elsewhere.

During autumn, most birds depart from the continental United States by mid-September, probably flying across the Caribbean, with some going around the Gulf of Mexico, but details are unknown. One nestling banded in Florida was shot approximately 3,720 miles away in Brazil about six months after being banded. Several sightings are also reported in December and January in Florida.

POPULATION Swallow-tailed Kite populations declined sharply during much of the twentieth century, with considerable range retraction from as far north as Minnesota (nesting there in 1886 and 1887). The overall population estimate in 1990 for the southeastern United States was 800 to 1,150 nesting pairs, with 450 to 750 in Florida. Populations were stable in Alabama, Mississippi, and South Carolina, but unknown in Georgia, Louisiana, and North Carolina. Information was not available in 1990 for the other southeastern states. These estimates, however, now may be low. The Swallow-tailed Kite population estimate throughout its entire New World range is several hundred thousand birds.

White-tailed Kite (*Elanus leucurus*)

The White-tailed Kite is a falconlike raptor that displays gull-like flight and colors and is very rare in eastern North America.

A White-tailed Kite. *Photo by Wade L. Eakle.*

HABITAT Agricultural, grassland, savannah, and marsh landscapes as well as riparian woodland areas constitute the habitats utilized by White-tailed Kites. Nests are placed in single trees or shrubs ranging in height from more than 164 feet tall to less than 9.8 inches high, respectively.

DISTRIBUTION In eastern North America the White-tailed Kite occurs mainly in southern Florida. The species is much more common in western North America.

Occasionally postbreeding dispersal produces sightings of kites elsewhere in eastern North America, including Illinois, Indiana, Maryland, Massachusetts, Minnesota, New York, Tennessee, Virginia, and Wisconsin.

FOOD HABITS White-tailed Kites feed on small mammals such as meadow voles, along with insects (beetles and grasshoppers), and frogs, lizards, and small snakes.

NESTING AND LIFE CYCLE Female White-tailed Kites select their nest site approximately at the time when copulation commences. Usually a new nest is constructed each year, by the female, although occasionally refurbished nests are used. Although males also begin nest building early in the season, the female rejects them in favor of her own structure.

An immature Golden Eagle.
Photo by Donald S. Heintzelman.

An adult Sharp-shinned Hawk during autumn migration. *Photo by Donald S. Heintzelman.*

Nestling Osprey along coastal New Jersey. *Photo by Donald S. Heintzelman.*

Broad-winged Hawk roosting on a dead tree for the night at Bake Oven Knob, Pennsylvania. *Photo by Donald S. Heintzelman.*

Immature Broad-winged Hawk during autumn migration. *Photo by Donald S. Heintzelman.*

Nest and eggs of a Broad-winged Hawk in Vermont. *Photo by Donald S. Heintzelman.*

Broad-winged Hawk nestling. *Photo by Donald S. Heintzelman.*

Male American Kestrel nestling. *Photo by Donald S. Heintzelman.*

Male American Kestrel with abnormal tail. *Photo by Donald S. Heintzelman.*

Barn Owl. *Photo by Donald S. Heintzelman.*

A red-morph Eastern Screech-Owl.
Photo by Donald S. Heintzelman.

A gray-morph Eastern Screech-Owl.
Photo by Donald S. Heintzelman.

A gray-morph Eastern Screech-Owl.
Photo by Donald S. Heintzelman.

Young Eastern Screech-Owls perced in a tree beside a city street.
Photo by Donald S. Heintzelman.

A Great Horned Owl—a top trophic level predator in the habitats in which it lives. *Photo by Donald S. Heintzelman.*

Eye-to-eye with a Great Horned Owl. *Photo by Donald S. Heintzelman.*

A nestling Great Horned Owl. *Photo by Donald S. Heintzelman.*

A Northern Saw-whet Owl. *Photo by Donald S. Heintzelman.*

Student hawk watchers on the South Lookout at Bake Oven Knob, Pennsylvania.
Photo by Donald S. Heintzelman.

Nestling Osprey in a coastal New Jersey nest. *Photo by Donald S. Heintzelman*

White-tailed Kite clutches consist of four white or creamy white eggs largely marked with brownish coloration. The eggs are deposited on alternate days with incubation lasting 30 to 32 days. The female performs the incubation while the male hunts and provides some nest defense. The eggs do not hatch at the same time.

Nestling White-tailed Kites fly when about 4 to 5 weeks old, with their parents teaching them how to fly and hunt. Juvenile birds will sometimes join their parents in the hunt.

The oldest known White-tailed Kite lived 5 years and 11 months.

BEHAVIOR White-tailed Kites use various types of flight typically consisting of slow wing beats, as well as kiting (remaining stationary while aloft without flapping). Leg hanging occurs when they engage in flutter and some other flight styles, including when pairs of birds dive at each other. Hovering is also used when hunting.

Kites are monogamous, with some pair bonds remaining intact year-round, and the birds staying on their breeding territories. Females apparently select nests consisting of small twigs and hay, grass, and leaves. Dummy nests are constructed, and nest building requires seven to 28 days. Before eggs are deposited, males may offer females prey—sometimes via spectacular aerial displays.

White-tailed Kites are agonistic toward large birds such as soaring hawks and crows when they enter kite nest territories and similar reactions also occur after the breeding season. Turkey Vultures, however, are never assaulted by these kites—probably because vultures are scavengers and do not prey upon the kite's exposed nestlings.

The species is moderately social, and communal roosts are sometimes used. These kites commonly make *kewt* or *keep* calls along with various other vocalizations.

MIGRATION Little is known about the movements of White-tailed Kites in eastern North America, but the species appears to be nomadic in the West.

POPULATION The primary focus of White-tailed Kite populations in eastern North America is in Florida, where they were nearly extinct by the middle of the twentieth century. By the 1960s, however, they increased in numbers in central Florida, and from 1973 to 1990 most sightings (plus thirteens nests) were in the eastern Everglades. Since 1991, an increase in reports came from central Florida. By 1996, the kites began renesting for the first time in the region in 66 years. It is unknown why these population increases are occurring, but the birds may be expanding their breeding range into northern Florida.

Alabama and Louisiana are two additional states that have increasing kite populations. The bird's status in Arkansas and Mississippi is unknown, and information is unavailable regarding White-tailed Kite populations in the other southeastern states. The White-tailed Kite population estimate throughout its entire New World range is hundreds of thousands of birds.

Snail Kite (*Rostrhamus sociabilis*)

This medium-sized, highly gregarious raptor, formerly called the Everglade Kite, is a central and southern Florida specialty. It is federally endangered and one of the rarer raptors in eastern North America.

HABITAT Snail Kites occupy large flooded freshwater marshes, shallow edges of lakes, and sometimes the banks of canals in central and southern Florida, where apple snails live and upon which these birds feed. Willow thickets typically exist in most of these habitats. Sometimes kite areas are occupied,

A pair of adult Snail Kites in Florida. The female is on the left, the male on the right. *Photo by Helen Cruickshank.*

abandoned, then reoccupied. Some Snail Kite habitats in Florida are isolated islands of wetlands, but others are connected with each other.

DISTRIBUTION Snail Kites in Florida extend from the St. Johns River headwaters, and the Kissimmee River basin, southward across shallow freshwater lakes and marshes through Lake Okeechobee and the northern Everglades. These kites also occur in small near-coastal freshwater wetlands in central Brevard County, southward to central Palm Beach County. Some Snail Kites also occur in the eastern Big Cypress area. When drought or other low-water levels occur, Snail Kites scatter across the peninsula.

FOOD HABITS Snail Kites are skilled specialists in capturing apple snails. As specialists, the kites are unable to adapt to changing environmental conditions or make changes in their food habits. In Florida, Snail Kites feed almost exclusively on apple snails. However, during drought conditions or unusually cold weather, the kites will eat similar-looking snails, crayfish, snakes, several species of small turtles, and speckled perch.

NESTING AND LIFE CYCLE Most Snail Kites begin breeding when two years old. This species nests mostly from December to June in southern Florida, and from March to August in the northern central part of Florida. Little or no nesting occurs when severe drought conditions occur. Some Snail Kites build nests as single structures away from other nests, while other kites construct their nests in loose colonies with two or more nests placed no more than 984 feet from another nest.

Usually a new nest is constructed each year by the male, with limited maintenance assistance provided by the female, but occasionally old nests are refurbished and reused. The nest is made of dry sticks formed into a loose, flat, bulky structure with a cup made of fine material such as green plants. The nest is placed over water on willows, cattails, sawgrass, and bulrushes. Artificial nests, in the form of baskets, are used by raptor conservationists to help these birds maintain improved numbers. Snail Kites also nest as solitary pairs or loose colonies—sometimes in close association with nesting colonial water birds.

Three (sometimes one to six) dull whitish eggs with brown splotches are deposited and incubated by both parents for 24 to 30 days. Females remain on the eggs at night. Both parents care for their young, which remain in the nest for 23 to 34 days. After the young fledge, their parents continue feeding them for up to 10 weeks.

Pair bonds generally last between 8 and 16 weeks during the nesting season. However, when apple snails are plentiful, and Snail Kites are nesting, one parent may desert the nest when the young are 3 to 6 weeks old, and start another nest. The parent remaining at the first nest then assumes all the duties of parenthood. This process is called "mate desertion."

The oldest known Snail Kite lived for 17 years. Nearly two dozen additional known-age individuals lived for at least 13 years.

BEHAVIOR After nesting is completed, Snail Kites tend to gather in flocks that often use communal roosts at night, often in association with colonial waders. Sometimes several hundred kites occupy roosts that are always over water, usually in willow thickets. During the day, however, these flocks of kites leave their roost and fly fairly long distances to foraging areas.

Snail Kites tend to display relatively non-aggressive agonistic behavior although their nest territories are defended by trying to drive another bird such as a Turkey Vulture away. Making *ka-ka-ka-ka-ka-ka* alarm calls is a common form of vocal aggression when defending nests or perches. Kites sometimes but not always defend foraging areas and feeding sites.

The kites typically capture apple snails by flying slowly over a marsh at very low altitudes, casting back and forth, searching for prey. When a snail is spotted, the kite drops on it and grabs it with its talons. The kite then flies with the prey to a feeding perch where the snail is removed from its shell and swallowed whole. When water temperatures drop below 50° Fahrenheit, apple snails bury themselves, thus making them unavailable to Snail Kites as food. This snail behavior may also explain why Snail Kites are restricted to central and southern Florida, why seasonal changes exist in kite distribution, and increases occur in kite nesting behavior.

Adult Snail Kites make several vocalizations including a cackling-like *ka-ka-ka-ka-ka-ka* rattle, often near nests in the presence of intruders, *k-a-a-a-a-a-a* during courtship, and *ker-wuck* when near other Snail Kites at roosts or when a kite is disturbed.

MIGRATION Snail Kites are seminomadic raptors that do not exhibit seasonal migrations. Rather, they roam for varying time periods over their geographic range and spend time in freshwater wetlands with adequate supplies of apple snails. Some movements occur after breeding and during cold winters when kites move farther south in Florida.

POPULATION Snail Kites vary from scarce to locally common depending on water levels in the wetlands in which they occur, and on the availability of apple snails. Populations show the ability to rebound from very low levels to more substantial numbers when water conditions improve. Snail Kite populations ranged from 65 birds in 1972 to 996 in 1994. Their populations have been increasing since 1969.

Mississippi Kite
(*Ictinia mississippiensis*)

The Mississippi Kite is another raptor of the southeastern United States that also tends to occur as a vagrant in many parts of eastern North America.

HABITAT Mississippi Kites nest along edges of large, lowland, undisturbed deciduous

A Mississippi Kite. *Photo by Allan D. Cruickshank.*

forest and riparian woodland. Old growth trees forming patches of 198 or more acres are desirable nesting locations in the eastern United States—conditions that are increasingly rare. Currently, they also occur in suburban and urban areas, including Gainesville and Tallahassee, Florida, and Memphis, Tennessee. Golf courses are favorite suburban and urban nesting areas.

DISTRIBUTION The current breeding range of the Mississippi Kite extends into parts of South Carolina, Georgia, Florida's panhandle and a portion of the northern peninsula, and portions of Alabama, Mississippi, and Louisiana. They also nest northward along the Mississippi River valley to parts of Tennessee and Illinois. A few kites nest in isolated pairs in breeding islands in Virginia, North Carolina, and Illinois.

Extralimital Mississippi Kite records in eastern North America are reported from Connecticut, Delaware, Illinois, Indiana, Kentucky, Maine, Maryland, Massachusetts, Michigan, Minnesota, New Jersey, New York, Ohio, Pennsylvania, Rhode Island, Virginia, Wisconsin, and in Canada from Nova Scotia and Ontario.

The winter range of Mississippi Kites in South America is poorly known. That is why two sightings of an adult Mississippi Kite in early February in Georgia are of considerable interest. The first was seen on February 2, 1991, over Statesboro, Georgia; the second, also an adult, on February 5, 1998 near Statesboro. It is unknown if these birds wintered in North America, or were very early spring migrants returning from South America.

FOOD HABITS Mississippi Kites feed on insects (large beetles, cicadas, dragonflies, locusts, and grasshoppers), frogs and toads, small turtles, lizards, small snakes, small birds, and mammals (mice, ground squirrels, rabbits, white-footed mice, bats). Carrion (road kills) is also consumed.

NESTING AND LIFE CYCLE Mississippi Kites are monogamous. They build nests from mid-May to mid-June, but sometimes reuse old nests of other birds. In Louisiana, Mississippi Kites appropriated an old Swallow-tailed Kite nest in a loblolly pine and used it as a nest site. Both adults participate leisurely in nest building or refurbishment, but the circular or oval stick nests are flimsy. Nevertheless, the inner cup is lined with fresh willow, oak, walnut, sumac, or other leaves that cover decaying prey remains. However, the exact purpose of the leaves is unknown. Sometimes Mississippi Kites also repair and reuse a previous year's nest, and some of these kites will nest in loose colonies.

Two (occasionally one) dull white eggs, sometimes with pale brownish stains, are deposited from the third week in May to early June in Illinois, with incubation requiring about 30 days. Overall, the female does much of the incubation. After hatching, the helpless nestlings are brooded and fed by their parents. The young birds remain in the nest, or move to nearby tree limbs, for 30 days. By 30 to 35 days, they fledge completely and are capable of flight, but they dislike flying until they are about 50 days old. Sometimes fledged kites return to their nest as long as 10 days postfledging. After about age 50 days, the juveniles engage in insect catching in association with their parents, and in another 14 days join their parents in foraging. If a nesting attempt fails early in the nesting season, some Mississippi Kites nest again during the same year.

The oldest known Mississippi Kite lived for 11 years and 2 months.

BEHAVIOR It is common to find other animals living in close proximity to Mississippi Kite nests. Included among these neighbors are Mourning Doves, Blue Jays, Northern Mockingbirds, Brown Thrashers, House Sparrows, and wasps. There is a report of a Mississippi Kite and a Northern Mockingbird nesting in the same tree. Both species defended their nest tree, which essentially represented joint territories. In another odd case, a nestling kite fell into a Brown Thrasher's nest and the parent thrashers cared for the misplaced kite.

Sometimes food scraps fall onto the ground beneath Mississippi Kite nests and other animals, including box turtles, feed on them.

Mississippi Kites are very gregarious when involved in foraging, migrating, and roosting. On the ground, Mississippi Kites walk and hop while foraging, and sometimes even venture into shallow water in search of food. They are aggressive toward Cooper's, Red-shouldered, Red-tailed, and Swainson's Hawks, as well as Great Horned and Barred Owls, and even humans.

The flight of Mississippi Kites is varied. Thermal soaring accompanied by flapping flight is used during the hot hours of the day, while hovering or slower flight is used when strong winds prevail. When capturing prey, Mississippi Kites exhibit graceful and acrobatic flight resembling that of the Swallow-tailed Kite. Prey is usually captured while the kite is aloft, but sometimes kites take prey from fence posts or other elevated and exposed perches. Actual capture can be rapid by grasping prey from the air, or it can require longer and more erratic flight until the prey is grasped by the kite's feet. Whatever the capture method, most prey is eaten by kites while they are in flight.

Hundreds of kites may also form hunting flocks during the breeding season, capturing prey close to nest sites or far away. Kites are social birds at their roosts and when aloft and hunting. Small flocks are seen commonly, but sometimes during migration much larger groups may occur containing more than one hundred individuals.

Mississippi Kite vocalizations include the *phee-phew* whistle when in flight, and the *phee-ti-ti* associated with courtship and breeding. There are variations of these, along with other lesser-utilized vocalizations.

MIGRATION Most kites from eastern North America funnel through southern Texas and Mexico into Central and South America, but a few stragglers sometimes appear in winter in Florida.

During spring, limited numbers of Mississippi Kites arrive on their eastern United States breeding grounds during March and April. Some extralimital individuals also appear at locations north of their southeastern breeding range. For example, on March 17, 1991, in Springfield Township, Erie County, Pennsylvania, just east of the Ohio border, a Mississippi Kite (the third record for western Pennsylvania) was reported. On March 31, 1991, at the Tuscarora Summit hawk-watching site in Pennsylvania, another Mississippi Kite was reported.

Sometimes Mississippi Kites are seen as late summer or very early autumn vagrants far north of their normal breeding range as, for example, on August 6, 1994, in Roseau, Minnesota.

POPULATION Populations of Mississippi Kites reached a low point around the beginning of the twentieth century, when shooting, egg collecting, and loss of narrow riparian habitat and nest trees contributed to the decline.

Mississippi Kites began to repopulate former areas in the 1950s and thus expand their population in the southeastern United States. In 1990, ten or twelve southeastern states reported nesting Mississippi Kites, with stable populations reported in Florida and Mississippi. Populations of Mississippi Kites were also increasing in South Carolina and Tennessee, but the status of populations in other southeastern states was unknown. In Illinois, in the early 1990s, between thirty to fifty nesting pairs of Mississippi Kites were identified, but similar data are not available for North Carolina. Much better population data are needed for the entire eastern United States. Presently, the Mississippi Kite population estimate throughout its entire New World range is at least 27,000 birds.

9

EAGLES

Eagles are large, powerful birds of prey. Two species occur in North America.

Bald Eagle (*Haliaeetus leucocephalus*)

The Bald Eagle, the national bird of the United States, is one of the most majestic raptors in North America. Ornithologists and hawk watchers look forward to seeing, and sometimes photographing, these wonderful birds wherever they are found.

HABITAT Breeding Bald Eagles in eastern North America are birds of major river systems, large lakes, reservoirs, coastal areas, and other large wetlands where they can find suitable nest sites and adequate supplies of fish on which to feed. Nests are constructed in trees in wooded areas adjacent or fairly close to aquatic areas. However, locations that have increasing human disturbances or housing developments along their shorelines—such as parts of Florida, Minnesota, and the Chesapeake Bay in Maryland and Virginia—are of less value for Bald Eagles because food supplies are located farther from their nests.

During winter, Bald Eagles seek areas with open water, plenty of fish, and suitable nearby perching and roosting trees. The Mississippi, Ohio, Tennessee, and Wisconsin rivers, with open water below dams and near power plants, are common Bald Eagle habitats in winter. Coastal areas of New Brunswick, Nova Scotia, and Maine are also eagle wintering habitats. Other wintering areas include inland lakes, reservoirs, and the Connecticut, Delaware, and Susquehanna rivers.

For roosts, eagles require large, old, deciduous or coniferous trees with very accessible canopies. Roosts are also sheltered from prevailing winter winds and can be associated with aquatic ecosystems. Roosts are often farther from feeding areas than nests, some as much as a mile from food sources. In the

An adult Bald Eagle. Its white head and tail are distinctive. This eagle is the national bird of the United States of America. *Photo by Ron Austing.*

Chesapeake Bay area, eagles prefer to roost away from roads, human habitats, and other development such as large forested areas with open flight corridors to the bay. Relatively little is known about Bald Eagle stopover habitats other than that they require an adequate food supply and must be relatively free of human disturbances.

DISTRIBUTION Bald Eagles are distributed in discontinuous population pockets throughout eastern North America, extending roughly south of Hudson Bay northeastward through northern Ontario, the southern two-thirds of Quebec, part of southern Newfoundland, and throughout most of Atlantic Canada.

Northern Bald Eagles breed north of 40° North, and migrate southward from December into January in part of the eastern United States. Southern Bald Eagles breeds south of 40° North all the way into Florida. Juvenile and immature Bald Eagles disperse from their natal locales, are nomadic, and wander widely.

During winter, Bald Eagles are distributed throughout eastern North America from extreme southern Ontario and Quebec southward to Florida and the Gulf Coast.

FOOD HABITS Bald Eagles are opportunistic foragers and feeders. The birds hunt from perches and while in flight. Flight capture is spectacular when an eagle effortlessly plucks a fish out of water. Their preferred food is fish—sometimes stolen from Ospreys. Eagles also eat birds (loons, cormorants, Canada Geese, Mallards, other ducks, coots, gulls, terns, and even Wild Turkey), mammals, reptiles, and a few invertebrates. In Minnesota, an immature Bald Eagle killed a Great Egret in flight, then carried it to the ground. During winter, carrion (dead white-tailed deer) is consumed extensively. In Minnesota, in late December, an immature Bald Eagle arrived in a backyard, remained for several days, and ate suet (beef fat) from a feeder. The eagle was later captured and relocated along the Mississippi River.

NESTING AND LIFE CYCLE Bald Eagles are monogamous and probably mate for life. They usually prefer and seek nesting areas removed from human development and activity.

Courtship flight displays are spectacular. Two birds lock talons high overhead and tumble in cartwheels toward the ground. The eagles release each other at the final moment before hitting the ground. Other flight displays are also used during courtship.

Nest construction begins about one to three months prior to egg laying. In Florida, nesting activities begin during late September and early October, while in Ohio and Pennsylvania these activities typically begin in February.

Nest trees usually are very large with sturdy limbs capable of supporting the large eagle nests. The nests are built in the upper quarter of the tree near the trunk and under the crown. Both sexes participate in nest construction or repair. Nests can take from four days to three months to complete and are built from sticks taken from the ground and broken from trees.

Completed Bald Eagle nests are huge and are said to be the largest made by birds. A very famous Bald Eagle nest in Ohio, weighing about two tons, was used for 34 years. An even larger nest in Florida was about 9 feet in diameter and 18 feet high! When gypsy moths defoliated one eagle nest tree in the Chesapeake Bay area, the eagles abandoned their nest and built another in a pine tree that provided more shade.

In 1986, a pair of Bald Eagles nested on an electrical power pole near Outing, Minnesota.

This was the first documentation in that state of such a structure used for eagle nest placement. Occasionally Bald Eagles will build a second, so-called frustration nest if a prior nesting attempt fails. An example was seen in Connecticut at the Barkhamsted Reservoir.

Twelve Bald Eagle nests in Minnesota were adorned with sprigs of fresh white pine needles that were not part of the nest's integral structure or lining. The purpose of the sprigs, which are replaced from time to time, is not known.

One to three (usually two) dull, rough white eggs are deposited in Bald Eagle nests. They are incubated for about 35 days, mostly by the female, but with occasional assistance by the male.

Young eagles pip and break free of the shells without assistance from their parents. Adults continue to incubate all unhatched eggs while brooding their first emerged nestlings, until all the young have hatched. During the first 2 or 3 weeks of the nestlings' lives, the adult female spends most of her time at the nest attending to them, while the adult male spends more time away from the nest securing food. However, at least one parent attends the young almost continuously for the first several weeks of their lives.

Both sexes secure food and feed their young. In Connecticut, at two separate Bald Eagle nests, a third adult Bald Eagle was also observed helping to feed eagle nestlings. In Wisconsin, Bald Eagles make an average of 5.2 daily deliveries of prey to each nest.

The young eagles will practice wing flapping and flight over their nests and onto adjacent tree branches before fledging. Some nestlings fall to the ground, where they may remain for weeks and become vulnerable to predators, but most are fed by their parents until they are again able to fly.

Departure from nests takes place when the young are between 8 and 14 weeks old de-

pending upon the sex of the nestling (males fledge first), amount of parental attention they received, local weather conditions, and the geographic area in which the nest is located. The parents sometimes fly with prey around the nest to encourage their nestlings to fledge. However, the juvenile eagles still remain in the vicinity of the nest for several weeks, using it as a feeding platform while they are developing increased flight and hunting skills.

Bald Eagles require 5 years to acquire full adult plumage. However, in areas with high eagle concentrations, younger Bald Eagles may not begin breeding until they are 6 or even 7 years old.

The oldest known Bald Eagle lived for 29 years and 7 months.

BEHAVIOR Bald Eagles walk awkwardly on the ground, but rarely hop except when "power-hopping" off a log or rock. Their flapping flight is powerful with slow wing beats, but much of their flight consists of thermal soaring and gliding or a combination of the two—occasionally with a few slow wing beats included. Bald Eagles will also float and row if they are in water that's too deep for wading, but they do not actually swim.

Communal roosting is common, with some large roosts containing hundreds of eagles. There is a good deal of social interaction between nonbreeding adults and immatures at communal roosts and feeding sites. As with Black Vultures, communal roosts may serve as an information exchange center. For example, eagles learn where the best feeding places are located by following other eagles to those sites the next day. Bald Eagles are more active during summer than winter when they become somewhat sedentary in cold weather to conserve energy.

Bald Eagles become aggressive when defending nests and at communal feeding sites.

Eagles are also agonistic when seeking use of favored roosts and tree perches. Most physical contact between Bald Eagles is avoided by using vocal and visual displays.

During winter, the Mississippi River near Red Wing, Minnesota, is an important wintering and feeding area for dozens of Bald Eagles, provided the water remains open for hunting and fishing. Most eagles hunt from favored perches on trees near the river or, if possible, from trees with branches that extend over the water.

For at least 12 days during December 1993, between 350 and 500 Bald Eagles concentrated along the Mississippi River between Reads Landing and Lake City in Minnesota, where they fed on gizzard shad and freshwater drum before the river froze. Sometimes groups of 20 to 30 eagles flew over the water and caught fish. The eagles also engaged in frequent midair tussling for fish. Some four thousand Common Mergansers were fishing in the same stretch of water, and sometimes the eagles stooped on mergansers, which dove underwater to escape. The eagles then plucked fish from the surface of the water, with the mergansers nearby.

Bald Eagles are famous for robbing Ospreys of fish they are carrying. The eagles then catch and claim the fish for themselves. As many as four Bald Eagles have been seen in flight fighting over a fish taken from an Osprey.

In Minnesota, an adult Bald Eagle was seen attacking two large Osprey nestlings in a nest. The eagle grasped one of the nestlings, carried it from the nest, and hit the water with the young fish hawk. The eagle then released its grip on the nestling, which began floundering on the water's surface. The bird was rescued by a birder, and two puncture wounds (one on each side of the back) were noted. The Osprey was bleeding slightly, and appeared to be in shock. An attempt to save it failed. The next day a similar incident occurred. The reason for the Bald Eagle's agonistic behavior toward the Osprey nestlings is unknown.

In central Florida, interactions have been reported between Bald Eagles and Black Vultures and Turkey Vultures. Bald Eagles (one adult, one immature) flew low above the ground toward a few Black and Turkey Vultures standing on the ground near a carcass, causing the vultures to depart. The eagles did not feed on the carcasses, but two Black Vultures returned and began to feed.

Occasionally, Bald Eagles engage in cooperative hunting. In a quarry pond in Pennsylvania, for example, two subadult eagles repeatedly dove at, and eventually captured, a merganser. However, the two eagles did not willingly share the prey immediately, and eventually one eagle secured only a small portion of the prey. Other interactions have been reported elsewhere between Bald Eagles and Golden Eagles, a Wild Turkey, Northern Harriers, Northern Goshawks, and a Snowy Owl. Bald Eagles also have been seen engaged in behavior that seemed like play, such as six eagles passing sticks while aloft, and eagles picking up and manipulating objects.

Bald Eagles make surprisingly weak vocalizations, such as high-pitched wails or peals, and a *kah-kah-kah* alarm call.

MIGRATION Spring migrations of Bald Eagles begin in late January or early February and build up through March. Northern Bald Eagles are back on their breeding grounds between January and March, as soon as food and other environmental conditions permit. Southern Bald Eagles that nested in Florida migrate northward in a postbreeding dispersal pattern between February and July, with some individuals reaching the Great Lakes states, Maine, and even parts of Atlantic Canada. However, some immature Bald Eagles also remain in Florida. Apparently Bald Eagles from other southeastern states (e.g., South Carolina) migrate northward along the Atlantic Coast into Maine, but return southward along the inland Appalachian ridges. In spring Bald Eagles also move up the Mississippi River.

Southern Bald Eagles return to their Florida breeding grounds beginning in early August, with large numbers appearing at Pennsylvania migration watch sites along the Kittatinny Ridge from late August through September and lesser numbers in October. Southbound migrations of smaller numbers of Northern Bald Eagles appear at the Pennsylvania migration watch sites in November and December.

The migratory movements of Bald Eagles during autumn along the Kittatinny Ridge in eastern Pennsylvania do not follow an obvious gliding and soaring pattern along the length of the ridge. Rather, a third or more of the eagles observed at Bake Oven Knob are not observed downridge at Hawk Mountain. Hence eagles have limited flight-line fidelity to the Kittatinny Ridge. Instead, they migrate over a broad front and ridge-hop southward to the Kittatinny, follow it for varying distances, then drift southward.

At the Hawk Ridge Nature Reserve in Duluth, Minnesota, in 1994, hawk watchers counted 4,368 Bald Eagles. On October 31, 410 eagles were counted, followed by 578 on November 19 and a whopping 743 on November 22. The November 1994 Bald Eagle count at Hawk Ridge was 2,600 birds.

Along the Kittatinny Ridge in Pennsylvania, Bald Eagle migration counts are much smaller. At Hawk Mountain the highest autumn Bald Eagle count was 189 in 1999, whereas at Bake Oven Knob the highest Bald Eagle autumn count was 175 in 2001.

One Bald Eagle banded as a nestling in Minnesota was found dead 1,185 miles away near Llano, Texas, and another nestling banded in Minnesota was recovered approximately 1,260 miles away near Matador, Texas.

POPULATION Few raptors in North America during the twentieth century demonstrated a population change as dramatic as that of the Bald Eagle. The population crash of breeding Bald Eagles occurred in the late 1940s and the following two decades, when DDT was used indiscriminately across the landscape.

The ban on the use of DDT in Canada and the United States in the early 1970s, enactment of the federal Endangered Species Act, reintroduction programs, increased protection for habitat and eagles, and the ban of lead shot used by hunters have made great strides in the recovery of Bald Eagle populations.

In Minnesota, by 1990, there were 437 breeding areas for Bald Eagles—an increase from 115 identified breeding areas in 1973. In addition, these eagles have expanded their breeding range throughout much of the state, including some habitats not used for more than 100 years. Similarly, in Wisconsin, since 1980, there was almost a threefold expansion of occupied Bald Eagle nest territories.

By 2002, more than six thousand nesting pairs of Bald Eagles were known from the contiguous United States.

White-tailed Eagle
(Haliaeetus albicilla)

The White-tailed Eagle is an accidental visitor to eastern North America with a single report of an individual near the Nantucket Lightship off the Massachusetts coast.

Golden Eagle (Aquila chrysaetos)

Golden Eagles are rare in eastern North America. The species is our only representative of the so-called booted eagles whose legs are feathered to their toes.

A Golden Eagle. These birds are relatively rare in eastern North America. *Photo by Ron Austing.*

Massachusetts reservoir and in coastal areas from New Jersey southward into the southeastern states. In 1998, in Kentucky, a midwinter eagle survey produced seven Golden Eagles (and 162 Bald Eagles). Golden Eagles in Georgia are rare transients with occasional sightings reported during winter. Very rarely these eagles are seen as far south as the Florida Keys.

FOOD HABITS Golden Eagles in eastern North America eat red foxes, mink, muskrats, woodchucks, snowshoe hares, and cottontails as well as Common Loons, American Bitterns (especially young), American Black Ducks, Red-shouldered Hawks, Broad-winged Hawks, Barred Owls, Common Ravens, nestling American Crows, and domestic geese. A leopard frog was also brought to a nest while still alive.

Golden Eagles also eat carrion, especially during winter. In some coastal marshes they consume waterfowl, dead or alive.

NESTING AND LIFE CYCLE Golden Eagles appear on their breeding territories between 4 and 7 years of age. The birds engage in several types of courtship displays such as the sky dance, tumbling (with talon grasping), and other types of behavior.

Nests are constructed of large, broken sticks carried with their beak or feet to the nest site. The inner cup is made of roots, moss, leaves, and similar fine materials. White pine sprigs are added to nests in northeastern North America. Some nests in trees are 8 feet in diameter. Other nests, including several in northern New England, are placed on cliffs, preferably with overhead shelter. Alternate nests are commonly constructed but not used annually. Nevertheless, several northern New England Golden Eagle nests are "ecological magnets" to generations of eagles, with their use doc-

HABITAT In eastern North America, Golden Eagles breed in remote tundra with cliffs, escarpments, or bluffs that substitute for trees, and in mountains, uplands, foothills, bogs and wetlands adjacent to waterways, pond and lake shorelines, and similar areas.

During winter, however, Golden Eagles occur in open agricultural landscapes, remote reservoirs, and coastal marshes (such as national wildlife refuges), where crippled or dead waterfowl serve as food.

DISTRIBUTION Little is known about the current breeding distribution of Golden Eagles in eastern North America. Given the numbers of migrant eagles counted during autumn at eastern inland and Great Lakes watch sites, small numbers of Golden Eagles must still nest in remote parts of Ontario, Quebec, and Labrador, perhaps in remote parts of Maine, and a few in remote mountains in southern Appalachia.

Golden Eagles in eastern North America winter in very limited numbers at a remote

umented for centuries (from 1689 in one case).

Repeated copulation takes place on the tree nest, at cliff eyries, or elsewhere in open areas. Infertile or nonviable eggs are common in Golden Eagles. For some days even before eggs are deposited, the female engages in incubation-like behavior while sitting on the empty nest.

From one to three creamy white eggs (some with brown blotches) are deposited during March and April, several days apart, in nests in northeastern North America. Incubation lasts for 43 to 45 days, with the female doing most of it. The male hunts and delivers food to the female, fairly early in the morning, and she flies to a nearby plucking spot. Often the male returns around noon and the female quickly departs, a process repeated later in the day. However, the female remains on the eggs at night, and the male roosts nearby. The eaglets hatch from late May to early June, requiring more than one day to hatch. The young eagles remain in the nest for at least 9 weeks, and generally fly for the first time when 65 to 70 days old. Often, fresh green sprigs of vegetation are taken to the nest during the nesting period.

Parental Golden Eagles sometimes "assist" their recently fledged young by flying below the young eagle and allowing it to land on its back for brief periods, before "dumping" the juvenile eagle and watching it fly lower and lower, only to repeat the process. This dramatic behavior was observed several times by reliable observers in Maine, New York, Utah, and California.

The oldest known Golden Eagle lived for 23 years and 10 months.

BEHAVIOR Various types of hunting behavior are used by Golden Eagles. They prefer to hunt from aloft, attacking upwind and sometimes stooping and dropping vertically, soar-ing, or chasing when the sun is relatively low in the sky, during the early morning and evening. It is not uncommon for these birds to fast or feast as opportunities occur. After capturing prey, an eagle is likely to perch for several hours.

Sometimes they hunt from perches. Cooperative hunting by mates, sometimes including immature birds, also occurs after the nesting season is completed. Sometimes a young or inexperienced Golden Eagle experiences a "hunger panic" and attacks prey regardless of danger to itself. There are also reports of young eagles attempting to capture prey that is too large, powerful, or dangerous for them to handle—such as cattle, deer, and porcupines. Golden Eagles eat approximately one pound of food daily.

Female Golden Eagles are capable of carrying prey weighing about 7 pounds, at least for short distances, whereas a small male eagle can carry prey weighing less than 5 pounds.

Golden Eagles are hostile toward other raptors—especially when one or both species are territorial and enter each other's space. Among raptors killed by Golden Eagles are Ospreys, Bald Eagles, Northern Goshawks, Red-shouldered Hawks, Red-tailed Hawks, Rough-legged Hawks, Gyrfalcons, Peregrine Falcons, and Great Horned Owls.

Golden Eagles are usually not heard vocalizing but sometimes make several yelps, shrill *ki-ki-ki-ki* screams, and several other sounds.

MIGRATION In spring, Golden Eagles migrate from February to May. Along the southern shoreline of Lake Ontario at Derby Hill, New York, the largest numbers occur from late March to late April. As many as 166 migrating Golden Eagles have also been reported during spring at Tussey Mountain in central Pennsylvania.

Autumn migratory movements of Golden Eagles during autumn along the Kittatinny

Immature Golden Eagles have a distinctive white basal area on their tail, and a conspicuous white patch on each wing. *Photo by Ron Austing.*

Ridge in Pennsylvania are complex. At Hawk Mountain, most of these eagles appear between mid-October and mid-November, with similar time periods occurring upridge, at nearby Bake Oven Knob.

A comparison of age and time records of Golden Eagles observed at Bake Oven Knob and Hawk Mountain, from 1968 through 1981, demonstrated that 133 (35.1 percent) of the 378 Golden Eagles observed at the Knob were not observed downridge at Hawk Mountain.

Although Golden Eagles are now observed in satisfying numbers at the raptor migration watch sites along the Kittatinny Ridge in Pennsylvania, the largest annual count along the ridge occurred in 2000 at Waggoner's Gap, when 221 Golden Eagles were seen. A record seasonal count of 144 was reported in 1998 at Hawk Mountain, and 93 Golden Eagles were reported in 1999 at Bake Oven Knob. At the Holiday Beach Migration Observatory in southwestern Ontario, the largest annual autumn count was 130 Golden Eagles reported in 1999.

POPULATION Estimates of North American populations of Golden Eagles suggest that there are about 70,000 individuals—mostly in western North America. Probably not more than several hundred Golden Eagles live in eastern North America at any given time.

The most recent examination of status and trends of Golden Eagle populations in the United States and Canada indicate the eastern population declined significantly during the period 1934–1972, was fairly stable between 1973 and 1986, and seemed to be increasing from 1987 to 1999.

A complex statistical analysis of autumn counts of migrating Golden Eagles passing Hawk Mountain shows a decline in immatures from 1940 through 1960. Hawk Mountain ornithologists also contend a severe decline in immatures occurred from 1934 to 1948—a period largely *before* the widespread use of DDT. The lowest seasonal Golden Eagle count reported at Hawk Mountain was 16 reported in 1966, and the highest count was 148 reported in 1998.

At Bake Oven Knob, autumn migration count data for Golden Eagles exist from 1961 to the present. A graph of annual percentages of immature and adult Golden Eagles counted at this watch site shows relatively low percentages of immatures in 1966, approaching the danger point signaling widespread reproductive failure. Hence, some reproductive failure may have occurred in the Golden Eagle breeding population in eastern North America—but not nearly as severe as that experienced by Bald Eagles.

10

ACCIPITERS

The genus *Accipiter,* containing the forest-loving hawks, is found worldwide although only three species occur in eastern North America: Sharp-shinned Hawk, Cooper's Hawk, and Northern Goshawk.

Sharp-shinned Hawk
(*Accipiter striatus*)

The Sharp-shinned Hawk is the smallest and most common of our accipiters or bird-eating hawks.

HABITAT Sharp-shinned Hawks breed in mixed deciduous-coniferous woodland, or just coniferous woodland, but during migration they fly over a wide range of wooded habitats and open areas. Stopover habitats are wooded areas with a varied vegetation composition. During winter, males prefer mixed deciduous-coniferous woodland or coniferous woodland and small woodland patches, while females prefer continuous deciduous woodland. These hawks also visit backyards with bird feeders, where concentrations of small birds are potential prey.

Sharp-shinned and Cooper's Hawk nest-site habitats in Wisconsin show differences between the species. Sharp-shins use younger tree stands containing smaller and shorter trees than do Cooper's Hawks. Sharp-shins also use a more restricted array of tree species, but in locations with mixed hardwood and coniferous trees, they select more tree species in which to place nests than do Cooper's Hawks. In general, in Wisconsin, Sharp-shinned Hawk nest sites have more coniferous elements than do Cooper's Hawk sites, which have more deciduous elements.

DISTRIBUTION Sharp-shinned Hawks breed in eastern North America from the southern third of eastern Canada southward through the northern Great Lakes states and the Ap-

An adult Sharp-shinned Hawk. These accipiters are woodland hawks. *Photo by Ron Austing.*

palachian Mountains. In Georgia, they were reported nesting in the Piedmont National Wildlife Refuge, the most southern nesting record for the species in eastern North America.

Sharp-shins winter south of their eastern North American breeding grounds in areas along the Atlantic and Gulf Coasts of the United States, or farther south to Cuba and Central America.

FOOD HABITS Small birds (adults and nestlings) are the primary food of Sharp-shinned Hawks, with adult prey size ranging from hummingbirds to grouse, and an occasional small mammal, reptile, or insect is also eaten. Birds taken include grouse, sandpipers, swifts, hummingbirds, woodpeckers, flycatchers, nuthatches, chickadees, mockingbirds, catbirds, thrashers, robins, bluebirds, creepers, kinglets, vireos, wood warblers, grackles, orioles, blackbirds, juncos, and sparrows. Occasionally an immature Sharp-shin attempts to capture larger prey such as a Wood Duck.

NESTING AND LIFE CYCLE Sharp-shinned Hawks probably are monogamous, and are largely solitary. Females begin breeding between 1 and 2 years of age. The pair bond is formed when the male, then the female, circles in undulating flight and dives above the nest. Copulation follows.

Nests are broad, flat, stick structures composed of dead evergreen twigs with some bark flakes lining the interior. The nest is built by the female, but both sexes gather nest materials. Nests usually are placed about 35 feet above the ground on horizontal limbs in the crown below the canopy of a conifer, although some are placed in deciduous trees.

Four or five white eggs, blotched with brown or violet colors, are deposited in the nest on alternate days. The incubation period is approximately 30 days. The female Sharp-shin incubates the eggs. The male roosts nearby and provides his mate with food at the nest. Eggs hatch within 2 days of each other, and sexual dimorphism in size is visible when the nestlings are a few days old. Differences in plumage growth appear within a week of hatching. The adult female broods her nestlings for 16 to 23 days. In New Brunswick, Canada, male nestlings departed from the nest when about 24 days old, nestling females when 27 days old.

The young hawks make their first flights to nearby trees below the forest canopy. Both parents provide food to them by passing it in midair. Juveniles capture their own prey when about 40 days old. Some recently fledged Sharp-shins vocalize in close proximity to other raptors such as Northern Harriers, Broad-winged Hawks, and Red-tailed Hawks.

The oldest known Sharp-shinned Hawk lived for 19 years and 11 months.

BEHAVIOR Sharp-shinned Hawks are opportunistic hunters in prey selection and use rapid, brief aerial pursuits that are soon successful or halted. These hawks hunt while in flight or when perched, darting after prey for brief periods of time. Migrating juvenile male Sharp-shins tend to choose smaller prey than juvenile females, but adults do not exhibit this difference in prey selection.

Sharp-shinned Hawks also occasionally walk or hop when trying to capture prey on the ground. The prey is then taken to a plucking stump, where feathers are removed prior to eating it, and where interactions between males and females may occur.

Accipiters have distinctive overhead flight silhouettes—relatively short rounded wings and a long, rudderlike tail. Sharp-shinned Hawks typically employ a flap-flap-flap-glide flight style but also use thermal soaring and sometimes dive steeply in pursuit of prey along migration routes. The Sharp-shin's wing-beat rate is more rapid than that of Cooper's Hawks and Northern Goshawks.

Ornithologists and hawk watchers sometimes witnesses vigorous, even dramatic, interactions between Sharp-shinned Hawks and other raptors during autumn migration. For example, on October 6, 1997, at Bake Oven Knob, Pennsylvania, I observed a Sharp-shin (age undetermined) dive four or five times on an adult Red-tailed Hawk. The Red-tail was twice forced to perform a 360 degree lateral roll, reaching upward with its legs and talons while upside-down, in failed attempts to grasp the persistent Sharp-shin. Each lateral roll lasted about 2 or 3 seconds, and the overall episode lasted about 2 minutes. It was not clear if the birds were engaged in play or interspecies strife.

One report has Barn Swallows attacking and pestering a Sharp-shinned Hawk and forcing it to fly higher and higher into the sky like a soaring hawk, until it finally departed the area. The hawk made no attempt to attack the swallows.

Sharp-shins migrate as individuals (as opposed to forming "kettles" or flocks like Broad-winged Hawks), sometimes in a seemingly endless stream. It is not unusual, however, to see a few of these hawks among other raptor species in thermal soaring.

Vocalizations of Sharp-shinned Hawks include *kek-kek-kek* alarm calls, and multiple *kip* sounds. Much remains to be learned about their vocalizations.

MIGRATION Sharp-shinned Hawks are fairly long distance migrants. They tend to follow leading lines during migration, especially during autumn, but also in spring along the southern shorelines of some of the Great Lakes such as Lake Ontario in New York.

Spring Sharp-shinned Hawk migrations occur from late March to early May, but mostly during April, over a broad front with temporal adjustment for the geographic locations of watch sites. Key spring watch sites include Whitefish Point in Michigan and Braddock Bay and Derby Hill in New York. Lesser spring sites exist along the Atlantic coastline, but no major spring watch sites are known inland along mountains such as the Kittatinny Ridge in Pennsylvania.

During autumn, Sharp-shinned Hawks migrate southward over a broad front but do so in combination with several major flyways: (1) the Atlantic coastline from Atlantic Canada southward to the Florida Keys; (2) the Kittatinny Ridge extending across parts of New York, New Jersey, and Pennsylvania (and to a lesser extent other mountain ridges); and (3) the northern and western shorelines of the Great Lakes. Much smaller numbers are seen during autumn elsewhere in eastern North America.

Autumn migration begins in the northern part of the Sharp-shin's geographic range during early August, but at Bake Oven Knob and Hawk Mountain in Pennsylvania peak Sharp-shin flights occur from early to mid-October or slightly later. Immatures occur mostly from early to mid-September, and adults appear from mid-September to mid-October.

High daily migration counts of Sharp-shinned Hawks include 2,407 on October 17, 2001, at Holiday Beach Migration Observatory in Ontario, and 1,623 on September 10, 1991, at Hawk Ridge Nature Reserve in Minnesota. Farther east, hawk watchers counted 1,265 on October 13, 1979, at Bake Oven Knob, 2,620 on October 8, 1979, at Hawk Mountain, Pennsylvania, 11,096 on October 4, 1977, at Cape May Point, New Jersey, and 3,842 on September 29, 1995, at Kiptopeke, Virginia.

On Grassy Key, Florida, during the autumn of 1995, a seasonal count of 1,499 Sharp-shinned Hawks suggests some migrant

Sharp-shins from eastern North America extend their autumn migration at least as far as southern Florida.

POPULATION The effects of DDT pollution on Sharp-shinned Hawk reproduction may have caused population declines from the 1940s to the 1970s. Population rebounds then seemed to occur after the ban on the use of DDT.

Hawk Mountain's ornithologists initially believed Sharp-shins were suffering reproductive failures due to increased levels of chemical contaminants. Nevertheless, in 1993 and 1994, normal age classes were reported for autumn Sharp-shin migration counts at Bake Oven Knob, Pennsylvania.

In 1996, Hawk Mountain's ornithologists suggested declining Sharp-shin migration counts were caused by short stopping, with increasing numbers wintering north of Pennsylvania. Possible reasons included climate change and increased use of bird feeders by small birds visiting backyards in New England during winter. After December, however, declines are reported in Sharp-shins visiting New England backyard habitats.

Autumn Sharp-shinned Hawk migration counts (birds per hour of observation) from Bake Oven Knob, Pennsylvania, show relatively low counts for 1961 through 1976, then a dramatic increase from 1977 through 1981, after which a much lower annual rate of passage is documented—with 1992 and 2002 nearly as low as the 1960s counts. From 1982 through 1993, and even during 2002, however, normal age ratios for Sharp-shins were reported at Bake Oven Knob.

Monitoring autumn Sharp-shinned Hawk migrations at the Holiday Beach Migration Observatory in southwestern Ontario, Canada, exhibited no important declines in Sharp-shinned Hawk counts from 1976 through 1993. Age ratios also remained normal from 1988 through 1993. However, hawks migrating past Holiday Beach represent an inland population separate from raptors counted at Atlantic coastal and inland ridge watch sites. The Great Lakes hawks were subjected to different environmental conditions. In Wisconsin, Sharp-shinned Hawk numbers are also stable or perhaps increasing.

In Pennsylvania, this hawk is classified as "status undetermined."

Cooper's Hawk (*Accipiter cooperii*)

Cooper's Hawks are larger, more robust versions of Sharp-shinned Hawks, less dependent upon extensive woodland, and capture somewhat larger prey.

HABITAT Cooper's Hawk habitat includes large deciduous, coniferous, and mixed woodland and woodlots, edges of woodland, riverine groves, and suburban and urban locations with patches of suitable woodland habitat throughout most of eastern North America from southern Canada southward. These hawks also visit backyards with bird feeders during winter because of concentrations of small birds, which provide a food supply for these hawks. See the Sharp-shinned Hawk species account for comparisons of Cooper's and Sharp-shinned Hawk habitat requirements in Wisconsin.

DISTRIBUTION Cooper's Hawks breed widely from southern Canada (but not Atlantic Canada) southward nearly to the Gulf Coast and southern Florida north of the Everglades. Non-breeding birds occur along the Gulf Coast and in Florida's Everglades area. However, the Cooper's Hawk breeding distribution is dynamic, with these hawks sometimes invading new breeding areas.

Wintering Cooper's Hawks occur from Michigan, Minnesota, New England, New

An adult Cooper's Hawk. This species is slightly larger than the Sharp-shinned Hawk. *Photo by Ron Austing.*

York, Wisconsin, and in Canada from Ontario southward throughout eastern North America.

FOOD HABITS Cooper's Hawks are predators on small- and medium-size birds and mammals, reptiles, amphibians, and insects. Rarely carrion is eaten.

Typical avian prey includes Northern Flickers, Blue Jays, American Robins, European Starlings, Ring-necked Pheasants, Ruffed Grouse, American Crows, and Dark-eyed Juncos. Eastern chipmunks, gray squirrels, and even bats are included among their mammal prey.

On November 4, 2002, at a banding station in Selkirk Provincial Park, Ontario, an adult female Cooper's Hawk engaged in cannibal-ism. The hawk fed on a juvenile male Cooper's Hawk—eating the prey's head and neck, and remained for the next two days to feed on the remains of the prey.

On January 16, 1994, near Jersey Shore, Pennsylvania, an immature Cooper's Hawk fed on a road-killed rabbit. The hawk returned during the next two days and continued feeding on this food, perhaps the first record of a Cooper's Hawk feeding on carrion.

NESTING AND LIFE CYCLE Cooper's Hawks are monogamous. They usually begin breeding when 2 or more years old, but a few (6 to 22 percent) of immature females also breed successfully. Adult males sometimes bow (occasionally the display is reversed) before a female before nest building begins. Nests are constructed of sticks with a bark flake cup, and some green sprigs for adornment, placed in extensive woodland or large woodlots, rarely in isolated trees. Pine plantations are important Cooper's Hawk nesting sites in the Midwest. Clear-cuts are often a habitat feature in wooded areas where these hawks nest.

Three to five dirty white eggs with a bluish tinge are deposited from late April to early May in nests in New York, Wisconsin, and Ontario. Incubation lasts for 34 to 36 days and is performed mostly by the female. The male provides most of the food for the female and young. Adults also cache prey on tree branches for later use.

Young male Cooper's Hawks leave the nest when 30 days old, females when 34 days old. However, the juveniles return to their nest for prey and roosting for another 10 days. Juvenile hawks also continue receiving prey from their parents for another 7 weeks.

The oldest known Cooper's Hawk lived for 13 years and 10 months.

BEHAVIOR The flight style of Cooper's Hawks consists of several flaps followed by a glide, with the wing beats somewhat slower than those used by Sharp-shinned Hawks but more rapid than those used by the Northern Goshawk. These are subtle differences, but expert hawk watchers include them among the identification characteristics they consider when identifying accipiters in flight. Occasionally these hawks also thermal soar, or use flapping and gliding and thermal soaring.

When hunting, Cooper's Hawks usually dart through woodland near the ground or under the forest canopy. They also capture prey outside of woodland during migration or in backyards at bird feeders. Sometimes Cooper's Hawks will walk or run when pursuing or retrieving prey, or when gathering nest materials from the ground. When eating prey, Cooper's Hawks tend to be bold and sometimes remain with their prey even when people approach within 10 feet. Occasionally immature and adult Cooper's Hawks visit backyard bird baths to bathe.

Cooper's Hawks often are attacked by groups of American Crows, which may force the hawk to seek shelter in a nearby wooded area. On the other hand, when Cooper's Hawks attack crows the result frequently is the death of the crow. Eastern Kingbirds also are bold and do not hesitate to attack and drive Cooper's Hawks away—as they sometimes also do with Red-tailed Hawks and other raptors.

More than seventy-five different vocalizations are used by Cooper's Hawks of various ages, with the *cak-cak-cak* alarm call especially well known. Males commonly use *kik* vocalization near the nest to indicate their presence; females use this same sound much less frequently. The *whaaa* vocalization is used frequently by females in relations with the males.

MIGRATION Spring Cooper's Hawk migrations occur from mid-March to early May.

Males migrate northward before females, and adults arrive before the previous year's young—which reverses the pattern documented during autumn (at least insofar as age classes are concerned).

Autumn migrations of Cooper's Hawks are far better studied than spring migrations. In autumn the hawks use the same migration flyways as Sharp-shinned Hawks, but their numbers are much smaller. Along the Kittatinny Ridge in Pennsylvania, migrating Cooper's Hawks appear from early August to late November or early December, with most counted during early to mid-October. Cooper's Hawks from the more northern part of the breeding range are more migratory than southern birds.

Many more Cooper's Hawks are seen during autumn along the Atlantic Coast than inland along the Kittatinny Ridge. Examples of maximum autumn migration counts of Cooper's Hawks include 2,950 in 1987 at Cape May Point, New Jersey, 1,121 in 1998 at Hawk Mountain, Pennsylvania, and 1,083 in 1991 at the Holiday Beach Migration Observatory in Ontario. At Grassy Key, Florida, during the autumn of 1995, only 185 Cooper's Hawks were reported, but this watch site is located at the southern edge of the geographic range of this species in eastern North America.

One juvenile Cooper's Hawk banded in September 1993 at Lehigh Furnace Gap on the Kittatinny Ridge in Pennsylvania was found injured on January 7, 2000, below a power line in St. John, New Brunswick, Canada. The hawk was taken to a rehabilitation center, where it died.

POPULATION As with the Sharp-shinned Hawk, Hawk Mountain's ornithologists detected a decline, and later a recovery, in Cooper's Hawk populations.

Nevertheless, Cooper's Hawk population trends based on Christmas Bird Count data from Pennsylvania suggest a population rebound that was slower than that of Sharpshins. There were also less apparent regional differences in Cooper's Hawk populations. Cooper's Hawks are classified as vulnerable in Pennsylvania.

Northern Goshawk
(*Accipiter gentilis*)

The Northern Goshawk is the largest and rarest of the North American accipiters. As breeding birds, these bold, powerful hawks are confined largely to forested areas.

HABITAT Large coniferous, deciduous, or mixed forests in Canada and the northeastern United States with small open foraging areas are the habitats generally used by Northern Goshawks. In mixed coniferous-deciduous forests, they tend to select deciduous trees in which to build their nests. Less shrub growth exists in some forest habitats used by Northern Goshawks as breeding sites, perhaps because it is easier for these big accipiters to fly rapidly through these areas.

In New York and New Jersey, Northern Goshawk nest sites are found at higher elevations in large forest blocks away from human habitation and roads. Nests in the Pocono Mountains in Pennsylvania have been located in extensive forests where small to medium dead tree branches litter the forest floor. In comparison, in southern Vermont, goshawk nests were found close to forest openings and rural roads not too distant from summer cottages (probably unoccupied when nesting began in early spring).

DISTRIBUTION Northern Goshawks breed in coniferous, deciduous, or mixed forests, with nests sometimes located near woodland edges or openings, throughout forested Canada and northern Minnesota, Wisconsin, and Michi-

An adult Northern Goshawk. They are the largest of the three species of accipiters found in North America. *Photo by Ron Austing.*

gan eastward throughout the northeastern United States and southward in the Appalachian Mountains to West Virginia and western Maryland. These hawks are expanding their breeding range southward.

Northern Goshawks sometimes appear during winter in city and suburban parks or backyard habitats with bird feeders. Occasionally they venture far south of their normal geographic range into Georgia, the northern portions of the Gulf states, west-central Florida, and even Bermuda.

FOOD HABITS Birds are the primary food of Northern Goshawks, with the species taken depending on sex of the hawk, season, and location. Ruffed Grouse and American Crows are typical prey, but ducks, Northern Bobwhite, Sharp-tailed Grouse, Greater Prairie Chickens, Ring-necked Pheasants, Rock Doves, Mourning Doves, Barred Owls, Blue Jays, grackles, blackbirds, and sparrows are also food items. Before they became extinct, Passenger Pigeons also were taken by Northern Goshawks. Chipmunks, squirrels, mice, rabbits, snowshoe hares, and sometimes other mammals are also eaten by goshawks. Rarely, during Northern Goshawk invasions in Maine, domestic dogs were attacked by these hawks. Additional odd food items include snakes, insects, and an occasional invertebrate. Carrion sometimes is also eaten.

The importance of Northern Goshawks as predators on Ruffed Grouse depends on location. Some individual goshawks apparently become habituated to particular prey. In Minnesota, for example, nesting Northern Goshawks were major predators on Ruffed Grouse living in marginal grouse habitat, but in New York and Pennsylvania grouse were not important prey in the diet of these hawks.

NESTING AND LIFE CYCLE Northern Goshawks establish pair bonds for life. Territorial displays occur annually. They include "high circling" and several other displays over the forest around the nest site and are a prelude to the "sky dance."

The female begins work on the nest in late February or early March. It is either new or refurbished from the previous year, constructed of sticks and twigs, and lined with fresh evergreen sprigs or green leaves. Nests are usually placed in the crotches of large hardwood trees. In Vermont, nests were found near small clearings or logging roads in mixed deciduous-coniferous forests. A plentiful supply of dead twigs and sticks often litters the forest floor. Nest construction requires about a week. Nests are reused for as long as 8 years (usually 3 or 4 years) in the northeastern United States, whereas in Michigan one Northern Goshawk nest was later used by Red-shouldered Hawks and Barred Owls.

Copulation takes place several times daily, usually on a branch near the nest, during nest construction and egg laying. Two or three eggs are deposited at 2-day intervals, and are incubated for 32 to 34 days. After hatching, the eggshells are carried away from the nest and discarded. If a clutch is lost, another is laid within a month.

Male Northern Goshawks feed their mate at the nest or nearby, using a plucking stump

Northern Goshawk nestlings in Vermont. *Photo by Donald S. Heintzelman.*

In the vicinity of their nests, Northern Goshawks sometimes are fierce and aggressive. *Photo by Ron Austing.*

to remove the prey's head and feathers from the body. Prey that is a nestling is usually not plucked before being eaten.

The female attends to the nestlings and the male secures food for his mate. After the nestlings are several days old, the male does not remain at the nest after delivering food, and the nestlings are fed after the male departs. Food is also cached for later use.

Nestlings leave the nest when 37 to 41 days old, males departing a few days before females. The juvenile hawks remain on tree branches near the nest for about a week, but spend nights in the nest. At this time, the parents deliver food to their young at the nest or nearby, but soon the juvenile hawks fly to their parents to receive food via an aerial pass. Sometimes live prey is provided. Juveniles become independent from their parents at about 70 to 80 days.

The oldest known Northern Goshawk lived for 16 years and 4 months.

BEHAVIOR Northern Goshawks are bold and fierce predators. They hunt low in the forest canopy while perched on a snag or tree limb.

Trees are spaced farther apart in goshawk habitat, making it easier for them to maneuver. Sometimes they hunt as pairs for squirrels. In Minnesota, the 988 acre primary foraging area for one pair of nesting Northern Goshawks was located 1.25 miles west of the nest site. The nest was on a ridge in a quaking aspen tree 328 feet from a lake in the Boundary Waters Canoe Area Wilderness near the Canadian border. There is even a report of two Northern Goshawks attacking Wood Duck decoys and trying to carry them away.

Northern Goshawks sometimes are extremely fierce and aggressive toward human intruders into nest territories or at nests, with some observers being attacked and injured. Not all individuals exhibit such aggressiveness.

Northern Goshawks roost alone deep within the forest canopy. A roost site may be used for several consecutive nights, or goshawks may use various roost sites.

Various vocalizations are utilized by Northern Goshawks, with cackling *ki-ki-ki-ki* or *cac-cac-cac* alarm calls used by both sexes in defense of nest territories.

MIGRATION Many Northern Goshawks in the northeastern states are largely non-migratory with hawks from the far northern regions accounting for birds seen in New York and New Jersey.

Spring Northern Goshawk migrations along the Kittatinny Ridge in Pennsylvania occur from late March through early April. Other watch sites approximate similar temporal patterns with adjustments for geographic locations and invasions.

Autumn Northern Goshawk migrations occur from early September through early December, depending on geographic location. A few appear annually at migration watch sites, but every 10 to 12 years these hawks experience peaks in population cycles, and numerous Northern Goshawks have major southward invasions. In the Toronto, Ontario, region, Northern Goshawk invasions have occurred about every 10 years since 1886, and at 9- to 11-year intervals in southern Canada and the northern and northeastern United States.

In the autumn of 1972, large numbers of Northern Goshawks appeared in the northern and northeastern United States. More than five thousand passed Hawk Ridge Nature Reserve in Duluth, Minnesota, and hundreds of goshawks passed Bake Oven Knob and Hawk Mountain in Pennsylvania. Most were adults.

An "echo flight" occurred in 1973 with fewer birds seen. More recently, Northern Goshawk invasions of varying magnitudes were detected from time to time at watch sites.

The probable causes of Northern Goshawk cycles include widespread shortages in food, but some ornithologists believe exceptionally strong cold fronts moving across the western Great Lakes region also cause goshawk invasions.

POPULATION Securing population estimates of Northern Goshawks is difficult. In New Jersey, however, ornithologists estimated only approximately twenty nesting pairs in the state.

Population trends of Northern Goshawks based on autumn migration counts at Hawk Mountain, Pennsylvania, increased during the years when Sharp-shinned and Cooper's Hawk population trends declined, then recovered. However, the exact geographic origins of the hawks counted at that watch site are unknown.

The U.S. Fish and Wildlife Service considers the Northern Goshawk a "species of concern." Maryland and Rhode Island consider it of "special concern." New Jersey also considers it "threatened," whereas Pennsylvania classified the species as "status undetermined."

11

SOARING HAWKS

Soaring hawks have broad wings and tails that readily enable them to use thermal soaring. Red-shouldered and Broad-winged Hawks are woodland examples, whereas Red-tailed, Swainson's, and Rough-legged Hawks are open-habitat birds.

Red-shouldered Hawk
(*Buteo lineatus*)

The Red-shouldered Hawk is one of the most colorful of our raptors. When adults are seen closely, they are the highlight of a day's hawk-watching activities.

HABITAT Red-shouldered Hawk habitat consists of mature bottomland and riparian woodland, deciduous swamps, wet hardwood forests, and mixed upland coniferous-deciduous forests.

DISTRIBUTION Red-shouldered Hawks breed from extreme southern Ontario and Quebec southward to the Florida Keys.

FOOD HABITS Red-shouldered Hawk food includes small mammals (chipmunks, voles, mice especially for nestlings), birds (Mourning Doves, House Sparrows, European Starlings), amphibians (frogs and toads) and reptiles (water snakes, garter snakes, turtles), insects (grasshoppers and crickets), and other invertebrates (crayfish).

An adult Red-shouldered Hawk was observed in Florida feeding on the remains of a Common Nighthawk carcass—one of the few records of this raptor utilizing carrion, and perhaps the first record of avian carrion.

In Maryland, an adult Red-shouldered Hawk visited a balcony bird feeder and daily ate large pieces of suet for 3 weeks during a period of extreme cold—remarkably adaptive behavior. When more normal temperatures arrived the hawk disappeared.

NESTING AND LIFE CYCLE Red-shouldered Hawks are monogamous (one nest in Florida had one female and two males in attendance). The hawks are already paired when they arrive on their nest territory in mid-February to mid-March. Males perform a "sky dance" over their woodland nest site, then copulate with the female for approximately 5 seconds. During this part of the nesting season, Red-shoulders are quite vocal, which is helpful in detecting their return and finding the approximate locations of nests.

Nest sites are placed in close proximity to a wetland such as moist hardwood forest, swamp, stream, or pond. Red-shouldered Hawks are strongly attached to their previous nest sites—even when disturbances occur at nest trees.

Nests are constructed new or refurbished before and to the end of courtship, often in

An adult Red-shouldered Hawk—among the most beautiful of our eastern North American raptors. *Photo by Ron Austing.*

a mature beech or oak tree. The nest is placed in coniferous or deciduous trees, below the forest canopy, in a crotch of the main tree trunk. Both sexes participate in construction or repair for 4 to 5 weeks, and nests are made of live and dead sticks and dead leaves. The inner cup is lined with flakes of bark, moss, lichens, and fresh conifer sprigs, the latter perhaps producing chemicals serving as an insecticide. Breeding Red-shoulders exhibit a high degree of nest-site fidelity, reusing nests and territories year after year, not unlike the so-called ecological-magnet attractiveness of many Peregrine Falcons toward prime cliff-nesting ledges overlooking rivers prior to their population crash in the mid-twentieth century in eastern North America.

Three or four (two in Florida) smooth white eggs with brown and lavender marks are deposited, with incubation starting before the clutch is complete. If necessary, a replacement clutch is deposited a month later. The adult female develops an incubation patch, which remains for more than 40 days, as she incubates her eggs for about 33 days. Several days separate hatching of some of the eggs, which soon becomes evident by the size differences (and sometimes behavior differences) of the nestlings.

Red-shoulder nestlings leave their nest in New York when about 32 days old, but their parents feed them for several more weeks. The juvenile hawks remain at, or close to, the nest for an undetermined time period and become independent when 14 to 16 weeks old. Juveniles become successful predators, however, when 10 to 13 weeks old.

Red-shouldered Hawks are at least a year old when they breed for the first time, although records exist of immatures (especially females) mated with adults. One pair of immature Red-shoulders also nested successfully.

In Wisconsin, several Red-shoulders banded as nestlings later nested only 15 miles from their natal locales, and one hawk ventured only a mile from its birthplace. Home ranges in Pennsylvania extended from 269 to 837 acres. During winter in Michigan, home ranges of four Red-shoulders covered up to 3.2 square miles.

The oldest known Red-shouldered Hawk lived for 19 years and 11 months.

BEHAVIOR Flight is the primary method of locomotion utilized by the Red-shouldered Hawk. When flapping flight is used, it resembles an accipiter's flight style by consisting of a series of flaps, followed by a glide. Sometimes thermal soaring is also used.

Red-shouldered Hawks use several methods of hunting. Sometimes they perch on branches of trees and hunt from there by watching the forest around them for prey. At other times, however, they hunt while in flight, see prey below them, and fly down and grasp the animal. Foraging is done in forested as well as open areas—usually those with some wet component.

Red-shouldered Hawks mob and chase Great Horned Owls that venture into the hawk's territory, sometimes actually striking the owl. Raccoons sometimes raid Red-shoulder nests and eat their eggs or nestlings.

Red-shouldered Hawks at one Massachusetts location used the same nest site annually for 26 years during the period 1882 to 1907. Presumably some of these birds were not those observed originally because this species is not known to live more than approximately 20 years. Logging, however, later disrupted use of the nest site by these hawks. Whether offspring from some earlier nests later returned and used their natal locale is unknown. Curiously, at the end of the long Red-shouldered Hawk usage period of that particular nest site, a pair of Barred Owls moved in and nested there—followed by a pair of nesting Red-tailed Hawks the next year. In Wisconsin, nest usage increased over the years to 150 nest sites with fifty to sixty nests now used annually.

At one Red-shoulder nest I visited in the Pocono Mountains in Pennsylvania, the nestlings exhibited considerable variation in aggressiveness. One smaller bird (perhaps the male) was exceptionally docile compared with its nestmates—a situation not uncommon with other raptors.

Red-shouldered Hawks make various vocalizations. *Kee-aah* is used commonly, *kip* when alarmed or excited, and *kee-ann-errr* when displaying to another Red-shoulder. Sometimes other vocalizations are also used. Blue Jays are able to imitate the vocalizations of Red-shouldered Hawks fairly well.

MIGRATION Red-shouldered Hawk migrations during spring occur across a broad front from late February through early April, with largest numbers seen from mid- to late March. The hawks divert along the southern shorelines of the Great Lakes to avoid crossing large expanses of open water.

During autumn, migrating Red-shouldered Hawks also tend to avoid crossing large bodies of open water such as the Great Lakes. Instead, they divert along major geographic features or leading-lines such as the Atlantic coastline, the Kittatinny Ridge in Pennsylvania, and the western and southern shorelines of the Great Lakes. Most autumn Red-shoulder migrations occur between late September and late November, with the bulk seen from mid-October to early November. The vivid coloration of adults makes these hawks spectacular ornithological and birding attractions.

POPULATION Analysis of Hawk Mountain autumn Red-shouldered Hawk migration count data suggest a long-term, nonsignificant population decline. A similar, long-term declining trend appears in Red-shoulder migration counts at Bake Oven Knob. In Minnesota, Red-shoulders also are declining. In Canada, however, the Red-shoulder population is estimated at two thousand to five thousand pairs and is stable or increasing.

Red-shouldered Hawks are classed as "endangered" in Illinois and New Jersey. Michigan, New York, and Wisconsin class them "threatened," and Connecticut, Minnesota, Mississippi, and Indiana consider them "of special concern." Red-shoulders are also on the "watch list" in Massachusetts and Maine, and in Pennsylvania this species is classified as "vulnerable."

Broad-winged Hawk
(Buteo platypterus)

Broad-winged Hawks are relatively tame woodland hawks and our most numerous migrant raptors.

HABITAT Broad-winged Hawks nest in large expanses of deciduous and coniferous-deciduous forest with nearby open areas and water. Nest sites in Ontario are typically young deciduous forest, whereas Minnesota sites are in woodland close to openings (roads, fields, trails) or wetlands (lakes, pools, wooded swamps, shallow or deep marshes). The Minnesota and Wisconsin nest sites utilize 35- to 50-year old managed, northern red oak and aspen woodland. In Maine and Vermont, Broad-wing nests are located in conifer-deciduous forests. In New York, sloped woodland with yellow birch trees is the preferred nest site. In Pennsylvania, I studied nests along the south base of the Kittatinny Ridge, and in deciduous mountain woodland within the city of Allentown. The latter was fairly close to human dwellings and roads.

DISTRIBUTION Broad-winged Hawks breed in deciduous and coniferous-deciduous forest and woodland from southern Ontario, Quebec, and Atlantic Canada southward to north-

ern Florida and the Gulf Coast. Occasional winter sightings are reported in eastern states, including Georgia, plus a few hundred in southern Florida and the Keys.

FOOD HABITS Broad-winged Hawks prey upon moth larvae, grasshoppers, locusts, beetles, dragonflies, ants, spiders, millipedes, earthworms, crawfish, crabs, fish, frogs, toads, lizards, snakes, more than thirty mammal species (shrews, voles, mice, chipmunks, squirrels, weasels, rabbits), and some twenty-five bird species (especially nestlings or fledglings), including Ruffed Grouse, Northern Flickers, Pileated Woodpecker, Blue Jays, Northern Saw-whet Owl, wood warblers, and sparrows. Measured in terms of biomass, birds usually represent about 22 to 38 percent, and mammals about 56 to 63 percent, of the diet of Broad-winged Hawks.

NESTING AND LIFE CYCLE Broad-winged Hawks are probably monogamous. Three types of courtship behavior are employed: high circling flights, sky dancing, and sky tumbling. Males engage in courtship feeding and bring food to the female at the nest.

In New York, nest construction begins from the third week in April to mid-May and lasts as long as 5 weeks. Occasionally, Broad-wings use nests of other birds such as hawks or crows, but considerable renovation is done. Broad-winged Hawks select a range of trees—including birches, maples, poplars, and occasionally pines—in which to construct their nests. Some nests are placed in the main crotch of a tree whereas others are put on a limb near the trunk. Both sexes build or renovate their nest using twigs, sticks, and sprigs of green vegetation. Construction requires 2 to 5 weeks to complete. Nests are reused only rarely in subsequent years. One Broad-wing nest high in a white pine tree along the south base of the Kittatinny Ridge in Pennsylvania was used the following year by a pair of nesting Great Horned Owls.

Observations of the copulation behavior of a captive Broad-winged Hawk revealed that the bird held its toes in a closed position, making it incapable of grasping or gripping—or harming a female with which a wild hawk would copulate.

Generally two or three white or creamy white eggs, with brown and lavender blotches and dots, are deposited early in May in Maryland, but a week or two later in Ontario. Incubation requires 28 to 31 days, is done by the female, and hatching occurs in mid-June. Food is provided to her by the male as she incubates the eggs.

The nestlings are also brooded by the female for longtime periods—usually for about 3 weeks. She feeds her nestlings with prey captured by the male, who takes the food to her at the nest, or drops prey on the nest if the female is absent. Broad-wings leave the nest when 29 to 31 days old, but remain nearby on tree limbs for several weeks before departing. During this period they obtain prey from

their parents away from the nest, or capture their own prey. Nevertheless, juveniles continue to remain near their parents for up to 4 weeks, and near their nest for as long as 8 weeks.

The oldest known Broad-winged Hawk lived for 16 years and 1 month.

BEHAVIOR Broad-wings commonly hunt from woodland perches in the bottom of the forest canopy, or the understory, and sometimes cache food. During migration, they occasionally pluck prey (probably butterflies and dragonflies) from midair. Little is known about their agonistic behavior, but these hawks seem relatively gentle.

Broad-winged Hawks use short gliding and flapping flight in forests, but also soar and flap low over the forests in which they nest. They are very thermal dependent during migration, but dislike flying in strong winds.

A two-year study of age-related differences in migratory behavior of Broad-winged Hawks passing Hawk Mountain, Pennsylvania, suggests that adults are more likely than

An adult Broad-winged Hawk and nestlings.
Photo by Ron Austing.

An immature Broad-winged Hawk on a woodland perch. *Photo by Ron Austing.*

their southern shorelines. At such times they often appear at lower altitudes, and in large numbers, at Whitefish Point in Michigan and at Braddock Bay and Derby Hill in New York.

Autumn Broad-wing migrations occur over a broad front, appearing from early August to mid-November, with most passing Mid-Atlantic states watch sites during the middle two weeks of September.

Although these hawks are very thermal dependent, enabling them to drift by the thousands across the landscape, they are also very susceptible to the influences of major geographic leading-lines, such as the northern and western shorelines of the Great Lakes, long and relatively unbroken inland mountains—especially those oriented in a northeast to southwest direction such as the Kittatinny Ridge in Pennsylvania—and, to a lesser extent, the Atlantic coastline from Atlantic Canada southward to the Florida Keys.

During autumn, Broad-winged Hawks are often very conspicuous. As many as 95,499 were counted on September 15, 1984, at the Holiday Beach Migration Observatory near Windsor, Ontario. More representative of Middle Atlantic migration counts are 5,655 Broad-wings reported on September 14, 1978, at Bake Oven Knob, Pennsylvania. These flights are modest, however, compared with hundreds of thousands of Broad-wings counted during autumn in southern Texas, Mexico, Costa Rica, and Panama.

Between 1961 and 1999, at Bake Oven Knob, Pennsylvania, there were 71 days when major autumn Broad-wing flights were reported of one thousand or more birds per day. An average of 1.82 major flights occurred per year. The seasonal high count in 1978 for Broad-wings at Bake Oven Knob was 15,599 and at Hawk Mountain 29,523. At Hawk Mountain, for the period 1936 through 1995 (no data were available for the war years

juveniles to form flocks. In mixed flocks of migrating Broad-wings, adults tend to be the lead birds as they glide out of thermals, perhaps suggesting adults lead juveniles south during a hawk's first migration to their wintering grounds in Central and South America. There also is evidence that juvenile Broad-wings are more likely to drift off course—which may explain why so many juveniles winter in Florida.

Vocalizations used by Broad-wings are varied, but a whistled *kill-e-e-e* or *pee-we-e-ee* are commonly heard when a hawk circles over its woodland home or at its nest. The male's version of these calls is an octave higher in pitch than that made by the female.

MIGRATION Spring Broad-winged Hawk migrations in eastern North America move over a broad front with the hawks generally flying higher than during autumn. However, when these hawks encounter major water barriers such as the Great Lakes, they divert along

1942–1945), 134 major Broad-wing flights averaged 2.4 major flights per year.

POPULATION Monitoring migrating Broad-winged Hawk numbers during autumn in Mexico indicates as many as 1.7 million individuals comprise their North American population. Some evidence also indicates that overall Broad-wing populations are stable or slowly increasing, but some local populations might be declining.

Hawk Mountain's Broad-winged Hawk autumn migration count trends, however, are not clear. Possible population declines "may be related to changes in wintering or migratory habitat," but long-term changes in Hawk Mountain's Broad-wing counts also may be influenced by changing weather pattern. During the 1990s, unusually low migration counts were reported at Bake Oven Knob and Hawk Mountain, but high counts were reported in 2002 at these watch sites.

Breeding Bird Surveys demonstrate slight population increases in four of five northeastern states.

Adult Short-tailed Hawks (light morph on top; black morph on bottom) in flight. *Drawings by Rod Arbogast.*

Short-tailed Hawk
(*Buteo brachyurus*)

This small, crow-sized soaring hawk is a rare Florida specialty.

HABITAT Habitat of the Short-tailed Hawk in Florida consists of savanna and mixed woodland with roosts located in patches or islands of mature woodland (pineland, cypress, swamp hardwood, or mangrove) adjacent to large areas of open landscape. Cypress and mangrove areas are especially important nesting habitats.

DISTRIBUTION The entire eastern North American population of Short-tailed Hawks occurs within Florida. From late February through early October, they are seen in central and southern Florida (rarely in the northern part of the state), but from mid-October through early February these hawks migrate southward entirely within the state to the extreme southern Florida mainland. About two hundred Short-tailed Hawks winter within and close to Everglades National Park.

FOOD HABITS Short-tailed Hawks are specialists in hunting small birds. They prey on Northern Bobwhites, Mourning Doves, gnatcatchers, wood warblers, Eastern Meadowlarks, and Red-winged Blackbirds. There is also a record of this hawk taking a Sharp-shinned

Hawk, and a few records of small rodents and a small snake.

NESTING AND LIFE CYCLE Early February to mid-March is prime Short-tailed Hawk nest-building time in Florida. Preliminary nests are built prior to the final nest, the latter sometimes reused in following years. Nest sites are stands of tall trees in upland or flooded areas adjacent to small woodland clearings. Nest trees are taller than others forming the woodland canopy. Nest materials are collected by the male, but the female does most of the nest construction with small woody sticks, green cypress twigs, Spanish moss, leaves, and other materials. Nests are placed in tall, straight trees near a major fork of the major trunk or side branch from 25 to 90 feet above the ground (one nest was 8 feet above the ground).

Two dull white eggs (sometimes one or three), sometimes marked with small brownish spots, are deposited from early March to late May, but mostly from mid-March to mid-April. After the first egg is laid, the female carries green branches to the nest nearly daily (several times each day when young are in the nest). Incubation, by the female, lasts for about 34 days. Nestlings are brought food two or three times each day by the female. The age at which nestlings depart the nest is unknown.

BEHAVIOR Male Short-tailed Hawks engage in agonistic behavior with other raptors such as Red-shouldered Hawks. However, females tend to be docile, allowing close human approach.

Hunting habitat used by Short-tailed Hawks in Florida generally has a long edge of woodland adjacent to tall cypress belts bordering creeks with surrounding open country, and islands of pine or cypress surrounded by marshland or pastures with open landscape areas much more extensive than wooded areas. Hunting is done by hanging in midair (similar to Red-tailed Hawks) where deflective updrafts occur, or slow soaring along a straight line. Hunting from perches is done rarely.

Breeding displays of Short-tailed Hawks consist of a male engaged in high circling above a nesting area, sometimes with a female perched in treetops below, between February and May but especially during March. Other displays include the sky dance and tumbling. Nest construction takes place from early February to mid-March, and copulation takes place in late March.

Short-tailed Hawk vocalizations are markedly different from those of other raptors in Florida. They include a high pitched *keeeea*, four or six high-pitched *keee* or *klee* calls (similar to the Osprey's call) used by males perched alone in woodland, and some other vocalizations.

MIGRATION Little is known about Short-tailed Hawk intra-Florida migrations, although occasionally small groups of eight to eleven individuals are seen within kettles of migrating Broad-winged Hawks. However, most Short-tailed Hawk sightings are of one or two hawks.

Migrations are entirely within Florida, with Short-tailed Hawks in the north-central part of the state flying southward to the Big Cypress Swamp and Everglades National Park in southern Florida. A few also continue into the Florida Keys. Hawks nesting in the Lake Okeechobee area apparently are resident year-round. The entire length of the intra-Florida migration is 155 to 372 miles.

POPULATION Populations of Short-tailed Hawks in Florida number fewer than five hundred hawks.

Swainson's Hawk (*Buteo swainsoni*)

The Swainson's Hawk's is a bird of open plains, grasslands, and agricultural areas in the West. Its status is marginal in eastern North America.

HABITAT Grassland is the primary breeding habitat (mainly in Minnesota) of the Swainson's Hawk in eastern North America. In Minnesota, Swainson's Hawks place nests in tall trees in small woodlots, shelterbelts, or isolated trees in close proximity to intensive agricultural activities where wheat and alfalfa are grown. Nests are placed in cottonwood, ash, box elder, spruce, and red pine trees.

DISTRIBUTION Swainson's Hawks reach the eastern limit of their breeding range in Minnesota (28 nests in eight counties from 1996 to 1997), with the easternmost nest in Winona County just north of the extreme southeastern border of the state. A few individuals also breed in northern Illinois.

Extralimital records are reported from Indiana, Maryland, Massachusetts, Michigan, New York, North Carolina, Pennsylvania, Virginia, and in Canada from Nova Scotia, Ontario, and Quebec.

FOOD HABITS Swainson's Hawks feed upon insects (grasshoppers, dragonflies), rarely fish (white suckers, whitefish), a few amphibians (salamanders and toads), reptiles (snakes including rattlesnakes), rarely a few birds (Mallards, American Kestrels, Sage Grouse, young Short-eared Owls), and mammals (bats, voles, deer mice, gophers, ground squirrels).

NESTING AND LIFE CYCLE Swanson's Hawks are monogamous (polyandry is reported a few times) and maintain long-term pair bonds for 10 or more years. They begin breeding when three or more years old, sometimes 5 to 18.6 or more miles from their natal locales (but one Swainson's Hawk dispersed 192 miles to establish its nest, and two others dispersed 118 and 124 miles from their natal locales).

Nest sites range from a single tree to a tree line or grove near a stream, with the comparatively flimsy nest usually placed near the top

An immature Swainson's Hawk. *Photo by Fred Tilly.*

of the tree. Occasionally nests are placed on utility poles or towers.

It takes a pair of Swanson's Hawks nearly two weeks to build or repair their bulky, exposed stick nest placed below the tree canopy. The male collects the nest material and does most of the preparation work, but both pair members take green sprigs of vegetation to the nest. In prime breeding habitat, nests are separated by up to 1.5 miles.

One to four (often two or three) unmarked dull white eggs are deposited at 2-day intervals and are incubated by the female for 34 to 35 days. When the female is away from the nest, the male covers the eggs for short time periods. He also brings prey to the female, frequently transfers food to his mate away from the nest, but occasionally carries prey to the nest. The female eats the prey away from the nest. Adult hawks defecate from perches several hundred feet from the nest (nestlings defecate over the edge of the nest).

The female broods her nestlings during the day for approximately 9 days. Nestling Swanson's Hawks remain fairly inactive for their first 8 to 10 days, then begin standing, and are aggressive when 27 to 30 days old. Nestlings also begin feeding themselves at the latter age.

There are a number of records of Swanson's Hawk fratricide among nestlings 15 to 30 days old. The youngest nestlings are killed by their older siblings. It is unknown why these hawks engage in this behavior.

The male parent secures food for his mate and the nestlings, although the female also hunts when the nestlings become older. Prey is ripped apart at the nest, and pieces are fed to the nestlings. When the nestlings are 23 to 26 days old, they feed themselves, sometimes with some assistance from the female.

Nestlings leave their nest when 27 to 33 days old although they remain nearby and perch on branches, from which they take flight when 38 to 46 days old. After depart-

ing the nest tree they range up to 0.6 mile away but continue associating with their parents and siblings for another 30 days, during which the parents feed the juvenile hawks. One brood of nestlings is produced per year.

The ornithological record of Swainson's Hawk breeding in Minnesota for 1981 to 1996 produced 16 nesting records. Another 28 nests were found in 1996 and 1997 (one nest was used twice). Added to 27 nests from 1879 to 1981, there are 43 Swainson's Hawk nests known for Minnesota since 1879. Productivity for Swainson's Hawks nests in Minnesota in 1997 was 76 percent successful. The nest density and rate of productivity in Minnesota are expected for a species at the extreme edge of its breeding range.

The oldest known Swainson's Hawk lived for 19 years and 7 months.

BEHAVIOR In Idaho on a warm summer day, 128 nonbreeding Swainson's Hawks were seen bathing in a reservoir, after which the hawks perched and preened until sunset. One hundred or more nonbreeding, and premigratory, hawks also were reported using communal roosts in shelterbelts or similar places, compared with an average of 2,300 Swainson's Hawks using nocturnal roosts on their Argentine wintering grounds. Another roost in South America reportedly contained 12,000 Swainson's Hawks.

Because Swainson's Hawks arrive on their North American breeding grounds after other raptors, Swainson's Hawks defend their previous year's nests against White-tailed Kites and Red-tailed Hawks who now use them. Swainson's Hawks also sometimes dislodge kites and Red-tails from nests. In addition, Swainson's Hawks defend their nest territories against Turkey Vultures, Northern Harriers, Golden Eagles, American Kestrels, Great Horned Owls, and Long-eared Owls.

Swainson's Hawks are opportunistic hunters and use thermal soaring over open country, with hawks foraging on the edges of cultivated agricultural fields (grain and hay fields), grassland, and shrub steppe in North America. When strong winds occur, the hawks may hang in midair, or even hover briefly, when foraging. They also follow farm equipment engaged in soil or crop preparation preying on rodents and insects. It is not unusual for adults and juveniles to walk or run on the ground seeking insect prey, and these hawks also flush prey by jumping on the ground and flapping their wings.

The flight styles of Swainson's Hawks consist of strong flapping flight and thermal soaring. The wings are held in a slight Turkey Vulture-like dihedral when thermal soaring.

These hawks roost at night in groups of more than one hundred individuals, resuming migration the next favorable day using mostly thermal soaring although flapping flight is also used. In Minnesota, during September, a mixed group of about fifty Swainson's Hawks and a few Red-tailed Hawks was observed on the ground in a harvested soybean field adjacent to some plowed land.

Adult Swainson's Hawks make various vocalizations including a plaintive *kreeeee* or *kree-e-e* alarm call, and a high-pitched *keee-oooooeee* or *keeeoooo* during prey delivery at the nest or when people approach nests. Other vocalizations include an odd gurgling sound during the sky dance.

MIGRATION Swainson's Hawks are diurnal migrants that depend heavily on thermal soaring. Thermal streets give large numbers of these hawks the ability to soar and glide for many miles with effortless flight.

Swainson's Hawks are famous long-distance migrants—traveling up to 12,400 miles round-trip—with most of the North American population wintering in the southern South American pampas.

Spring Swainson's Hawk migrations arrive in North America in large numbers during April, with most hawks arriving in Minnesota by late April.

Autumn migrations begin in late August and vacate North America by late September. About 25,000 Swainson's Hawks are seen per day at coastal Texas watch sites. Hundreds of thousands of Swainson's Hawks are counted in early to mid-October at Veracruz, Mexico, and other Central American watch sites.

A few stragglers appear during autumn in Georgia, Indiana, Maryland, Massachusetts, Michigan, New Jersey, New York, North Carolina, Pennsylvania, and Virginia and occasionally in Ontario, Quebec, and Nova Scotia. However, Swainson's Hawks are fairly common autumn migrants in the Florida Keys.

Satellite tracking of two adult female Swainson's Hawks from nest territories in Minnesota followed their migration routes into South America. Migration began during the third week in September, with one hawk flying to Bolivia, where contact was lost. The bird flew 5,213 miles in 60 days, an average of 87 miles per day. The hawk failed to return to Minnesota during 1997 and was presumed dead.

The second Swainson's Hawk arrived in Argentina on November 18, 1996. She traveled 6,224 miles in 48 days, averaging 136 miles per day. She wintered in Argentina, then moved north during the fourth week of February 1997, arrived in Minnesota early in May, averaging 85 miles per day during her northward migration. This hawk nested at the same site she used the previous year.

POPULATION No consistent estimate of Swainson's Hawk populations in North America is available, but more than 845,000 were counted in 1996 during autumn migration in Veracruz, Mexico. No accurate population trends are available for this species. Probably not more than several hundred live in eastern North America.

Zone-tailed Hawk
(*Buteo albonotatus*)

The Zone-tailed Hawk is an accidental visitor in Nova Scotia and Louisiana.

Red-tailed Hawk
(*Buteo jamaicensis*)

Red-tailed Hawks are common and particularly beautiful birds, a favorite of many people. Eastern Red-tails are extremely vari-able in color, including nearly all-white and pure albinos and melanistic individuals.

HABITAT Red-tailed Hawks are birds of agricultural and old field ecosystems, woodland edges, woodlots, prairie groves, roadsides, mowed medial strips of super highways, and plains. They are adapting to changes in land-use patterns in southeastern Pennsylvania, however, and also are common in areas with medium- to high-density human dwellings as well as college campuses, cemeteries, and reservoirs. In Allentown, Pennsylvania, a Red-tail is as likely to be perched on a light standard beside a highway as on a tree in a cemetery, park, college campus, or circling aloft over dense urban development. Red-tailed Hawks also nest successfully on ledges of apartment buildings adjacent to Central

An albino Red-tailed Hawk. These strikingly beautiful birds are rare, but illustrate how variable Red-tail plumage can be. Melanistic birds are also known. *Photo by Ron Austing.*

A pair of adult Red-tailed Hawks. Red-tails are among our common soaring hawks. *Photo by Ron Austing.*

rion (such as dead chickens discarded on a farm field).

A disabled Red-tailed Hawk with a seriously deformed foot visited a backyard bird feeder and ate suet and beef heart during an unusually cold period in the state of Washington. The following November, the same hawk apparently returned and spent the winter visiting the hawk feeder, dining on beef heart and taking shelter in an adjacent wooded area.

There is one remarkable record in California of an adult Red-tailed Hawk grasping and removing a Bald Eagle chick from a nest while an adult female eagle was present. The eagle immediately flew after the hawk, soon returned with the then dead eaglet in its talons, and placed the eaglet on the edge of the nest. Shortly thereafter, the Red-tail again attempted unsuccessfully to take the dead eaglet from the nest. Finally, the female eagle fed part of the dead eaglet to another eaglet in the nest and consumed part of the dead bird itself.

Park in New York City. These hawks hunt in Central Park.

DISTRIBUTION Red-tailed Hawks are among the most widely distributed and commonly seen soaring hawks. They breed throughout much of Ontario, Quebec, and Atlantic Canada, south through the eastern United States to the Gulf Coast and peninsular Florida, with occasional stragglers seen in the Keys.

FOOD HABITS The diet of Red-tailed Hawks varies considerably depending upon geographic location and season. They feed largely on medium and small mammals, birds, and reptiles. Mammals include meadow voles, mice, rats, muskrats, squirrels, fox squirrels, chipmunks, cottontails, pocket gophers (Minnesota), and even house cats. Avian prey includes Ring-necked Pheasants, Northern Bobwhites, crows, and small birds. Sometimes snakes are eaten. Red-tails also eat fresh car-

NESTING AND LIFE CYCLE In Minnesota, Red-tailed Hawk courtship displays occur in early March with two hawks circling and diving at each other, then locking bills and descending to the ground. Sky-dancing (a series of steep, fast dives from high altitudes) and other displays are also used. Red-tails exhibit considerable differences in nesting behavior, some much more aggressive than others. In southern Minnesota, for example, these hawks generally are tolerant of other birds, including other Red-tails coming fairly close to nests without defending nest territories. However, some Red-tails engage in vigorous defense of nest territories. Birds have had wing feathers broken or pulled out, and one Bald Eagle was grasped by a Red-tail's talons when the eagle flew too close to the hawk's nest.

Red-tailed Hawk nest construction occurs from late January to early March, depending on location. Nests are placed high and exposed in a tree's canopy in a dominant tree such as a basswood, elm, or oak. In Minnesota, nests were placed 41 to 86 feet above the ground, averaging 58.5 feet, whereas in Massachusetts nests ranged from 35 to 48 feet above the ground. Nests in Minnesota tended to be on slopes facing east, with one nest on a slope facing northwest and another west. Many nests have been in view of highways, and in Wisconsin some nests are located in open areas.

Both adults participate in nest construction or refurbishing, using twigs and sticks of deciduous trees. The female is especially concerned with construction of the inner cup and uses bark strips, catkins, and similar materials. Green conifer sprigs are placed on the outer rim of the nest. Nest construction is completed within four to seven days.

Red-tail eggs are white with dark brown, reddish brown, or purple markings. The two or three (sometimes four) eggs are deposited on alternate days. In Minnesota, they are deposited from mid- to late March to early April, with incubation lasting for nearly 34 days. The female does most of the incubation, but the male helps. Eggs hatch between mid-April and early May. The male Red-tail provides most of the food required by the female during the nesting period, although she also does some hunting. Cannibalism (adults feeding on dead nestlings) is reported at some nests in New York.

The nestlings are brooded for several hours each day, and are preened by the female until

An adult Red-tailed Hawk attending to its young at the nest. *Photo by Ron Austing.*

they are up to 35 days old. Nestlings leave the nest when approximately 42 to 46 days old, but remain near the nest for another 25 days. During this time their parents bring food to them or entice them to get food that's delivered nearby. In Wisconsin, juvenile Red-tails remain associated with their parents for as long as one-half year. Juveniles migrate before adults.

Nestling Great Horned Owls in southern Minnesota fledge at approximately the time Red-tailed Hawks eggs are hatching. This prevents serious, simultaneous, inter-species competition for food supplies when the two species live near each other.

The oldest known Red-tailed Hawk lived for 28 years and 10 months.

BEHAVIOR Red-tailed Hawks are large, opportunistic, generalist predators with the possibility of high dietary overlap with Great Horned Owls because they occur in similar habitats. However, the two species utilize different prey in the localities in which they live. This results in "distinctive tropic characteristics" for the hawks and owls—especially in the western United States, but less so in eastern North America.

From the viewpoint of their ecology, Red-tailed Hawks and Great Horned Owls seem similar, with the hawks active during daylight and the owls active at night. Hence, the notion developed among ornithologists that Red-tailed Hawks and Great Horned Owls are diurnal-nocturnal dietary counterparts.

Red-tailed Hawk locomotion includes slow, awkward walking on the ground when feeding on carrion, and hops when chasing insects. Much Red-tail hunting is done from perches in trees or other elevated structures from which the hawks carefully observe the surrounding landscape for available prey.

Roosting generally is done alone in trees with dense foliage. Red-tail roost sites are used for a period of days or even weeks. The hawks sleep while standing (often on one leg) with their eyes closed. These hawks also bathe.

Red-tails steal prey from other Red-tails and other raptors, including Northern Harriers and Rough-legged Hawks. Sometimes when hunting squirrels, two Red-tails hunt cooperatively on different sides of a tree. Prey can be eaten on the ground, or taken to a perch.

During autumn migration, Red-tails commonly soar on deflective updrafts along the Kittatinny Ridge or other mountains, with flapping flight used less frequently, and thermal soaring, or thermal soaring and flapping flight, used occasionally when strong surface winds are poor or lacking. It is not unusual to see these hawks "hanging" motionless in midair for a few seconds as they intently watch the forest or ground below for prey—then drop like a stone to capture whatever prey they were targeting—or gliding or soaring to another nearby spot to repeat the performance.

Sometimes odd Red-tailed Hawk behavior is observed, as when an immature Red-tail spiraled aloft in a thermal to approximately 1,000 feet above the Kittatinny Ridge at Bake Oven Knob, then folded its wings, and, in a tear-drop shape, plummeted toward the forest below; but it pulled out of its stoop and, using a U-shaped pattern, glided straight upward. The hawk repeated its roller-coaster performance six times, then disappeared downridge. The flight was similar to the sky dance but the season, situation, and hawk's age were wrong. Occasionally Red-tails also engage in "dogfights."

Red-tailed Hawks will also engage in play-like behavior. A hawk near Glenmoore, Pennsylvania, carried a stick, then a twig, and finally a leaf while aloft. It landed in a tree and seemed to try to break off a branch as if playing with these objects, and then watched them fall. At Bake Oven Knob, I also watched an immature Red-tailed Hawk carrying a small stick in its talons. Several times the hawk reached down with its bill and attempted to pull the stick from its talons, eventually doing so. The stick fell 2,000 feet to the forest floor. The hawk then soared higher in a circle, and flew out of sight. It was not my perception, however, that this was play behavior.

Individual Red-tails sunbathe by perching and facing toward the sun. This allows observers to spot them fairly easily and at considerable distances, by looking for what I call "white blobs" on tree branches—actually the white undersides of the hawks. This provides raptor biologists with a helpful census technique.

Red-tails make various vocalizations with a *kee-eee-arrr* scream commonly uttered when in flight and widely recognized by outdoor people.

MIGRATION Most Red-tailed Hawks do not leave the eastern half of North American during migration. Rather, hawks from northern areas migrate to the southeastern and Gulf Coast states. Red-tails from the southern part of the continent remain there and share habitats with the northern birds. During very mild winters migrant Red-tails stay on their southern wintering grounds for relatively short time periods.

Spring Red-tail migrations begin in early February with the largest numbers moving north across a broad front from mid-March through April.

Autumn migrations occur from early August through mid-December, sometimes even into January, with the largest flights seen from mid-October through mid-November. Major autumn migration routes occur along the Kittatinny Ridge in Pennsylvania (and ad-

jacent ridges to the north) and along the northern and western shorelines of the Great Lakes. Lesser numbers of Red-tails migrate southward along the Atlantic coastline.

On October 24, 1994, at the Hawk Ridge Nature Reserve in Duluth, Minnesota, 3,988 Red-tailed Hawks migrated past that watch site, with 3,488 more counted the next day. At the Holiday Beach Migration Observatory in Ontario, 3,002 Red-tails were counted on November 11, 1994—that site's largest one-day flight of these hawks. These are the largest daily autumn migration counts of Red-tails in eastern North America. At Bake Oven Knob in Pennsylvania, the largest single-day Red-tail count was 700, reported on November 2, 1980. A record seasonal (autumn) count of 3,843 Red-tails was reported in 1999 at Bake Oven Knob. The highest autumn Red-tailed Hawk count at Hawk Mountain was 6,208, reported in 1939.

POPULATION Trends in breeding Red-tailed Hawk populations increased from 1965 to 1979 in eastern North America—especially in Kentucky, Minnesota, Ohio, and Wisconsin. Christmas Bird Counts of Red-tails from the 1970s through the early 1980s reflected a 33 percent population increase, although Red-tails in Illinois declined during the twentieth century.

According to a food habits and population trend study of Red-tailed Hawks in Pennsylvania, based on Christmas Bird Count (CBC) data from 1970 to 1985, Red-tails exhibited a 5.8 percent annual increase in numbers in the southeastern section of the state, but those in northwestern Pennsylvania showed no significant population trend. The increasing southeastern Pennsylvania trend is similar to increases reported for this species in Breeding Bird Surveys.

Migrating Red-tailed Hawks during autumn at Hawk Mountain from 1972 through

1986 showed a declining population trend. Hence, the two information sources are contradictory, and a meaningful conclusion can't be achieved, although, from a *regional* perspective, Red-tails are exhibiting an increasing trend in winter numbers in the southeastern part of Pennsylvania.

The estimated North American population of Red-tailed Hawks ranges from 300,000 pairs to as many as one million individuals.

Ferruginous Hawk (*Buteo regalis*)

Ferruginous Hawks are the largest buteos found in North America, and breed in western North America. They do not breed in the eastern half of the continent, although they occasionally occur there—mostly in Minnesota and Wisconsin. Additional records are reported from Alabama, Florida, Illinois, Indiana, Michigan, Mississippi, New Jersey, Ohio, Tennessee, Virginia, and Ontario.

Rough-legged Hawk
(*Buteo lagopus*)

Rough-legged Hawks are soaring hawks from far northern latitudes. They periodically leave their Arctic breeding grounds and invade southern Canada and the northern and northeastern United States during some autumns and winters.

HABITAT Rough-legged Hawks breed on open tundra, with nests placed on escarpments, ledges or depressions in steep cliffs, rocky outcroppings or columns, hillocks, eroded banks of rivers, and near the tops of trees.

During winter in southern Canada and in the northern and northeastern United States, these hawks perch on trees, poles, or other elevated structures bordering agricultural

A dark-morph Rough-legged Hawk (left) compared with a light-morph Rough-legged Hawk (right). *Photo by Ron Austing.*

fields, old fields, marshes, prairies, coastal dunes, and even garbage dumps.

DISTRIBUTION Rough-legged Hawks breed in the North American Arctic, including the southern edge of Hudson Bay. During winter, when they move southward, they reach southern Canada. During invasion years these fascinating hawks sometimes even reach southern Virginia and Tennessee, but the area between Cape Cod and Chesapeake Bay especially receives many Rough-legs. One hawk was even observed near Cobb, Sumter County, Georgia.

FOOD HABITS Rough-legged Hawks feed on small and medium-size mammals (moles, shrews, mice, voles, rats, lemmings, ground squirrels, hares, house cats), a few birds (crippled ducks, Sharp-shinned Hawks, grouse, shorebirds, Short-eared Owl, sparrows, buntings), amphibians (frogs, toads), reptiles (lizard), fish, insects (grasshoppers and crickets), other invertebrates (crabs and shellfish), and carrion.

NESTING AND LIFE CYCLE There is evidence of long-term Rough-legged Hawk pair formation with pairs perched together on their wintering grounds and during spring migration. Rough-legs also use various pair displays, including high circling and a sky dance similar to that used by Red-tailed Hawks.

Rough-legged Hawk nests are bulky. Construction or refurbishment is carried out by the female using sticks, twigs, bones, and other materials provided by the male. Grasses, twigs, sedges, feathers, and fur from small mammals serve as lining materials. Alternate nests sometimes are located near active nests, indicating that each is not used every year, although some nests are especially favored and used year after year. In locations where lemming populations are very low, Rough-legs defend nests but fail to breed, and those nests are abandoned early when the hawks depart their breeding grounds. Nesting and hunting territories extend over areas as large as 3 square miles.

Clutches of two to five or six pale blue or green eggs, quickly fading to white and blotched with browns, are deposited during May or June. The eggs are incubated for approximately 31 days by the female, with occasional minor assistance from the male. During the incubation and nestling periods, these hawks decorate their nests with "greenery" consisting of willow and birch twigs and other fresh vegetation.

At least 85 percent of Rough-leg eggs hatch, and the nestlings exhibit a 20- or 22-day growth spurt after which their maturation slows. The nestlings tear apart their prey when they are 25 to 27 days old, prior to which they swallowed whole prey. During years with abundant prey, extra food is stockpiled on the nest. Nestlings leave the nest when about 31 days old and fly fairly well when 36 days old. Juvenile Rough-legs fly well.

The oldest known Rough-legged Hawk lived for 17 years and 9 months.

BEHAVIOR On their Arctic breeding grounds, Rough-legged Hawks sometimes are evicted from cliff nest sites by Peregrine Falcons. Rough-legs, however, usually find replacement nesting sites although they may not be on cliffs.

Rough-legged Hawks are fairly unwary when they come into contact with people because few people populate the remote parts of North America in which they nest. This makes these birds delightful to observe, but makes them vulnerable to shooting.

Rough-legs are crepuscular hunters that hover over open fields or other areas while hunting prey. On cloudy days with light or no winds, they sometimes hunt earlier in the day. A Rough-leg in Wisconsin was seen eating dead fish (alewives), and plunging into water to capture a live fish—not unlike an Osprey's fishing behavior.

During the winters of 1960–1961 and 1961–1962, I observed Rough-legged Hawks on agricultural lands near Allentown, Pennsylvania. Generally, one hawk was on a hunting perch and several more individuals perched nearby on trees. When disturbed, all the hawks departed and landed as a group in a distant tree line or group of trees. Rough-legs sometimes roost communally during periods of prey abundance. Winter hunting territories are also established and maintained.

Rough-legged Hawks tend to be silent birds, but when alarmed at their nests they make a *kee-eer* whistling sound.

MIGRATION This species is thought to engage in periodic southward invasions with a periodicity of 3 or 4 years, sometimes concurrent with Snowy Owl invasions. In recent decades in Pennsylvania, however, these periodic cycles have been much less marked.

Spring migrations of Rough-legs begin in February and peak from March through early April. By the end of April, most Rough-legs are on the way to their Arctic breeding grounds, although some linger at least into mid-May. As many as 253 were seen on April 23, 1979, migrating past Whitefish Point, Michigan. Additional Rough-legs tend to divert along the southern shoreline of Lake Ontario at Braddock Bay and Derby Hill in New York.

A remarkable count of 1,011 Rough-legged Hawks migrated past the Hawk Ridge Nature Reserve in Duluth, Minnesota, in the autumn of 1994. Apparently 1994 was an invasion year for these hawks. In comparison, the 1994 migration season at the Holiday Beach Migra-tion Observatory in Ontario produced only 80 Rough-legs. Indeed, the largest Rough-leg count at Holiday Beach was 315 birds during the 1991 season.

POPULATION Periodic Rough-legged Hawk population cycles, linked with cyclical small mammal (lemmings) populations, have peaks occurring roughly every 4 years. But not all ornithologists accept the existence of Rough-leg population cycles; some claim the rigorous periodicity that mathematics demands is not reflected in Rough-leg migration counts. Nevertheless, biological and ecological systems do not always reflect rigid mathematical rigidity, and most raptor biologists accept periodic Rough-legged Hawk population cycles. It is, however, difficult to detect and establish long-term population trends for these hawks.

12

CARACARAS AND FALCONS

Crested Caracara
(*Caracara cheriway*)

The Crested Caracara is a medium-size, monogamous, territorial raptor restricted in eastern North America to south-central Florida, where it remains year-round on its nest territory. Caracaras are included in the falcon family but are sufficiently distinct to be placed in their own subfamily.

HABITAT Florida's habitat for the Crested Caracara includes pastures (in cattle ranches), prairies, open grassland, and brushland with a small stream, some ponds, sloughs, and river channels. Vegetation patches with taller

vegetation such as cabbage palm, live oak, saw palmetto, Australian pine, black gum, tall native pines, and mangroves are useful potential nest sites.

DISTRIBUTION The distribution of the Crested Caracara in the eastern United States is south-central Florida. Hence a Crested Caracara reported in Minnesota is most unusual.

FOOD HABITS Both a carrion-eating scavenger and a predator, the Crested Caracara is a generalist feeder. Its food consists of carrion and live prey that it kills. Caracaras regularly harass Turkey Vultures at carcasses, causing them to disgorge food that's eaten by the

An immature Crested Caracara.
Photo by Allan D. Cruickshank.

caracaras. Sometimes caracaras also steal food from vultures, other raptors, Brown Pelicans, and other caracaras, occasionally grasping the food in midair. Caracaras also feed on insects found on carcasses.

Mammals in the caracara diet include young rabbits, Florida water rats, spotted and striped skunks, mice, and squirrels. Birds eaten include Cattle Egrets, American Kestrels, Florida Scrub Jays, Eastern Meadowlarks, Indigo Buntings, and House Sparrows. Eggs and nestlings are also consumed.

Other dietary animals include fish, young American alligators, turtles, snakes, lizards, and frogs as well as grasshoppers, beetles, millipedes, snails, worms, crayfish, and freshwater crabs. Vegetation includes grass, leaves, and seeds—the latter perhaps swallowed accidentally.

NESTING AND LIFE CYCLE Caracaras are monogamous within a breeding season and remain on breeding territories year-round. Their home range extends from 1.25 to 1.8 miles from the nest, although birds sometimes venture as far as 5 to 5.5 miles away. A small amount of territorial overlap sometimes exists.

A link exists in Florida between caracara nesting and precipitation. Most nesting occurs during the dry season (November through April). As the breeding season approaches, a pair engages in allopreening, food sharing, and perching near each other.

The Crested Caracara gathers nest materials and constructs a nest (unlike other members of the falcon family), with both sexes participating in nest repair or building which requires 2 to 4 weeks.

These birds place their nests in tall vegetation. One nest in Florida contained two nestlings, about 4 weeks old, in the top of a cypress tree in a pasture beside a major road near a residential area—apparently the first time a cypress was used by caracaras as a nest site. Approximately 2 weeks after the nestlings fledged, the wind blew the nest down.

Within 2 months of nest preparation, many caracaras begin egg laying. Some deposit eggs from mid-September through December (early season nesters), others between January through March (middle season nesters), and still others between April and mid-July (late season nesters).

Two or three eggs (often two) are deposited. They are vivid cinnamon brown, heavily blotched with brown. Both sexes participate in incubation which lasts for 32 to 33 days. The nestlings hatch 1 or 2 days apart. Generally, more eggs hatch in first clutches than in second clutches.

Newly hatched chicks wear pinkish yellow natal down, which changes to grayish to dark brown down when the nestlings are 4 weeks old. Nestlings remain in the nest for 7 to 8 weeks and are fed by both parents. Fur, feathers, pellets, and unconsumed food accumulate in the nest. Nestlings that depart from their nest run rather than fly. Some remain near their nest, fed by their parents, for another 2 months.

Some Crested Caracaras nest twice during the same year. The length of breeding season, and availability of food, are related to double brooding. Those caracaras produce many more young than single-brooded pairs. Adult Crested Caracaras show strong fidelity to their nest sites although some turnover occurs.

The oldest known Crested Caracara lived for 17 years and 7 months.

BEHAVIOR Spacing of caracaras across the landscape is accomplished by establishing nesting territories that remain intact year-round.

Little social behavior is exhibited by adult Crested Caracaras, but among immatures of mixed age groups as many as 30 birds forage together and engage in aerial displays. Sometimes as many as 178 gather in communal roosts.

Caracaras become active in the early morning or late afternoon and fly low over pastures, marshes, and roads searching for food. Sometimes they walk slowly looking for prey and make numerous stops looking in various directions. When prey is seen, caracaras run or fly to reach the animal and capture it. Not uncommonly, they walk beside cattle in pastures and remain alert for insects. The birds also walk behind tractors plowing fields. In the wake of prairie fires, groups of up to ten caracaras follow behind the fire edge and feed on dead animals. Cooperative attacks are reported, and caracaras occasionally raid songbird nests to capture nestlings. There are also examples of food storage by caracaras near their nests.

Crested Caracaras usually are silent except when disturbed at nests or nest territories. Sounds that are made include rattles, cackles, and other calls, including *cre-ak cre-ak, cro-ak cro-ak,* and *wuck, g-wuck.* Sometimes bill clacking is used if an intruder approaches a nest. Flapping in flight also produces a loud sound.

MIGRATION Crested Caracaras do not engage in migrations, remaining on their nest territory year-round.

POPULATION There are various estimates of the population size of Crested Caracaras. From 1971 to 1991, between 196 and 312 adult birds were reported, with a stable adult population of about 300 birds utilizing 150 territories. During the same time period, 100 to 200 juveniles were thought to be present each year, resulting in an overall population of about 400 to 500 birds. From 1994 through 1996, there was a 100 percent occupancy of known territories, and a 99 percent breeding rate.

Ornithologists believe the population of Crested Caracaras in Florida is stable, although their geographic range has contracted and is fragmented. If additional caracara habitat is lost due to conversion of land for development, a decline in the population may occur.

Eurasian Kestrel (*Falco tinnunculus*)

The Eurasian Kestrel is an accidental European visitor in Massachusetts, New Jersey, New Brunswick, and Nova Scotia.

American Kestrel (*Falco sparverius*)

The American Kestrel is the smallest, most common, and most colorful falcon in North America. It is the only kestrel native to the New World.

HABITAT American Kestrels are habitat generalists. As breeding birds they occur in

A pair of American Kestrels. The male is on the left, the female on the right. *Photo by Ron Austing.*

agricultural fields and pastures, exposed hilltops, old fields, open urban and other parkland, cemeteries, vegetated medial areas and sides of superhighways, rural and suburban roadsides, and similar habitats. Additional important features of these habitats include tall trees and/or utility wires and poles suitable for perches.

Winter habitats used by American Kestrels in Berks and Lehigh County, Pennsylvania, indicate that males and females prefer open habitat, but with gender-related differences in the types of habitats used. Females prefer areas with shorter vegetation more suitable for foraging than habitat selected by males. Females also prefer more pasture habitat, whereas males used areas containing less foraging opportunities and higher potential predation risk.

DISTRIBUTION American Kestrels breed from south of Hudson Bay southward through Florida. Males occupy a winter range farther south of the range used by females.

FOOD HABITS Prey taken by American Kestrels depends on season of the year, geographic location, and availability and vulnerability of potential prey species. Their diet consists of noninsect invertebrates (centipedes, spiders, crayfish, earthworms), insects (beetles, grasshoppers and crickets, dragonflies, butterflies, moths, and ants), fish (trout), amphibians (tadpoles, frogs, toads), reptiles (lizards, small snakes), birds (quail, doves, hummingbirds, larks, flickers, swallows, wrens, thrushes, wood warblers, grackles, meadowlarks, blackbirds, cowbirds, and sparrows), and mammals (shrews, bats, squirrels, chipmunks, wood rats, cotton rats, mice, voles, and rabbits). Occasionally carrion is consumed, and consumption of bread was reported in one study.

NESTING AND LIFE CYCLE American Kestrels generally are monogamous, even through several breeding seasons, although rarely a third kestrel is known to help at a nest. Males usually arrive on their nesting areas before females. Pair bonds last at least for the duration of a nesting season although a new partner is secured if one dies.

American Kestrels are secondary cavity nesters but readily use nest boxes. The male inspects potential nest cavities in trees, but the female makes the final selection. Nest box utilization in the Hawk Mountain area of Pennsylvania reaches 53 percent, with annual reproductive success up to 82 percent.

Either sex initiates copulation, which often occurs spontaneously, at least twice a day, or between 330 and 690 copulations per egg clutch. Copulation occurs only rarely outside the pair bond.

No nest construction material is used, but if material is inside a cavity in a tree or nest box, the female deposits eggs on that material. Otherwise, eggs are laid on the wood floor of a nest box or tree cavity. Four or five creamy white or pale reddish brown eggs blotched with browns, violet, and other colors are deposited on alternate days, with the female doing most of the incubation. If a clutch is lost or destroyed, the female deposits a replacement in an alternate nest cavity or, if necessary, in the same cavity.

Incubation lasts for 29 to 31 days. A few eggs are infertile. Hatching success varies seasonally, geographically, and sometimes depending on weather conditions. In eastern Pennsylvania, 78 percent of the eggs hatched in one study, but lower and higher percentages are also reported. Sometimes the female assists a nestling breaking out of its shell.

Nestlings are brooded by the female for about 10 days, after which she broods the young at night. Nestlings leave the cavity or nest box when 28 to 31 days old, but may roost in the nest cavity or box for another 12 days. The parents continue feeding the juvenile kestrels for another 12 to 14 days. During this time the juvenile falcons remain close to each other, but they gradually learn to survive on their own.

Generally, one brood is reared each breeding season but occasionally a second is produced. Double brooding tends to occur in Florida, but is also reported in Pennsylvania and Ontario.

The oldest known American Kestrel lived for 14 years and 8 months.

BEHAVIOR Agonistic or aggressive behavior used by kestrels includes elevating back feathers, grappling with bills and feet, and making the *klee* call when losing. The "false eyes" formed by feathers on the back of the head and neck are a form of protective coloration.

During winter (the nonbreeding season) American Kestrels roost in protected sites but generally not in nest boxes. In the rolling hills and farmland of Berks and Lehigh Counties in Pennsylvania, possible winter roost sites include branches of trees (maple, eastern white pine, and oak), natural cavities, eaves under roofs, and buildings such as barns and silos. Sixty-eight percent of roost sites are man-made structures (eaves and buildings), 24 percent are trees, and 8 percent are tree cavities. These findings are similar to American Kestrel roosting behavior documented in Missouri (nest boxes there were used for roosting during one winter), and in Louisiana, where man-made structures (buildings) were used for roosting purposes.

American Kestrels hover when hunting over fields lacking high perches. At other times they use flapping flight, and soar and glide.

Several ornithologists suggested it is unusual for American Kestrels to capture flying prey, except when grasshoppers are captured after they take flight at field fires. Nevertheless, one kestrel was observed leisurely gliding and plucking a bat from the air, and another kestrel captured a Ruby-throated Hummingbird, suggesting that the ability of kestrels to capture flying prey is greater than is currently known.

Capture success rate varies depending on the type of prey, season, geographic location, and hunting skills of individual birds. The prey capture success rate ranges from 22 to 90 percent, but a 50 to 65 percent capture success rate is more representative.

In Minnesota, an American Kestrel feeding on a meadow vole discarded the prey's intestines and pieces of fur before eating the vole. It is unknown why the falcon discarded the intestines. American Kestrels also cache surplus prey for later use, although this is uncommon. Cache sites used include clumps of grass, hollows in tree limbs and even railroad ties, and building gutters.

American Kestrels make various vocalizations including the commonly heard *klee-klee-klee-klee-klee* used when a bird is alarmed or excited. When the two sexes interact they use a *chitter* at frequent intervals.

MIGRATION Most American Kestrels are migratory, except for the resident kestrels in the southeastern states. Some individuals occupying far northern parts of their range migrate as far south as peninsular Florida.

Spring American Kestrel migrations disperse over a broad front, with the largest numbers appearing at watch sites from late March through much of April.

During autumn, American Kestrels migrate in largest numbers along the mid-Atlantic Coast of the United States. The largest numbers are seen at Cape May Point, New Jersey, and lesser numbers occur farther south at Grassy Key, Florida. Much smaller numbers are also counted along the Kittatinny Ridge in

Pennsylvania, and the northern and western shorelines of the Great Lakes. During autumn, peak American Kestrel migrations occur from early September through mid-October at Hawk Mountain, Pennsylvania.

Some high daily counts of autumn migrating American Kestrel are 1,105 reported on October 17, 1989, at Holiday Beach Migration Observatory in Ontario, and 25,000 reported on October 16, 1970, at Cape May Point, New Jersey.

POPULATION American Kestrels are the most common falcons in eastern North America. In 1982, one continentwide population estimate was more than 1.2 million pairs, and in 1990 a winter population estimate in the United States and southern Canada was 236,000.

Migration data from Bake Oven Knob, Pennsylvania, demonstrate that these falcons exhibit population cycles with a periodicity (population low) of 10 to 12 years. Graphing these data for 1961 through 2001 reveals population lows in 1963, 1972, 1984, and 1996. The North American population of American Kestrels in 1982 was estimated at about one million individuals, and in 2001 the population of this species throughout its entire range was projected as high as four million individuals.

Merlin (*Falco columbarius*)

Merlins are slightly larger falcons than American Kestrels. They are most commonly seen at raptor migration watch sites, especially along the Atlantic Coast at places such as Cape May Point, New Jersey.

HABITAT Patchy boreal forests are the preferred habitats of Merlins. They establish nesting territories along forest edges, bogs, islands, and lake shorelines in Minnesota's boreal forests, and in similar Canadian habitat. Merlins also nested in Minneapolis, Minnesota.

In winter in the Middle Atlantic states, Merlins live in some urban parks and cemeteries. The falcons exhibit no concern about nearby human activities. A wintering roost of Merlins was also documented at Sandy Hook, New Jersey, and four Merlins roosted in winter at Bath, Ohio. In addition, four Merlin were seen together on March 10, 1996, in Northampton County, Pennsylvania. It is not known if these latter birds were early migrants or falcons overwintering.

Three background trends help explain winter roosting of Merlins in Pittsburgh: (1) a general northward expansion of the winter range from former Gulf states limits, (2) evolved Merlin behavior to accommodate urban environments and breeding with increasing frequency in some Canadian cities in Ontario and Quebec, and (3) an increasing population trend for Merlins.

Otherwise during winter, Merlins occur along Atlantic and Gulf coastal areas.

DISTRIBUTION Merlins breed in eastern Canada with a few pairs spilling across the Canadian-United States border into Minnesota.

Most Merlins are seen in the eastern United States as autumn migrants at Atlantic Coast and Great Lakes watch sites—especially along the Atlantic Coast—but a small number also migrate along the Kittatinny Ridge in Pennsylvania.

Merlins winter along the Atlantic Coast from Long Island southward to Florida, and in southern parts of the Gulf Coast states.

FOOD HABITS Merlins feed extensively on small to medium-size birds (storm-petrels, swifts, hummingbirds, swallows, shrikes, jays, flickers, creepers, kinglets, gnatcatchers, wax-

A Merlin. *Photo by Ron Austing.*

wings, wood warblers, sparrows). Very rarely larger prey is taken, including young ducks, Green-winged Teal, Red-tailed Hawk, Willow Ptarmigan, Rock Doves, Mourning Doves, American Woodcock, and Black-bellied Plovers.

A few mammals also serve as prey (shrews, bats, voles, mice, ground squirrels), as do a few reptiles (small snakes and toads). Insects, too, provide some prey (butterflies, moths, beetles, grasshoppers, cicadas, crickets, and dragonflies), as well as spiders and crayfish.

Merlins in New Jersey and on Fisher's Island, New York, feed on a few mammals, many more birds, and large numbers of insects. In Ontario, birds formed nearly 90 percent of the prey of Merlins, with some insects also eaten.

NESTING AND LIFE CYCLE Merlins generally breed when 2 years old, although sometimes they are younger. Their courtship displays include high-perching, power-flying (to better exhibit feathers), power diving (comparable

to sky dancing in soaring hawks), and high circling. Copulation occurs frequently.

Some Merlins reuse abandoned nests of crows, ravens, jays, squirrel nests, natural tree cavities, and secondary cavities made by Pileated Woodpeckers. Merlins also use ground nests, cliff aeries, and others placed on the ground under stunted trees or overhanging brush (in Newfoundland). Greenery taken to the nest is obtained nearby.

Four to six rusty-brownish eggs with chestnut or brownish marks are deposited at 2-day intervals, from mid-May through June, depending on geographic location. Incubation lasts for about 32 days, and broken eggshells are discarded and/or eaten.

The adult male hunts for food but the nestlings are fed by the female. She flies from the nest to receive food via aerial transfer, although sometimes the male brings food directly to the nest where the female receives it in her bill. From 22 to 28 days of age, nestlings venture onto nearby branches to exercise their wings, then leave the nest when 29 to 34 days old. By day 32 (for males, and 34 for females), juveniles are able to fly, although a week passes before they engage in extended flight, during which they playfully chase various birds—including small raptors.

The oldest known Merlin lived for 11 years and 11 months.

BEHAVIOR Juvenile Merlins departing their nesting areas are social and usually remain in a sibling group at least until they begin their autumn migration, and perhaps even during the beginning of the migration period. At this time there are sometimes loose foraging flocks of half a dozen individuals. In Newfoundland, loose groups of juvenile Merlins and Sharp-shinned Hawks were seen migrating together over water to Nova Scotia. The juvenile raptors then continue south along the Atlantic Coast of the eastern United States.

Merlins are relatively inefficient predators, with their hunting success rate ranging from about 5 to 30 percent. They hunt from perches, but sometimes fly (and even glide) low over the ground, taking advantage of protective cover until ready to capture prey. The falcons then take their prey to a plucking stump or spot where the head is eaten first, followed by the rest of the plucked prey. Rarely, cooperative hunting is employed. A Northern Harrier occasionally serves as a "beater" by flushing prey captured by a Merlin.

It is unusual to see a Merlin capture prey along the Kittatinny Ridge in Pennsylvania, but on November 15, 1998, at Bake Oven Knob, a migrating Merlin, without altering its flight path, captured an unidentified songbird in flight. Along the Atlantic Coast, migrating Merlins fly very late in the day after other raptors stop flying—apparently it is part of their hunting strategy. Merlins also cache food, and ornithologists estimate one Merlin eats between 800 and 900 birds per year.

Merlins make higher-pitched and more rapid vocalizations than those of Prairie or Peregrine Falcons. *Ki-ki-kee* is used in aggressive and territorial interactions with other birds, and a repeated *tic* accompanies most displays involving interactions with each other or other birds. Merlins also mob Great Horned Owls in nonpredatory behavior.

MIGRATION In spring, Merlins migrate northward very rapidly—sometimes within 15 days from late April to early May in New Jersey.

During autumn, Merlins scatter and migrate over a broad front but concentrate in largest numbers along the Atlantic Coast. They readily cross the Great Lakes and the Gulf of Maine. At Hawk Mountain in Pennsylvania, the highest counts occur from late September through late October.

Some record autumn migration counts include 102 reported at Bake Oven Knob in 2001, and 168 at Hawk Mountain in 1995 and 2000, as well as 121 at the Holiday Beach Migration Observatory in Ontario in 1995. In the late twentieth century (1976–1992), annual autumn Merlin migration counts at Cape May Point, New Jersey, varied widely (562 to 2,876 per year) but declined slightly during the last five years of that data set. In 1996, at Grassy Key, Florida, the gross seasonal high Merlin count was 689 birds.

POPULATION Accurate population data on Merlins in eastern North America are unavailable, but ornithologists believe their population is increasing.

Gyrfalcon (*Falco rusticolus*)

The Gyrfalcon is the largest, and one of the world's most beautiful, falcons. It occurs in several colors (called morphs) of which white birds are the most prized by everyone who sees them.

HABITAT During the breeding season, Gyrfalcons prefer Arctic and sub-Arctic tundra in close proximity to rocky outcroppings near costal areas, rocky seacoasts, and offshore islands. Other landscape features can include inland cliffs with a recess and a rooflike overhang that provide shelter from inclement weather; river bluffs; escarpments; and tundra lakes and rivers along the edge of the taiga. Above timberline, mountain landscapes with rocky crags and cliffs are the third habitats used by Gyrfalcons. Locations with plenty of waterfowl, or colonial seabird nesting colonies, are additional wildlife features of Gyrfalcon breeding habitats.

DISTRIBUTION Gyrfalcons are Arctic breeding falcons that usually are permanent resi-

A gray-morph Gyrfalcon. *Photo by M. Alan Jenkins.*

dents in Canada at 70° to 60° North—far from civilization. They winter in small numbers in southern Canada and in the northern and northeastern United States. When major incursions occur at irregular intervals, some Gyrfalcons fly farther south to the northern limit of the southeastern states.

Spectacular white birds typically come from Canada's Arctic islands and northern Greenland, while the darkest-plumaged falcons come from Labrador, Quebec, and perhaps southern Greenland. White Gyrfalcons tend to be more common in colder areas.

FOOD HABITS Gyrfalcon food favorites are largely geese, ducks, puffins, murres, guillemots, dovekies, Rough-legged Hawks, grouse, pheasants, ptarmigans, gulls, terns, kittiwakes, jaegers, shorebirds, Short-eared Owls, ravens, crows, Snow Buntings, Lapland Longspurs, redpolls, and sparrows.

Some mammals are also taken (shrews, mice, voles, lemmings, ground squirrels, hares). Occasionally carrion is consumed by young birds. Changes in diet occur annually, seasonally, and geographically, but vulnerability (rather than abundance) determines which prey is taken.

NESTING AND LIFE CYCLE Gyrfalcons are monogamous and apparently pair-bonded for their lifetime. They breed when 4 years old (occasionally at age 3). Pair bonding occurs with behavior displays at nest ledges, as well as aerial displays including food transfers near the nest site. Copulation occurs as long as 29 days prior to egg laying and continues through the egg-laying period. Pair bonds remain intact until the nestlings fledge and disperse.

Gyrfalcons use old nests of other birds, such as those of Rough-legged Hawks, Golden

Eagles, and ravens, and shallow scrapes on ledges. They may add some sticks in the nest, although they prepare no inner nest lining. Up to three alternative nests are placed near an active nest. Three or four white eggs, spotted with cinnamon, are deposited and incubated by both parents—especially the female—for 35 to 36 days.

During hatching, and after nestlings are free of the eggs, they are brooded 80 percent of the time until 10 to 15 days old. Food is taken to nestlings soon after hatching, with the adult female feeding the nestlings almost until they fledge. The male hunts and delivers prey for the first 2 or 3 weeks, then some hunting is done by the female. Food caching is used by adult Gyrfalcons until the nestlings are about 29 days old. Gyrfalcons leave the nest when 45 to 50 days old, but are dependent on their parents for about a month. They are independent and gone from their natal locales within a month to 6 weeks.

The oldest known Gyrfalcon lived for 13 years and 6 months.

BEHAVIOR Gyrfalcons are masters of flight. Compared with Peregrine Falcons, they are less agile and more buoyant but can maintain sustained flight for longer periods of time— and are surprisingly faster than Peregrines. In addition to flapping flight, Gyrfalcons use soaring and quartering flight. These large falcons also fly at night.

Sometimes local populations of Gyrfalcons develop a special dependency on select prey species. Hence, on some Canadian Arctic islands, Arctic hares form most of the falcons' diet.

Gyrfalcons bathe in water (baths last as long as 17 minutes), in snow, and in dust. Juveniles and immatures engage in play by attacking objects or make false attempts at attacking live prey.

Agonistic behavior is used by Gyrfalcons when chasing or striking other Gyrfalcons or other birds. Other than for prey, birds killed by these falcons include Rough-legged Hawks, Peregrine Falcons, and Common Ravens. Other agonistic behavior includes threat and appeasement displays.

Some examples of Gyrfalcons interacting with other raptors are worthy of note. On Amherst Island, Ontario, a dark-morph Gyrfalcon made a flight directly toward a Snowy Owl perched on a rock. The falcon did not touch the owl, coming only very close. The owl awkwardly fluttered into the air, then returned to its rock perch. Meanwhile, the falcon departed. About 10 minutes later, a second Snowy Owl was perched on a 6.5-foot pole in a pasture. Unexpectedly, what probably was the same Gyrfalcon reappeared flying low above the ground directly toward the second Snowy Owl. The owl remained perched, and the falcon disappeared from view.

A juvenile Gyrfalcon in Alaska was observed stooping at raptors and other birds, and similar interactions were documented between a Gyrfalcon and a Snowy Owl in winter in Newfoundland. Some ornithologists believe this behavior might involve protecting food or defending winter territories although others consider it play behavior.

In the harbor area at Duluth, Minnesota, a Gyrfalcon was forced to drop its prey (a pigeon) when a Bald Eagle and Red-tailed Hawk swooped into view toward the falcon.

Gyrfalcons are more vocal than Peregrine Falcons. They make a variety of vocalizations, especially during the breeding season, using a guttural *kak-kak-kak* when alarmed or being mobbed when aloft, perched, or at the nest. Other vocalizations are used depending on season and circumstances.

MIGRATION Little spring migration information for Gyrfalcons is available for eastern

North America, but the few falcons that are in the eastern United States and southern Canada during winter return to their Arctic breeding grounds by mid-March. Adult male Gyrfalcons remain on territory during the winter. Subadults and immatures may be more migratory, with a possible female bias in respect to individuals that migrate.

By late August or September, Gyrfalcons that migrate are engaged in southward movements, with the birds typically arriving on southern wintering grounds in southern Canada and the northern United States in October and November.

Southward migration routes for Gyrfalcons from eastern Canada follow the east coast of Labrador and the Gulf of St. Lawrence, both sides of Hudson Bay, and through the Labrador peninsula's interior. Juvenile birds migrate southward between 558 and 1,488 miles during their first winter. However, by January through March, rarely as late as May, they return to their breeding grounds in Canada's remote far northern areas.

Occasionally, when significant winter influxes of northern owls occur in Great Lakes states such as Minnesota, and if they are linked with cyclical population lows in ptarmigans, limited numbers of Gyrfalcons also appear. During the northern owl influx of 2000–2001, for example, ten Gyrfalcons were reported in Minnesota from early November to mid-March 2001. Previous northern owl influxes in the early 1990s in Minnesota also produced fourteen and fifteen winter records of Gyrfalcons. Curiously, only one Gyrfalcon is reported (November 1991) from the Holiday Beach Migration Observatory in Ontario.

Along the Kittatinny Ridge in Pennsylvania, a few Gyrfalcons were reported at Bake Oven Knob (mostly during November) and Hawk Mountain (mostly during October and November), over a period of four to six decades. All Gyrfalcons reported in Pennsyl-

Gyrfalcons, such as this gray morph, are Arctic falcons that rarely venture into the eastern United States. *Photo by Donald S. Heintzelman.*

vania during the twentieth century were seen in seventeen counties, many concentrated in a five county core area along and near the Kittatinny Ridge east of the Susquehanna River. Three Gyrfalcons wintered in Lancaster County, Pennsylvania, for two successive winters in the early 1980s.

POPULATION In 1994 ornithologists reported 10 to 12 Gyrfalcon pairs in Labrador, and more than 1,000 pairs in Quebec. Worldwide, ornithologists estimated 15,000 to 17,000 pairs.

Peregrine Falcon (*Falco peregrinus*)

The Peregrine Falcon is the most famous and spectacular falcon in the world, and one of the fastest-flying birds on earth. Since antiquity, these birds have been legendary among falconers. Modern hawk watchers and ornithologists are no less enthralled by them.

HABITAT Tundra, coastlines, open areas, cliffs overlooking rivers, and urban areas (tall

A Peregrine Falcon with eggs in a cliff nest. *Photo by Ron Austing.*

buildings and large bridges) in close association with aquatic ecosystems are Peregrine breeding habitats. Migratory birds appear over lakes, ponds, marshes, rivers, and Atlantic and Gulf Coast areas with waterfowl, shorebird, and other small and medium-size bird concentrations. They also migrate along the Kittatinny Ridge in Pennsylvania.

DISTRIBUTION Peregrine Falcons breed in the Canadian Arctic and Greenland (Tundra Peregrines). In addition, captive-bred reintroduced falcons (some sedentary) also breed in limited riverine wilderness areas in New England and New York, and in many urban areas in southern Canada and the eastern United States. Some Peregrines winter along the Atlantic and Gulf Coasts whereas Tundra Peregrines winter deep in South America.

FOOD HABITS The diet of the Peregrine Falcon consists mostly of birds—especially waterfowl and shorebirds—although they sometimes dine on herons, gulls, terns (young), grouse, doves, cuckoos, flickers, Blue Jays, Belted Kingfishers, swallows, nighthawks, nuthatches, American Robins, tanagers, wood warblers, grosbeaks, and sparrows. An immature Peregrine Falcon in Minnesota killed and ate an adult female Sharp-shinned Hawk. There is also a report of a Peregrine killing a Red-shouldered Hawk and Snowy Owls. Occasionally a Peregrine's diet includes mammals (shrews, bats, meadow voles, lemmings), fish (pirated from Ospreys), insects (beetles, grasshoppers, crickets, butterflies, dragonflies), and other invertebrates (slugs, fiddler crabs). Carrion is eaten rarely.

Peregrine Falcons in urban environments hunt Rock Doves (pigeons), which form much of their diet, in addition to European Starlings and sparrows. In New Jersey, the diets of three reestablished pairs of Peregrine Falcons nesting along the Atlantic Coast included prey representative of thirty-seven avian species. Migratory birds formed much of their diet, although the falcons nesting closest to the ocean preyed on more migratory birds than falcons nesting farther inland. In addition, transient migrants (migratory birds that do not nest in New Jersey) formed 44 percent of the diet of Peregrines nesting closest to the ocean, while a falcon pair farther inland utilized only 12 percent of transient migrants. Apparently, differential migration flight lines of avian prey influence how many transient migrants are captured by Peregrines.

NESTING AND LIFE CYCLE Peregrine Falcons are monogamous. Polygamy occurs very rarely. Many begin breeding when they are 2 years old, some sometimes older, and some individuals never breed. Various displays are used during the breeding season, such as high circling, high perching, and, early in the season, the ledge display. Sometimes the female begs for food. Copulation is encouraged by the female.

Selection of a nest site by an adult Peregrine is strongly influenced by the type of nest site from which it fledged. This influence, however, is not rigid or irreversible, and females are more flexible than males in their choice of a nest site. Varying the nest site helps maintain an adequate gene flow among Peregrines.

A Peregrine's cliff aerie is analogous to a Red-tailed Hawk's stick nest. The best are sometimes called "ecological magnets" because they are irresistible to generations of Peregrine Falcons. Some North American nesting sites have been used for more than a hundred years (in Great Britain as long ago as the thirteenth century!). Some substitutes for cliff ledges include bridges, ledges on tall buildings in cities, quarries, and elevated platforms. Peregrines also rarely deposit their eggs in tree cavities.

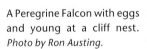

A Peregrine Falcon with eggs and young at a cliff nest. *Photo by Ron Austing.*

Females become listless about 5 days prior to egg laying, with the male bringing food to her. The eggs are deposited about every 2 days until a clutch contains three or four. They are a beautiful reddish brown in color, richly marked with more browns and reddish browns. Eggs are deposited between mid-March to early April, depending on geographic location. The female does most of the incubation which requires 33 to 35 days.

Nestlings leave their nest at different ages depending on their sex. Males depart when 39 to 46 days old and females leave when 41 to 49 days old. The nestlings are very noisy and restless just prior to departing. After departure they engage in practice flights, pursuit of each other, prey-capture, food passing, family hunting forays, play, and many other falcon activities.

The oldest known Peregrine Falcon lived for 19 years and 3 months.

BEHAVIOR Bathing is accomplished in several ways. Sometimes a falcon wades breast-deep into shallow water, puts its head into the water, and splashes water over the rest of its body. At other times, a Peregrine engages in flight bathing by striking the water at a low angle, causing water to splash onto its body, then rapidly swooping upward. Even dew on tall grass enables Peregrines to bathe, followed by sunning from a higher rock or branch.

As Peregrine Falcons of the Midwest reach carrying capacity and intense competition develops for nest territories, some birds will try to use all types of nest sites, including cliff nest sites along the Mississippi River (sites that remain unused by Peregrines because of predation activities by Great Horned Owls), thus assuring full diversification of nest site use among Midwestern Peregrine Falcons. Presumably this also applies to Peregrines in the northeastern United States and eastern Canada.

Peregrine Falcons use several types of hunting methods, with success rates varying from approximately 8 to 40 percent of the attempts made. Despite their fantastic flight abilities, Peregrine Falcons commonly hunt from perches on the tops of tall trees, cliffs, or other tall objects. When it sees prey lower than where it is perched, the Peregrine launches into flight above the prey, giving it considerable advantage over the prey. Nevertheless, sometimes several efforts, including high-speed stoops, are needed to successfully capture the prey.

Peregrine Falcons also engage in cooperative hunting, perhaps with the female positioning the prey and the male attacking and killing it. Sometimes these falcons use Northern Harriers as beaters to flush prey that is then killed by the Peregrines. Depending on prey size, two or more kills can be made daily. When attacking a land bird over water, however, the falcon may force the prey increasingly lower until it drops into the water. The Peregrine then circles and grasps the prey from the water.

Peregrines also hunt by soaring overhead and stooping at prey. When engaged in normal flight, Peregrines usually fly at about 40 to 55 miles per hour, but its flight speed sometimes exceeds 200 miles per hour in a stoop. Apparently the long rear toe and talon slashes through the victim's body, killing it immediately. However, some evidence suggests the toes are closed at impact, and the physical force resulting from such a high-speed impact either kills or stuns the prey, which falls to the ground. When on the ground at the prey, the falcon bites the back of the animal's skull, breaking the neck, and assuring the victim's death. Sometimes small prey is eaten in flight.

Peregrines are particularly fond of food hoarding during the breeding season. The incubating female sometimes caches food on the nest cliff if she does not want to accept it immediately.

Sometimes Peregrines exhibit odd behavior. At Bake Oven Knob, Pennsylvania, I watched an adult male Peregrine repeatedly stoop at a Turkey Vulture soaring on deflective updrafts. Although the Peregrine never touched the vulture, the latter twisted and turned much more rapidly than I had ever seen vultures do previously. I concluded the Peregrine was engaged in play.

When alone, Peregrine Falcons generally remain silent, but commonly make loud *cacking* vocalizations at their aeries as part of their defensive behavior. The female also makes a *chitter* sound when threatened. Other vocalizations are also used while nesting.

MIGRATION Radio and satellite tracking of spring and autumn migration patterns and routes of Peregrine Falcons captured at North American nest sites in boreal forest, low Arctic locations, and along mid-Atlantic and Gulf of Mexico coastlines demonstrates that Peregrines travel an average of 5,347 miles during southward migration, and 5,113 miles during northward migration. The falcons average 107 miles per day during autumn, and 123 miles per day during spring. Tundra Peregrines leapfrog over the former range of Eastern Peregrines, sometimes using stopover habitats along the Atlantic and Gulf Coasts and some Caribbean islands when migrating to their South American wintering grounds.

During spring, when Peregrines reach Padre Island, Texas, they disperse widely across the continent, with some falcons heading to central Alaska, and others venturing as far north and east as central-west Greenland. Peregrines do not follow the shortest routes to and from their breeding and wintering grounds.

During autumn, Peregrines use at least three broad, southward migration routes (coastal, midcontinental, and water-crossing over Hudson Bay, the Davis Strait separating West Greenland and Canada, and the Caribbean Sea), with some birds stopping along the mid-Atlantic Coast of the United States, others on some of the Caribbean islands, and still others continuing on to central Argentina.

Autumn migrations of Peregrine Falcons at the Holiday Beach Migration Observatory in Ontario are relatively modest. The largest seasonal count to date, eighty-two, was reported in 1995, and recent seasonal counts ranged from forty to sixty birds. These numbers are roughly similar to Appalachian Mountain Peregrine migration counts.

Apparently the Appalachian Mountains are a migratory divide, with some Peregrines moving along the Atlantic coastline and others west of the Appalachians going over midcontinental North America. This dispersed migration is confirmed by the limited numbers of Peregrines counted during autumn at Kittatinny Ridge watch sites in Pennsylvania—fifty-eight at Bake Oven Knob in 1999, and sixty at Hawk Mountain in 1997—compared with larger numbers counted at Cape May Point, New Jersey, and other Atlantic coastal watch sites.

Hawk watchers at the Florida Keys Raptor Migration Project on Grassy Key in Curry Hammock State Park, Florida, are making long-term efforts to count migrant Peregrines at that watch site which is one of the best Peregrine bottlenecks in southeastern North America. During the autumn of 2000, for example, 2,043 Peregrine Falcons were counted on Grassy Key.

POPULATION Historic records of breeding pairs of Peregrines in North America prior to the well-known decline of the species, roughly in the mid-twentieth century, indicate that approximately 8,775 territorial pairs existed on the continent, with about 22,000 historic breeding and nonbreeding Peregrine Falcons for all of North America. Approximately five hundred historic territorial pairs of Peregrines existed east of the Rocky Mountains, with approximately four hundred territorial pairs east of the Mississippi River and in southern Canada.

Emergency captive Peregrine breeding programs were begun in several parts of North America which, by 1994, resulted in 1,971 pairs of Peregrines on territories throughout North America. As of 2002, there were an estimated 7,169 pairs of Peregrine Falcons breeding in North America.

Prairie Falcon (*Falco mexicanus*)

Prairie Falcons do not breed in eastern North America. A few birds, however, sometimes occur east of the Mississippi River during winter. In northwest Georgia, on February 5, 1977, one individual was seen on the Lookout Plateau, and there are three additional Georgia sightings of Prairie Falcons. Prairie Falcons may be extending their winter range into the southeastern United States.

13

BARN OWLS

Barn Owl (*Tyto alba*)

Barn Owls are strikingly handsome but some-times elusive birds, with an amazingly keen ability to hear very low intensity sounds, making them especially efficient predators on meadow voles, even on moonless nights.

HABITAT Barn Owls are birds of open land-scapes such as agricultural areas, meadows, marshes, and grassland. Sometimes they live in cities if nesting and hunting areas are available. Availability of nest sites may be the limiting factor that determines which other-wise suitable habitats are utilized by these owls.

DISTRIBUTION Barn Owls are cosmopoli-tan—one of the most widely distributed birds in the world. They breed from south-ern Minnesota, Wisconsin, Michigan, and Ontario, eastward to eastern New York, western Vermont, and western and southern Massachusetts, then south and west contin-uously through all the states from the At-lantic and Gulf coasts to the Mississippi River.

Barn Owls in Minnesota nest as far north as Pine Island in Lake Vermilion west of Tower, near the Canadian border in Superior National Forest adjacent to the Boundary Waters Canoe Area, and in several locations in southern Ontario. Barn Owls have a dis-continuous distribution in the northernmost part of their range, but elsewhere they are dis-tributed very locally because of declining populations.

FOOD HABITS A range of food is taken and consumed by Barn Owls depending on geo-graphic location, season, and availability and vulnerability of prey. Microtine rodents, such as meadow voles, are especially important, but other prey mammals include shrews, moles, mice, bog lemmings, cotton rats, kan-garoo rats, rice rats, wood rats, Norway rats, muskrats, rabbits, hares, chipmunks, and ground squirrels. Avian prey includes Soras, marsh wrens, Yellow-rumped Warbler, Euro-pean Starlings, House Sparrows, blackbirds, meadowlarks, and sparrows. Barn Owls also capture reptiles, amphibians, and some in-vertebrates on rare occasions.

When voles were at a cyclical population peak, 96.9 percent of the diet of nesting Barn Owls in East Lansing, Michigan, consisted of meadow voles. Considered over a period of time, however, microtine rodents ranged from 57.6 to 92.5 percent of their diet.

When meadow vole populations crash, other small mammals—especially short-tailed shrews and deer mice—replace many microtine rodents in Barn Owl diets. Curi-ously, Norway rats do not form an important

A family of Barn Owls at their nest. *Photo by Ron Austing.*

part of the diet of these owls. Nevertheless, Barn Owls are allies with farmers—indeed, they are "flying mouse-traps" that help to regulate rodent numbers without the use of poisonous chemicals.

NESTING AND LIFE CYCLE Barn Owls usually are monogamous, but there are reports of polygyny. Although they breed during all months and seasons, depending on geographic location, most Barn Owls nest during spring or late summer and early autumn. Climatic conditions, however, can affect Barn Owl nesting activities.

Barn Owls do not build a nest but are very adaptable at selecting a nest site such as hollow trees, small caves, recesses on cliffs and holes in river banks, church towers, barns, silos, granaries, mills, attics, other buildings with sheltered nooks, and nest boxes (placed in barns or silos).

After the first egg is deposited, however, the female pulls apart some pellets she regurgitated and shapes the soft material into a nest. If the same nest site is used in following years, the female Barn Owl from the next nesting effort reuses the earlier nest structure (which may include decayed or decaying surplus animals that have an unpleasant odor in a nest site lacking good air circulation).

Barn Owls commonly deposit six or seven (range two to eighteen) dull white eggs. The female begins incubation starting with the laying of the first egg, and it lasts for about 30 days. The male feeds the female while she incubates. Nestling Barn Owls leave the nest when they are about 64 days old, but they are dependent on their parents for another 3 to 5 weeks, but only for food. The juvenile owls roost near each other for awhile after departing their nest.

Barn Owls are double-brooded, producing a second brood during the same year. Forty-six percent of females, and 4 percent of males, mate again with a new partner from 0.5 to 6 miles away from their first nest in the same season. There is no difference in nesting success between the two breeding efforts.

The oldest known Barn Owl lived for 15 years and 5 months.

BEHAVIOR Because Barn Owl eggs are deposited over a period of days and hatch at different times, the nestlings vary greatly in size. The last birds that hatch are very small compared with their much larger and somewhat older siblings. Nestling Barn Owls are also active, even from a fairly young age, and quickly become very aggressive when attempting to defend themselves by turning onto their backs and striking at intruders with their feet.

Barn Owls chase intruders from their nests, but when mobbed by crows they escape by flying to protective shelter or fly higher than the birds doing the mobbing. Their flight is buoyant, aided by slow wing beats. They also walk awkwardly, run (with flapping wings), and climb inside hollow trees containing nests.

Barn Owls roost in hollow tree cavities, buildings, nest boxes, and dense tree foliage during summer, and sleep soundly with their head hunched down. However, when night arrives they venture into the darkness to seek meadow voles or other prey in agricultural and old fields, meadows, around farm buildings, and in other suitable habitats utilized by voles, mice, and other prey.

The ears of Barn Owls are located at a slightly different position on each side of the head, allowing the birds to listen to the sounds made by voles and mice and to use triangulation to guide it to prey.

It is well known that Barn Owls capture more food than they need immediately, and store (or discard) the surplus supply at the nest—in one Michigan study, 186 meadow voles and a few other rodents. Curiously, eighty-six voles were beheaded, and some had their limbs removed, a potentially distorting factor in pellet analysis. Apparently the male owl was stockpiling the surplus vole supply while the female incubated her eggs.

After eating, these owls regurgitate undigested material (bones, fur, feathers, insect parts) through their mouth in the form of pellets—less than two per day—with an average of nearly three voles or mice remains per pellet. Hence, many Barn Owl food habit studies are based on dissection, identification, and analysis of bones, feathers, and other prey remains in pellets. Many school biology classes also use owl pellet dissection to teach students about owl food habits and predation ecology.

Much is written about the sounds of Barn Owls, but certainly their hair-raising *karr-r-r-r-ick* screams are famous—along with an assortment of other screeches, snores, hisses, and sneezes.

MIGRATION In eastern North America, Barn Owls north of 35° North apparently are migratory while those farther south are not. Nevertheless, studies of marked Barn Owls in North America do not demonstrate that these birds migrate. Moreover, juveniles disperse widely, sometimes as far as 1,200 miles from their natal locales. Hence, dispersing juvenile Barn Owls may be mistaken as migrants.

POPULATION From the late 1960s into the early 1970s, populations of Barn Owls declined seriously in some parts of eastern North America—especially the Midwest. Moreover, the population status of these owls varies substantially in different locations depending on season, habitat quality, and prey abundance. In Ohio, for example, they are nearly endangered, whereas in parts of the Midwest, including Illinois, Indiana, Michigan, and Wisconsin, they are endangered.

By the early 1980s, wildlife organizations and agencies began Barn Owl reintroduction programs in the Midwest, but they produced limited success. Ornithologists from Bowling Green State University then identified two basic requirements to sustain stable or thriving Barn Owl populations: (1) meadows and grasslands containing adequate to thriving populations of meadow voles (*the* major prey of these owls), and (2) an adequate number of natural nest sites.

14

OTHER OWLS

Eastern Screech-Owl
(*Otus asio*)

The Eastern Screech-Owl is our only small owl with prominent ear tufts. Three color morphs —red, gray, and chocolate—occur without a link to an owl's sex.

HABITAT Eastern Screech-Owls in urban and suburban-rural areas occupy a mosaic of habitats—shade trees along streets, parks, and other open areas containing maple, oak, and hickory trees. Open woodland near fencerows, meadows, old fields, orchards (apple), farmland, wooded wetlands, and pine plantations—especially if a small stream or larger river is nearby—are also suitable habitats. These owls tend not to occur in deep forests where Great Horned Owls live, or large swamps which are prime Barred Owl habitat. Water (such as creeks, streams, rivers, ponds, or lakes) is an important part of the breeding territories of Eastern Screech-Owls.

DISTRIBUTION Eastern Screech-Owls breed roughly from extreme southern and western Ontario and extreme southwestern Quebec southward to Florida and the Gulf Coast. They are absent in the northern part of the western Great Lakes states, northern Vermont, New Hampshire, and Maine.

FOOD HABITS The Eastern Screech-Owl utilizes a range of prey that's more varied and extensive than that taken by any other owl species in North America. What individual owls take, however, depends on geographic location, season of the year, and local prey abundance, availability, and vulnerability. Larger prey sometimes is cached in tree cavities for use later. Eastern Screech-Owls regurgitate pellets containing indigestible bones, fur, feathers, insect bits, and so on. During

An Eastern Screech-Owl at the entrance to its nest hole. *Photo by Ron Austing.*

winter, pellets are regurgitated inside their roost cavity, but at other times they are cast up at roosts amid tree foliage.

Eighteen mammal species are taken by these owls, especially in rural areas, including shrews, moles, bats, mice, voles, rats, squirrels, and rabbits.

Avian prey (especially ground-feeding species) form the most important urban diet of these owls. Birds are much more extensive in their diet than mammals—eighty-three species including small falcons, shorebirds, Rock Doves, doves, cuckoos, woodpeckers, owls (screech-owls included), flycatchers, swallows, jays, creepers, wrens, thrushes, mockingbirds, thrashers, waxwings, European Starlings, vireos, wood warblers, sparrows, House Sparrows, and finches.

Eastern Screech-Owls consume twelve species of amphibians—toads, frogs, tree frogs, newts, and salamanders—whereas reptile prey includes sixteen species such as blind snakes, garter, earth, and ground snakes, lizards, skinks, and geckos. Fish, including shad, minnows, catfish, and sunfish, are also taken.

A wide range of insects are also part of their diet, including beetles, moths, grasshoppers, crickets, and cicadas. Noninsect invertebrate prey includes spiders, millipedes, centipedes, pill bugs, snails, and crawfish.

NESTING AND LIFE CYCLE Eastern Screech-Owls usually are monogamous. From 77 to 91 percent begin breeding as yearlings (depending on sex and subspecies). They generally maintain pair bonds for life, breed annually, and share hunting, nesting, and roosting activities year-round.

Female Eastern Screech-Owls remain in their tree cavity or nest box for about 6 days prior to depositing their first egg. From mid-March to mid-May, depending on geographic location (earlier in Florida, later in New England), four or five (occasionally two to nine) white eggs are deposited. Smaller clutches are produced by smaller or younger females. When prey is abundant, clutch size tends to be larger. Incubation is by the female for at least 26 days, but can be 29 to 31 days, depending on clutch size and weather conditions.

The female broods her nestlings for up to 16 days. The male hunts, then delivers prey to his mate as she broods her young. The young owls leave the nest when approximately 28 days old, although this varies by a couple of days depending on location and subspecies. After leaving the nest, juvenile owls continue their dependence on their parents for as long as 10 additional weeks. It takes the juvenile owls at least several days to learn to fly adequately, and they often roost together and are fed by their parents.

The oldest known Eastern Screech-Owl lived for 13 years and 6 months.

BEHAVIOR Eastern Screech-Owl flight consists of rapid and uniform wing beats accompanied by little soaring. Occasionally adults hover when hunting. In woodland, they fly through or beneath the lower foliage of the canopy.

Pairs of Eastern Screech-Owls roost close to each other in the entrance to natural tree cavities, nest boxes, or sometimes branches of coniferous trees during winter; however, during the nesting season, these owls roost on braches of deciduous trees. They also engage in sunbathing when mild winter weather occurs.

Nesting Eastern Screech-Owls sometimes are displaced from their nests by Northern Flickers, who build nests over the owl eggs, and by fox squirrels that eat owl eggs. However, the owls sometimes wait until other birds or squirrels are finished nesting, then begin their own nesting. In northern Ohio, however, ornithologists believe that Eastern Screech-Owls prevent European Starlings from using Wood Duck nest boxes (which are used by the owls) located within the owls' feeding area. Moreover, ornithologists believe this exclusion of European Starlings from these boxes also enhances Wood Duck productivity because starlings sometimes bury Wood Duck eggs with their own nesting material.

In northern Ohio, causes of unsuccessful Eastern Screech-Owl nesting efforts included desertion or destruction for unknown reasons, predation by raccoons, failure of eggs to hatch, dead nestlings, and very rarely children taking one or more nestling owls.

In northern Ohio, fledged Eastern Screech-Owls tend not to use nest boxes very much for roosting until deciduous trees lose their leaves, but at that point in October the owls increase their roosting use of nest boxes. From November through January, however, these owls make substantial use of nest boxes for winter roosting and feeding-station purposes.

Various types of agonistic behavior are used by these owls. For example, in Georgia, an Eastern Screech-Owl attacked an observer because the bird had nestlings in a nearby nest box. The bird regularly and persistently engaged in attack (moaning and buzzing) behavior. In other cases, however, the owls become docile and seemingly habituated to people.

Eastern Screech-Owls make a horselike whinny during the nonbreeding part of the year, a rapid *who-who-who* quivering trill during the breeding season, and hoots, barks, yips, bill snapping, and other sounds. Bill snapping and barking, and trying to grasp an intruder with talons, are used when defending nestlings.

MIGRATION Eastern Screech-Owls are generally sedentary. During autumn, however, Eastern Screech-Owls in the northern portion of their geographic range wander short distances—typically 10 miles for adults, and 20 miles for young birds—from banding sites or natal locales. In the northeastern United States, juvenile Eastern Screech-Owls that disperse move in westerly and/or southerly directions.

POPULATION Some Eastern Screech-Owl subspecies exhibit population cycles with a periodicity of 4 years. Continuing local uses of nest boxes are helpful to these owls. In some areas, immigrating suburban populations contribute birds to other areas with less stable populations.

Great Horned Owl
(*Bubo virginianus*)

The Great Horned Owl is one of our most powerful, widely distributed owls. It is a top feeding-level nocturnal predator.

HABITAT Great Horned Owls occupy a range of habitats including old growth woodland, deciduous, coniferous, and mixed forests (especially secondary and open wooded areas), extensive woodland bordering upland and agricultural fields, woodlots of varying sizes, swamps, orchards, pastures, fragmented landscapes, cemeteries, and urban and suburban parks.

DISTRIBUTION Great Horned Owls breed from the northern limit of the tree line south throughout all of eastern North America.

FOOD HABITS The diet of Great Horned Owls reflects that of an opportunist, generalist hunter dependent on prey of widely varying sizes. The owls' numbers change according to region, season, and habitat type.

Great Horned Owls are powerful, top-level predators in the wildlife communities in which they live. *Photo by Donald S. Heintzelman.*

Mammals are the most important part of the diet of horned owls—typically representing 90 percent of their food. Species taken include Virginia opossums, rabbits and hares, skunks, woodchucks, raccoons, porcupines, ground squirrels, muskrats, and even house cats. Moles, bats, shrews, deer mice, voles, cotton rats, rice rats, wood rats, Norway rats, squirrels, chipmunks, and various other species are also prey items.

Avian prey normally represents about 10 percent of a horned owl's diet. Species taken include loons, Great Blue Herons, ducks, geese, mergansers, coots, Ring-necked Pheasants, Ruffed Grouse, Northern Bobwhite, Rock Doves, American Crows, and European Starlings. Raptors taken as prey include adult Ospreys, Northern Goshawks, Red-shouldered Hawks, Broad-winged Hawks, Red-tailed Hawks, Barn Owls, Eastern Screech-Owls, Barred Owls, Long-eared Owls, Short-eared Owls, and Northern Saw-whet Owls. They

will also occasionally take a domestic chicken.

Although reptiles, amphibians, fish, insects (beetles, grasshoppers, crickets), and other invertebrates (crayfish, earthworms) are eaten, they form a tiny part of the diet of these owls. During winter, when deep snow cover exists, Great Horned Owls also feed on carrion (road kills).

NESTING AND LIFE CYCLE Great Horned Owls are monogamous, some pair bonds lasting five or more years—if not a lifetime. These birds commonly remain on their breeding territory year-round. Horned owls are among the first birds to nest, in late January and February in the Middle Atlantic states, but as early as late November in Florida, and as late as mid-May in parts of Canada. One brood is reared yearly.

Male horned owls probably select and defend nest sites. Horned owls do not construct their own nests, instead repairing and using old nests of Ospreys, Bald Eagles, Red-tailed or Broad-winged Hawks, squirrels, or other stick nests. When a horned owl is settled into its nesting cycle in a Bald Eagle's nest before the eagle arrives back at its home, the eagle usually does not attempt to evict the owl—instead preferring to build or refurbish another nest. In Minnesota, a Great Horned Owl was found nesting in a Great Blue Heron colony within 10 feet of a Mallard nest, but without any indication the owls engaged in predation on the duck. Another Minnesota horned owl nest was in a shallow cavern in a rock face, and yet another nested on a shelf in a washout in bluffs. Other nests are in hollow tree snags.

Two white eggs form a clutch, although one to five sometimes are deposited, and are incubated for 30 to 37 days by the female. She seldom leaves the nest and is fed by the male who brings food to her at night. During snow storms she is covered with snow while incubating her eggs—occasionally in air temperatures below –20° Fahrenheit—a charming picture of a wild animal's bond to its forthcoming young. The eggs hatch as long as 2 days apart.

Nestling Great Horned Owls depart the nest when about 6 weeks old by venturing onto nearby tree branches. Within a week, they are able to fly short distances, and several weeks later their flight skills are much improved. During this period, the juvenile owls remain close by, but these family bonds gradually weaken and disappear as the birds venture farther away. Their parents continue to feed them as late as October, and defend them into early autumn, when the juveniles disperse. Most Great Horned Owls breed when about 2 years old, although occasionally a bird breeds when only a year old.

The oldest known horned owl lived for at least 27 years and 7 months.

BEHAVIOR Great Horned Owls are active from about an hour after sunset to just before sunrise, with their peak activity period just after sunset. They hunt mainly from perches, but also seek prey while in flight over a range of habitats (marshes, woodland edges, meadows). Juvenile horned owls, however, very slowly learn how to hunt effectively and even during summer remain on perches and practically beg their parents for food, which is brought to them. When the juveniles finally do capture their own prey, however, insects sometimes are the first prey they capture.

A Great Horned Owl nesting in a hollow tree snag. *Photo by Ron Austing.*

Great Horned Owls frequently hunt from perches on dead tree snags or fence posts near a roadside or clearing, watch for prey, then launch into a shallow glide and grasp and kill the prey with its powerful feet and talons.

Ornithologists group horned owl prey roughly into three categories. First are waterbirds roosting at night on open water, or engaged in incubation on nests. Second are moderate-size birds that tend to roost in open places, such as Rock Doves or European Starlings. Third are nestlings of larger birds, including some hawks, owls, and crows, that are preyed upon at night. Food caching is very rarely reported, but is known from the Yukon Territory, Canada.

At locations where large numbers of migrating songbirds are killed by striking the support cables of tall towers, Great Horned Owls are common consumers of these dead birds, an easy-to-secure food supply for the owls. Sometimes Eastern Screech-Owls that attempt to secure some of the dead songbirds are also killed by the horned owls.

Great Horned Owls usually use a favored roost for feeding where they take prey to be plucked, ripped apart, and consumed. They begin eating their prey with the head and continue with the body. Small mammals are swallowed whole, whereas birds are plucked before being eaten. Like their relatives, horned owls also regurgitate pellets containing indigestible prey remains such as fur, feathers, and bones.

Vigorous interactions occur between these owls and crows, which mob and harass the owls during daylight. Blue Jays, Northern Flickers, and Eastern Kingbirds also attack horned owls, as do raptors including accipiters, Red-tailed Hawks, Swainson's Hawks, and American Kestrels.

Great Horned Owls use roosting sites with a range of landscape features. A few examples include a large white pine in a grove of smaller white pines, another white pine amid pitch pines, and a pitch pine in a hemlock and white pine grove. Ornithologists believe the roost tree is selected by horned owls because the tree is distinctive among others growing nearby—perhaps making it easier for horned owls to distinguish its roost tree from nearby trees.

A range of vocalizations are used by Great Horned Owls, but deep-sounding hoots are commonly heard starting in late September or early October in New England and the Middle Atlantic states, especially from January through mid-March. These owls commonly snap their bill loudly when annoyed—an impressive defense display—and they will also hiss.

MIGRATION Most Great Horned Owls are permanent residents in their local habitats, but some owls from northern areas engage in occasional, unidirectional southeasterly irruptions in response to snowshoe hare population crashes. Sometimes these movements accompany Northern Goshawk invasions exhibiting a periodicity of approximately 10 years. One horned owl flew 1,276 miles from Alberta to western Illinois.

POPULATION Accurate information about Great Horned Owl populations is not available.

Christmas Bird Count (CBC) data from Pennsylvania for 1970 through 1985 indicated a gradual increase in numbers from 1973 to 1981, followed by a stable or slightly declining trend. In southeastern Pennsylvania, horned owls increased annually during winter by 7.7 percent, which conflicted with Breeding Bird Survey (BBS) trends for 1966 through 1985. Increases in Great Horned Owl population trends may have occurred only in urban and suburban parts of southeastern Pennsylvania.

Snowy Owl (*Nyctea scandiaca*)

Snowy Owls are beautiful, Arctic-nesting birds that are delightful to see when they venture southward from their Arctic homes.

HABITAT Snowy Owls nest on Arctic tundra where they sometimes spend winters when their lemming prey base makes food readily available. When lemmings are scarce, however, the owls engage in southward invasions into southern Canada and the northern and northeastern United States. There they appear along Atlantic coastal areas and in open fields (which simulate tundra), inland wetlands, marshes, harbors, shorelines of rivers and lakes, open areas on large airports, landfills, seashores, urban areas, and similar places.

DISTRIBUTION Snowy Owls are circumpolar in distribution, with owls in North America breeding north of the tree line in the Arctic and sub-Arctic. A few usually occur in southern Ontario, New England, and New York every winter.

During invasions, Snowy Owls especially are found along Atlantic coastal areas—sometimes as far south as Florida and the Gulf Coast. However, coastal areas north of New Jersey receive most of these owls. Moreover, sightings tend to be most dispersed in New York and Massachusetts, while elsewhere in New England most Snowy Owls occur along the coast and on offshore islands. Owls wintering along coastal Connecticut and Rhode Island may maintain home ranges if they remain for several weeks.

FOOD HABITS The prey of Snowy Owls includes lemmings and ptarmigan. Availability of food supply seems to be the limiting factor regulating when and where these birds live. During years of high lemming populations,

A female Snowy Owl in first winter plumage. *Photo by Ron Austing.*

the birds do not engage in southward invasions, but when lemming numbers crash every 3 or 4 years, Snowy Owls engage in invasions to southern Canada and the northern and northeastern United States.

After arriving on their southern wintering areas, Snowy Owls are opportunistic, preying on rats, mice, rabbits, Mallards, waterfowl, Ring-necked Pheasants, game birds, pigeons, waders and shorebirds, songbirds, fish, shellfish, and some invertebrates.

NESTING AND LIFE CYCLE Snowy Owls are usually monogamous although there are exceptions. Pair bonds develop either during winter or from late April to mid-May on the breeding grounds, using elaborate aerial courtship displays. The female constructs the nest by using her talons and body to form a shallow scrape in the ground. No nest materials are used, and some scrapes are reused for many years.

A Snowy Owl in flight. These lovely birds fly south from the Arctic when populations of their food supply crash. *Photo by Ron Austing.*

Three to five white eggs form a clutch when limited food is available, but when high lemming populations occur clutches increase to seven to eleven eggs, which the female incubates for 32 to 33 days. The eggs hatch at intervals of 2 days. The female broods the young owls during their nestling period, leaving her brood only to feed herself. The male secures food and brings it to her at the nest. She feeds her nestlings varying sizes of food depending on their age. The nestlings depart the nest between 14 and 26 days of age—often 25 to 26 days. However, their parents continue feeding the wayward owls for another 5 weeks as they develop flight skills, at which time the juveniles do their own hunting supplemented with some food provided by their parents.

The oldest known Snowy Owl lived for 10 years and 9 months.

BEHAVIOR Agonistic behavior by Snowy Owls varies, but some males react very ag-gressively at nests by dive bombing human intruders. Females are less aggressive, although some individuals will also strike at intruders.

When food (lemmings) is abundant, Snowy Owls cache it at a perch away from the nest, although the purpose of these caches is not understood.

During winter in Minnesota, Snowy Owls usually remain perched in one place for several hours, engaged in perch hunting. However, the owls are very active during daylight attacking, capturing, and eating prey.

For several decades during winter in Duluth, Minnesota, Gyrfalcons, Peregrine Falcons, and Prairie Falcons engaged in agonistic interactions with individual Snowy Owls in the Duluth-Superior harbor. Usually, a Gyrfalcon elicited more determined and vigorous reactions from an owl. Not infrequently, the owl held its wings up and partly spread, with head very low. Then, with feet extended toward the falcon, the owl jumped up toward the attacker as it flew over the owl. When Peregrines or Prairie Falcons attacked, the reaction of an individual Snowy Owl was less vigorous or intense. Sometimes an owl vocalized (screamed) when a falcon attacked. No Snowy Owls were killed, hit, or injured, although similar encounters elsewhere resulted in occasional deaths of these owls.

A Gyrfalcon's attacks on a Snowy Owl during winter may cause an owl to change its roosting behavior to utilize a site with more protection. Chunks of ice jumbled in shipping lanes provide additional protection for the owls, but there are also times when a Gyrfalcon's arrival in a Snowy Owl's winter territory causes the owl to "disappear" (an owl still utilizes its winter territory but is much more difficult to locate).

During the winter of 1999–2000, at the Duluth-Superior harbor, two Snowy Owls roosted as far as 3 miles from their hunting areas and were inactive almost until complete darkness arrived, due to a Peregrine Falcon that roosted on a bridge and had its center of activity there. Hence, even when a Snowy Owl is not injured, the presence of large falcons in an owl's winter territory initiates a change in owl behavior.

During early February in Minnesota, an immature Snowy Owl feeding on prey was observed leaving its prey to chase additional quarry. It quickly consumed a whole pheasant, with only the tail and flight feathers remaining.

Hoo-hoo and *hooooo* hoots, sometimes heard more than 2 miles away, are among the vocalizations made by male (rarely by female) Snowy Owls on their nesting territories—when these birds are most vocal. During winter, Snowy Owls are usually silent, but occasionally they will make a windy, high-piercing whistle similar to that made at the nests. Other wintering sounds include a faint grating in association with a screaming territorial display. When threatened, they hiss.

MIGRATION (AND INVASIONS) Snowy Owls are somewhat nomadic. Their migratory status is unknown in the northeastern United States, although some individuals may be irregular migrants. Nevertheless, their periodic or cyclical southward invasions are famous ornithological events. During invasion years, when lemming populations crash, Snowy Owls arrive in the northeastern United States early in November, and depart for their far northern breeding grounds in mid-March.

In an analysis of Snowy Owl invasion data from 1833 to 1987 into the northeastern United States, forty-seven invasions were identified. Periodicities with 4-year intervals occurred eighteen times, 3-year intervals ten times, 1-year intervals six times, 2-year intervals five times, 5-year intervals three times, and 6-year intervals once. Most Snowy Owls involved in invasions are juveniles.

In addition, studies at Kennedy International Airport indicate the male to female ratio there was 1:1.33, though no annual Snowy Owl migrations occur there.

POPULATION No adequate population status information is available for Snowy Owls in North America.

Northern Hawk Owl (*Surnia ulula*)

The Northern Hawk Owl is closer in shape to that of hawks (accipiters) than any other North American owl—a fact reflected in its name. However, much less is known about them than other owls.

HABITAT Habitats of Northern Hawk Owls include broken or boreal, and mixed coniferous-deciduous, forests close to open areas with hunting perches such as marshes or other wetlands, burned areas, roadsides, and even farmland essential for their foraging activities.

A Northern Hawk Owl. They're so named because of their rather hawk-like appearance. *Photo by Alan Wormington.*

DISTRIBUTION The year around and breeding distribution of the Northern Hawk Owl extends north to tree line across Canada's boreal forest from the southwestern shore of Hudson Bay eastward through Quebec and Labrador and Newfoundland. A few pairs also nest in the northern part of the western Great Lakes states and in the Gulf of St. Lawrence area.

During winter invasions Northern Hawk Owls rarely appear as far south as Long Island, New York, New Jersey, and Pennsylvania.

FOOD HABITS Summer food of the Northern Hawk Owl includes voles on which they depend for their survival. During winter, grouse and ptarmigan form part of their diet. Other prey includes shrews, hares, rabbits, mice, rats, lemmings, squirrels, Spruce Grouse, and a variety of other birds.

In Minnesota, the food of Northern Hawk Owls consists of meadow voles, red-backed voles, northern bog lemmings, short-tailed shrews, a few other small rodents, and a Ruffed Grouse—the latter unusual. Three-quarters of a mile from its nest, a hawk owl repeatedly swooped from a utility wire to capture rodents on the ground within 20 feet of a man, then flew to the nest to feed its young. The owl was not disturbed by the close presence of a person.

NESTING AND LIFE CYCLE Pair formation of Northern Hawk Owls begins in mid-February in Minnesota, with the male singing to attract the female. By mid-March, in Labrador, one female was observed sitting on her nest site atop a hollow snag.

These owls commonly nest on top of a hollow snag, in shallow cavities in decaying trees, old woodpecker holes, stick nests, cliff nests, or even nest boxes. No new material is added to the nest.

Seven white eggs typically form a clutch, but three to thirteen are known. Incubation lasts for 25 to 29 days, almost entirely done by the female. The male secures food for the female and gives it to her on a perch near the nest. Males are captivated and gaze at the eggs or nestlings.

The female broods her nestlings for up to 14 days, and the young owls depart their nest when 3 to 5 weeks old. At this stage they are flightless and merely capable of climbing on tree branches, walking, or hopping. The male secures food and feeds them at this age, without help from the female, and sometimes leaves his offspring alone to forage. Even up to 8 weeks of age, the young hawk owls tend to be found in the vicinity of their nest, but disperse and become independent when about 3 months old.

Northern Hawk Owls are known to live as long as 10 years in the wild.

BEHAVIOR Northern Hawk Owls engage in diurnal hunting, which explains why they are also known as "day owls." They dash rapidly through woodland dodging shrubs and other obstructions. The owls hunt for a high perch and swoop down fast and low onto prey. Occasionally, they hover when hunting. On rare occasions they use a waddling type of walk.

Hoarding or caching food in Minnesota (and elsewhere) occurs on conifer boughs about 10 feet above ground before and during the nesting season. The male caches, retrieves, and takes the food to the female, who is incubating her eggs or brooding her nestlings. After eating, the owls sometimes eat snow.

Roosting Northern Hawk Owls use a branch near the tree trunk, in the upper half of the canopy, hidden amid the foliage.

In Minnesota, Northern Hawk Owls sometimes linger in the areas in which they spend winters after an invasion. This resulted several times in postinvasion breeding. In 2001, for example, four nests of Northern Hawk Owls were found in Minnesota—an unprecedented situation.

Copulation is dramatic. In Minnesota, a large female Northern Hawk Owl flew to the top of a large spruce tree and landed there, accompanied by very loud screeching and cackling, and wings fluttering. Suddenly, a noticeably smaller male flew to and landed on the back of the much larger female and engaged in noisy copulation. The complete behavior lasted for only a couple of minutes. The male then flew into a nearby frozen bog, the screeching female quickly following her mate. The marked size difference between this particular pair of Northern Hawk Owls, however, is not always so distinctive.

Male Northern Hawk Owls are aggressive at their nests, but females incubate eggs or brood nestlings and usually do not participate in defense. In Minnesota, a male Northern Hawk Owls vigorously attacked a mounted (dead) Great Horned Owl to drive the larger predator away. Typically, the hawk owl bobbed its head and uttered a *shre-e-e-yip* alarm call, flew 40 feet over the mounted owl, and stooped at it. Vocalizations and stoops continued repeatedly until the owl finally perched on the edge of its nest territory some distance from the dead horned owl. Variations of this defense behavior, sometimes with preening included, were used by Northern Hawk Owls during several experiments.

A *rike-rike-rike-rike* or *kee-kee-kee-kee* alarm call is used by Northern Hawk Owls when in flight, with a screeching *screeeeee-yip* used at nests in the presence of an intruder. Many other calls are also made, often in association with courtship and nesting. Bill snapping is used when young and adults are threatened.

MIGRATION Northern Hawk Owls are nomadic, in response to changes in their food supply. They seldom venture very far south of the Canadian border, except to the Great Lakes states and perhaps to extreme northwestern New England—and then mainly during invasion years.

Occurrences of these birds in states as far south as Pennsylvania, for example, are rare and infrequent. A few nineteenth-century records exist, but the first documented twentieth-century Northern Hawk Owl record occurred on February 19, 1991, near Lookout, Pennsylvania. The owl arrived in October 1990, and was last seen on March 17, 1991. A few early nineteenth century records are also reported from New Jersey.

POPULATION Detailed information is not available regarding Northern Hawk Owl population trends, but their numbers apparently are linked (at least in part) to variations in prey densities. Overall, their numbers are thought to be stable in North America.

Burrowing Owl (*Athene cunicularia*)

Unlike most owls, the Burrowing Owl is largely terrestrial and active at night and during the day. It is the only North American owl that nests in burrows in the ground.

HABITAT Burrowing Owls live in short-grass prairies and treeless plains, especially where mammal burrows exist in Minnesota. Florida's Burrowing Owls, however, dig their own burrows on open, slightly higher and dry spots to prevent high water tables from flooding their burrows. Some are on airports, cemeteries, golf courses, overgrazed pastures, and similar places with mowed or short grass.

DISTRIBUTION In eastern North America, the Burrowing Owl's breeding range is peninsular Florida, and it is increasingly rare in the western prairie margin of Minnesota. Non-breeding Burrowing Owls occasionally venture beyond Florida. For example, one bird was observed at the airport in Gainesville, Georgia.

FOOD HABITS Food of Burrowing Owls consists of invertebrates (crustaceans, spiders, beetles, locusts, crickets, grasshoppers), mammals (shrews, mice, meadow voles), birds (Mourning Doves, Horned Larks, Bobolinks, Savanna Sparrows), reptiles (turtles, lizards, snakes), amphibians (frogs and toads), fish, and some fruits and seeds.

NESTING AND LIFE CYCLE Burrowing Owls usually are monogamous although cases of polygyny are known among western birds. Most Burrowing Owls in Florida exhibit very strong pair bonds.

In Florida, eggs are deposited between February and late May, especially in mid-March. The number of eggs varies within the geographic range of these birds, but seven to nine

A Burrowing Owl. In the eastern United States, their largest numbers are found in Florida. *Photo by Ron Austing.*

(but sometimes six to twelve) often form a clutch. The white eggs require 28 to 30 days of incubation by the female. Nestlings are brooded by the female and depart the nest when about 44 days old. They remain close to their parents and their nest burrow, however, where they participate in late-evening foraging flights.

The oldest known Burrowing Owl lived for 9 years.

BEHAVIOR Burrowing Owls use distinctly undulating flight, plus hovering, and they fly out to capture prey in a flycatcher-like manner. They also run, hop, and walk on the ground when pursuing insect prey. Juveniles improve their predation skills by jumping on live or dead insects delivered by their parents.

Burrowing Owls are active during the day and are semicolonial birds. Sometimes they are also crepuscular (active at twilight and dawn) and nocturnal. The birds roost and sleep at their burrow entrance, or occasionally at a nearby depression in the soil.

Burrowing Owls nesting in an urban development in Florida had a complex relationship between their population status and the amount of land developed. The largest number occurred when houses existed on 54 to 60 percent of an area. However, when housing covered more than 70 percent, Burrowing Owl productivity declined.

They are usually gentle birds and quite tame at their nest burrows, although they can be very defensive and will vigorously defend their nest territory by striking and chasing human or other intruders.

Burrowing Owls use more than a dozen different calls, generally near their nest burrows. Their alarm consists of a *cack-cack-cack-cack* sound, a screaming rasp, and a defense warble. A variety of courtship and other vocalizations are also used, along with bill snapping as a defensive tactic.

A Barred Owl. They are distributed widely in eastern North America. *Photo by Ron Austing.*

MIGRATION Burrowing Owls from the northern edge of their range in Minnesota are migratory. Florida's owls are mostly non-migratory.

POPULATION In Florida, ornithologists estimate that between 3,000 and 10,000 adult birds form that state's Burrowing Owl population. In the early 1920s, these owls were common nesting birds in the western counties of Minnesota, but the Burrowing Owl was listed as endangered in Minnesota in 1984. From 1986 to 1990, thirteen nests were found in Minnesota, with 38 percent of nest burrows in alfalfa fields, 38 percent in pastures, 13 percent in roadside ditches, and 13 percent in fence lines separating row crop fields.

Barred Owl (*Strix varia*)

The Barred Owl is a bird of extensive forests—especially deep swamps and riparian areas—but it also lives in extensive hemlock forests, and dense stands of pines, in upland landscapes.

HABITAT Barred Owls typically are birds of mature hardwood bottomland forests, but they also occur in much more open areas. In Massachusetts, they inhabit extensive white pine woodland as well as mixed pine and oak woods. In Florida, they are partial to living on prairies in mixed hammock shelters with live oaks and cabbage palmettos, especially in close proximity to marshes, sloughs, and similar wetlands with adequate food supplies.

DISTRIBUTION The Barred Owl breeds widely throughout eastern North America from boreal forests in southern Canada south to the northern Florida Keys and the Gulf Coast.

FOOD HABITS Barred Owls are opportunistic, nocturnal or seminocturnal predators. Their diet varies seasonally and geographically.

Nevertheless, small mammals constitute the largest portion of their prey, followed by birds, amphibians and reptiles, fish, and invertebrates. Undigested parts of prey such as bones, feathers, and insect fragments are formed into pellets and regurgitated through the mouth.

In Minnesota, Barred Owls prey on short-tailed shrews, meadow voles, white-footed mice, Norway rats, pocket gophers, house mice, flying squirrels, and red squirrels. Birds in their diet include Ruffed Grouse, Blue Jays, Common Grackles, in one case an adult Cooper's Hawk, and various small birds. Other prey includes snakes, skinks, crayfish, beetles, and grasshoppers. A Barred Owl in Duluth, Minnesota, apparently attempted to cache a rabbit.

The food habits of Barred Owls near Ann Arbor, Michigan, include meadow voles, deer mice, southern bog lemmings, meadow jumping mice, short-tailed shrews, and a few other mammal, bird, amphibian, and insect remains. Two Sharp-shinned Hawk remains were found in pellets. In Pennsylvania, Barred Owls are known to prey on Eastern Screech-Owls and other small owls. Food habits of Barred Owls in Florida also resemble those of their northern relatives, and also include cotton rats and fiddler crabs.

There also are two remarkable records in New England of Long-eared Owl remains found in the stomach's of two Barred Owls—and an Eastern Screech-Owl in the stomach of one of the Long-eared Owls. These are especially unusual examples of predators preying on other predators.

NESTING AND LIFE CYCLE Barred Owls are thought to be monogamous. Vocalization occurs most frequently during February and early March before eggs are deposited in March, and again in late summer and autumn. These birds are strongly attached to their nest sites, sometimes using them for many years. Nests usually are located in the interior of large woodlands, but occasionally they are placed in small woodlots or stands of young trees. The nest cavity is higher than 25 feet above ground, and occasionally it is a depression in a high tree stump. The owls also use nest boxes.

A unique Barred Owl nesting site (containing two white eggs) was reported on a ledge under the Sand Bar Ferry Bridge that was being dismantled on the South Carolina side of the Georgia-South Carolina border near Augusta, Georgia.

Two or three (sometimes one to five) white eggs are deposited on rotting wood chips and owl breast feathers. They are incubated by the female for 28 to 33 days, from late March to early April, and nestlings remain in the tree cavity until nearly full juvenile plumage is acquired.

In Minnesota, young owls leave their nest during the first half of June, within a few days of one another, usually at 4 to 5 weeks of age. The owls then stay near their nest for about 12 days, which is their preflight stage, with the adult female remaining nearby. If a bird falls to the ground, it laboriously climbs a tree with rough bark (such as basswood or ash) sometimes to heights of 47 feet to return to a large, horizontal branch at the bottom of the canopy.

Juvenile owls capable of flight roost during the day on the ground among tall grass near streams and woodland openings, or in trees in dense woodland or lowland areas. Parents feed their young during summer, but by August juveniles capture mice, small trout, and crayfish. By late summer, adult Barred Owls are active during the night and roost during the day. Family groups remain together well into autumn.

The oldest known Barred Owl lived for 18 years and 2 months.

BEHAVIOR The flight of Barred Owls is noiseless, buoyant, and light, which allows them to easily fly around trees in woodland that has an open understory but lacks numerous shrubs.

Barred Owls start hunting a few hours prior to sunset and continue to sunrise, but their most intense hunting activity occurs shortly after sunset, typically hunting from high perches on trees beside roads, in mature woodlots, and along streams and lowland areas—looking and listening for prey below them. Sometimes they also hunt from perches extending over water, which enables the birds to drop and catch fish; fish and crayfish also are captured by wading into shallow water. Barred Owls capture amphibian prey on the ground by running and pouncing upon the animals. In winter, they also may plunge into snow to capture small mammals.

After capture, Barred Owls usually take their prey to a feeding nest where the prey is swallowed whole, or ripped apart and consumed, with some parts of larger animals left for consumption later. The feeding nests usually are decorated with down feathers and are located near the nests the owls use for breeding.

Of the many vocalizations made by Barred Owls, the most famous is their loud *hoo-hoo-to-hoo-oo, hoo-hoo-hoo-to-whoo-oo* hooting, often translated in English as "who cooks for you? who cooks for you all?" Males have lower voices than females. Adults and young owls also engage in bill snapping as a form of agonistic behavior.

MIGRATION Barred Owls are nonmigratory although some birds from the northern edge of their range may move south in winter.

POPULATION Populations appear to be stable or perhaps increasing, although local declines due to forest clear-cutting are known for Tennessee, Ontario, and Atlantic Canada; 10,000 to 50,000 pairs are estimated to nest in Canada.

Great Gray Owl (*Strix nebulosa*)

The Great Gray Owl is one of North America's rarer, far northern owls. Although they appear large, much of the size is due to feathers. They are smaller than Great Horned Owls.

HABITAT Breeding birds prefer dense coniferous forests—but with bogs, muskegs, and other open areas—a limited combination in Canada.

During winter in Ottawa, Ontario, in the mid- to late 1960s and 1971, Great Gray Owls occupied open fields with large elm trees, along with shrubbery patches, areas with weeds, and fencerows overgrown with vegetation—in other words, abandoned shield farmland with poor soil. Small roads, mixed forests of considerable size, and scattered houses were adjacent to these areas. Large branches of elm trees served as roosts, with smaller trees and shrubs serving as hunting perches.

A Great Gray Owl that visited the Warren, Pennsylvania, area was observed in a cemetery, the grounds of a refining company, and along railroad tracks adjacent to the Allegheny River.

DISTRIBUTION The breeding distribution of the Great Gray Owl extends in boreal forest from extreme western Quebec westward through most of Ontario, south of Hudson Bay, and rarely in extreme northeastern Minnesota. During irruption years, however, these birds venture southeastward into New England, and the northern parts of the Great Lakes states. On rare occasions they reach Pennsylvania and Long Island, New York.

A Great Gray Owl. These boreal forest owls venture southward when their food supply is scarce. *Photo by Alan Wormington.*

FOOD HABITS The diet of Great Gray Owls varies with season, location, and with availability and vulnerability of prey. Microtine rodents are especially important food items.

Small mammals (meadow voles, red-backed voles, deer mice, jumping mice, shrews, moles, and others) are the primary food items captured and eaten by Great Gray Owls. Avian prey is relatively unimportant but includes ducks, Sharp-shinned Hawks, Broad-winged Hawks, Spruce Grouse, Gray Jays, and American Robins. Wood frogs are also taken.

The meadow vole is the primary food of Great Gray Owls during winter in Quebec. However, snowshoe hares are also taken, and a few short-tailed shrew remains were identified in pellets.

NESTING AND LIFE CYCLE Great Gray Owls are monogamous, although polygyny occurs rarely. Pair bonds are not long term in boreal forests, but the same mates may nest again in a subsequent year.

Great Gray Owls adopt old nests of other raptors or corvids, using them without refurbishment. The nest territory (but not the foraging territory) is defended via vocalizations made by the male. Great Gray Owls seem unconcerned when other raptors have nests at least 1,500 feet away. In Minnesota, Great Gray Owls retain a territory in the nest site area year-round, provided an adequate prey base exists.

Depending on the location, the female lays her eggs from late March to early June—or later. Two or three (rarely four or five) white eggs are incubated entirely by the female and hatch in 28 to 30 days. After hatching, the female broods her nestlings for 2 or 3 weeks, then roosts near the nest. The male captures prey and delivers it to the female, who feeds her nestlings. By the time the young owls are 3 or 4 weeks old, they depart their nest and roost on the ground or on nearby trees; they are able to fly after another week or two. Juvenile owls become independent in late summer and depart the area during autumn and winter.

The oldest known Great Gray Owl lived for 12 years and 9 months, although another banded bird was living still when at least 13 years old.

BEHAVIOR Great Gray Owl flight is mothlike, with deep, slow wing beats. They frequently hover prior to dropping onto prey.

These owls commonly hunt during early morning, and late afternoon, up to dusk. They typically use an exposed hunting perch that provides an excellent view in all directions, sometimes moving from one perch to another, while looking for vole activity under the snow. When a good spot is found, the bird gazes at the spot, then drops into the snow to capture the prey. When captured, it is briefly covered with the owl's umbrella-like out-spread wings, then consumed whole, head-first, within 2 or 3 seconds. If suitable hunting perches are unavailable, the owls hunt by standing in the snow. They can also walk and run on hard snow. Apparently these birds locate and capture their prey by using a keen sense of sound, but field observations also indicate that Great Gray Owls use very keen eyesight to spot movements of small prey such as voles.

A Great Gray Owl that visited Pennsylvania during winter was amazingly tolerant of people, even taking mice from people offering them, and capturing mice and voles in the snow—including one rodent captured at the feet of a birder!

Various agonistic Great Gray Owl behavior includes active defense of its nest territory by chasing, and sometimes attacking, other Great Gray Owls, Northern Goshawks, Broad-winged Hawks, and Great Horned Owls. During winter, owls also defend their territory against hawks and other owls. At other times, these owls simply fly deep into the safety of a forest when harassed. Spreading and drooping the wings, bill snapping, and spreading rictal bristles and feathers, constitute a low-level threat display.

During autumn and early winter, Great Gray Owls are solitary. During winter in Quebec, they established a home range within which they remained most of the time. One owl remained for 11 days almost entirely within an area of about 112 acres—showing how strongly these owls are attached to their winter range. These owls rarely engage in winter territorial confrontations.

Great Gray Owls prefer to roost on a tree branch near the trunk. They fold their facial disk to change their profile, which helps them blend into the bark of the tree.

Quebec studies of Great Gray Owls in winter revealed that these birds used two calls.

One was "a short, rasping 'e-e-e-e-e-e-ee-e-e'" with poor carrying power, the second "a quiet, drawn out 'Who-oo-oo-oo-oo-oo'" with excellent carrying power over long distances. Adults and young birds also use bill snapping, commonly accompanied by hissing.

MIGRATION Great Gray Owls are both resident and irregularly migratory depending on the availability of food. These so-called irruptions have occurred very roughly every 10 or 12 years (with echo flights sometimes appearing in following years) since as early as 1831. John James Audubon attempted unsuccessfully to see this owl alive along coastal Massachusetts, unknowingly becoming North America's first "bird chaser."

POPULATION The Great Gray Owl's population is estimated at 50,000 birds in North America.

Long-eared Owl (Asio otus)

Long-eared Owls are smaller, but look similar to, Great Horned Owls. They are distributed widely but are rarer than their larger cousin.

HABITAT Only once in my ornithological career, many years ago, did I discover an occupied Long-eared Owl nest in a pine woodlot near Trexlertown, Pennsylvania. The dense pine trees were approximately 15 to 20 feet high, but now have grown much taller, and a very extensive ground litter now exists throughout the woodlot. Long-eared Owls no longer exist there. Indeed, it is now a public park consisting of the pine woodlot, open grassy fields, and walking paths and trails.

During winter in the southern third of Minnesota, Long-eared Owls roost in dense pockets of eastern red cedars on sloping

A Long-eared Owl. They're smaller than Great Horned Owls, but also have "ear" tufts. *Photo by Alan Wormington.*

hillsides surrounded by semiopen habitat. Sometimes long-needled pine or spruce plantations provide roosting sites when the trees are intermediate in height (much taller coniferous trees are used by Great Horned Owls). Long-eared Owls have also roosted in dense, remote groves of long-needled pines ranging in height from 10 to 20 feet, *without* an understory in the pine grove. Open fields were located nearby, and prime Long-eared Owl habitat was located a considerable distance from roads on private property. If this pattern prevails elsewhere, it may provide helpful management implications for these owls.

A winter roost of Long-eared Owls near Seemsville, Pennsylvania, contained twelve owls and remained active for 68 days. It was in a line of six pine trees near a house and was visited by numerous birders (they kept a distance from the roost trees and birds and kept noise to a minimum).

Wintering Long-eared Owls in reclaimed strip-mine areas in western Kentucky roosted in a small stand of Virginia pines bordered by a pond, autumn olive, multiflora rose, and a grassland field. (Autumn olive and multiflora rose are highly invasive, nonnative plants

that are not recommended for habitat restoration or enhancement.)

DISTRIBUTION The breeding range of the Long-eared Owl extends in Canada from the lower three-quarters of Ontario, somewhat south of Hudson Bay, and lower one-third of Quebec, and southern Atlantic Canada, south through much of the Great Lakes states, most of Pennsylvania and New York, most of New Hampshire and Vermont, and all of Maine.

The Long-eared Owl's wintering range extends southward through most of the southeastern and Gulf Coast states, but they do not reach Florida. On March 28, 1988, for example, at Fernbank Forest, DeKalb County, Georgia, a Long-eared Owl was observed roosting in a juniper tree. These owls are rare winter visitors in that state.

FOOD HABITS Long-eared Owls are opportunist rather than specialist predators. Their diet consists largely of small mammals (meadow voles, other microtine voles, deer mice, house mice, young rats, moles, shrews, bats, young rabbits, weasels, red squirrels, and other species). Birds are rarely taken, but some lizards and snakes are captured.

Long-eared Owls in flight use deep wing beats. *Photo by Ron Austing.*

In Bloomington, Minnesota, Long-eared Owls in a winter communal roost site preyed on meadow voles, white-footed mice, and three short-tailed shrews. The food habits of other Long-eared Owls in Minnesota consisted mostly of meadow voles with a few deer mice, harvest mice, red-backed mice, masked shrews, birds, and insects also taken.

The Minnesota data are similar to Long-eared Owl food habit information from the vicinity of Ann Arbor, Michigan. Meadow voles, deer mice, southern bog lemmings, and small numbers of other mammals and birds constituted the diet of those owls.

Winter food habits of Long-eared Owls living on a reclaimed strip mine in western Kentucky consisted of prairie voles, southern bog lemmings, and a few mice, shrews, and birds.

Long-eared Owls roosting in trees at Seemsville, Pennsylvania, preyed on a few

A Long-eared Owl roosting. Their protective coloration makes them difficult to see. *Photo by Ron Austing.*

An adult Long-eared Owl using a spread-wing threat display. *Photo by Donald S. Heintzelman.*

shrews, numerous rodents, and heavily upon birds—perhaps because bird feeders were operated in backyards near the owls' roosting site. That would explain the avian prey composition at this site—House Sparrows, European Starlings, House Finches, White-throated Sparrows, Dark-eyed Juncos, and American Goldfinches, plus one Black-capped Chickadee and fourteen Northern Cardinals.

NESTING AND LIFE CYCLE Long-eared Owls are monogamous and sometimes nest in colonies. Pair bonding probably occurs early in the year. Courtship displays include aerial zigzag flights, with gliding and wing clapping, near and within the nest habitat. Vocalizations are used by both birds during pair formation, and the female sits on a nest (used previously by other hawks or corvids) she selects.

Long-eared Owls usually use an old crow nest in which to lay their eggs rather than building a nest of their own. Nevertheless, John James Audubon found a nest in Pennsylvania near the Juniata River that was built by Long-eared Owls using green twigs with

A nestling Long-eared Owl using a spread-wing threat display. *Photo by Donald S. Heintzelman.*

leaflets intact, and some sheep wool and fresh grass to line the nest.

Long-eared Owls usually do not nest on the ground. Occasionally, however, they do so, as in Spencer Township, Aitkin County, Minnesota. The owls selected their nest site in a small tamarack and alder bog, and built the nest of loosely arranged sticks placed "in the middle of the base of an alder bush." Another ground nest near Montreal in Quebec was near the border of a lake in a bog but well inside a black spruce forest. Twigs, flakes of bark, and leaves of Labrador tea lined the shallow depression in the ground below a young black spruce tree.

Four or five (sometimes three to eight) white eggs are deposited and incubated by the female for 25 to 30 days. She is diligent about her duties and leaves the nest for only brief periods at night. Because female Long-eared Owls have good protective coloration, however, they are difficult to see sitting on their nests.

The male takes food to the female at the nest. Upon hatching, the nestlings remain in the nest for about 21 days, then move to nearby tree branches and move around in them. The young owls develop an early flight capability when about 35 days old, but their parents still feed them until they are about 10 or 11 weeks old. The juveniles do their own hunting between 2 to 6 weeks after leaving the nest. Juvenile owls then move as far as 52 miles from their natal locale when they are between 9½ and 11 weeks old.

The oldest known Long-eared Owl lived for 11 years and 1 month.

BEHAVIOR Long-eared Owl flight is buoyant, light, and often agile when moving around many objects such as trees. Typically, the owls employ a series of long glides, with the wings held level, followed by deep wing beats. When prey is located, they commonly hover over the animal before dropping and capturing it.

An incubating female sleeps on her nest during the day while the male roosts in nearby trees. During the breeding season, some males (which generally are solitary) roost with other males from other nests in the area. During other seasons, from two to one

hundred Long-eared Owls roost communally. Sometimes, a few Short-eared Owls also roost with Long-eared Owls.

When threatened by a person, and perhaps by another animal, some Long-eared Owls use an impressive spread-wing display that makes them appear much larger than they are. Various vocalizations, and bill snapping, are used simultaneously in an effort to scare the person away.

Long-eared Owls usually are silent except during the breeding season, when their vocalizations are varied. Calls sometimes heard include a prolonged *quoo-oo-oo,* a soft, hooting *quoo-quoo-quoo,* and a soft *whoof-whoof-whoof.* They also make catlike and doglike sounds.

MIGRATION Much remains to be learned about the species' nocturnal migrations or nomadic movements. Nevertheless, they do undertake seasonal migrations, especially in northern states such as Minnesota, where 1,859 individuals were captured and banded (and many others observed) during autumn from 1972 to 1999 at the Hawk Ridge Nature Reserve in Duluth. However, the annual capture rate of Long-eared Owls at Hawk Ridge declined drastically—down to fifteen owls netted in 1998 and nine in 1999, compared with a long-term average of sixty-six netted per year. Several warmer winters might be responsible for the drop at Hawk Ridge of these owls—perhaps because adequate prey bases made it unnecessary for the owls to migrate. One Long-eared Owl banded at Hawk Ridge was recovered 1,922 miles away in Puebla, Mexico.

In the Middle Atlantic states, northward spring migrations of Long-eared Owls occur from mid-March to mid-April, whereas southward autumn migrations at Cape May Point, New Jersey, occur from mid-October to late November.

POPULATION Long-eared Owls are widespread in North America. They are designated "endangered" in Illinois, a "species of special concern" in Michigan, Wisconsin, and throughout New England (except Maine), and as "status undetermined" in Pennsylvania.

Short-eared Owl (*Asio flammeus*)

Short-eared Owls are more or less the crepuscular counterparts of Northern Harriers, with both species occupying similar habitats. They occur widely in temperate areas throughout much of the world.

HABITAT Short-eared Owls occupy a range of habitats including tundra, grassy plains, old fields, pastures, marshes, and sand dunes, but avoid wooded areas and forests.

On May 30, 1979 a Short-eared Owl nested in a reclaimed part of a strip mine in western Pennsylvania. The habitat was a sloped savanna covered with grass measuring about 8 inches high and scattered autumn olives (a very bad choice of invasive, nonnative vegetation) about 6 feet tall. The nest was lined with dried grass. These owls also occur in this reclaimed strip mine in winter. In addition, they nest in marshes near Philadelphia International Airport. Along the Ottertail River near Breckenridge, Minnesota, a Short-eared Owl nested in a denlike burrow in the river's bank about 8 feet above the surface of the river.

Short-eared Owls wintering in a reclaimed strip-mine area in western Kentucky roosted in a vegetated depression positioned between two low hills. A small, ephemeral pond containing phragmites and cattails was adjacent to the owl roost.

DISTRIBUTION The Short-eared Owl is distributed in eastern North America from southern Canada through Florida and most of

A Short-eared Owl. *Photo by Ron Austing.*

the Gulf Coast. The breeding range includes southern and Atlantic Canada, to the northern portion of the western Great Lakes states, and eastward into Pennsylvania, New York, and southern and coastal New England. In many areas, breeding is local and spotty, however. The extent of the winter range varies from year to year.

Changes have occurred in the Short-eared Owl's distribution. For example, on June 21, 1993, near Keewaydin, Pennsylvania, a Short-eared Owl was observed perched on a sign beside a road, then flew into a nearby depression in a reclaimed strip-mine area containing groves of young conifers and black locust trees. This may be an eastward extension in the summering and breeding range for these birds in Pennsylvania.

FOOD HABITS Short-eared Owls are opportunistic but somewhat specialist predators that feed very heavily on meadow voles and other microtine voles, plus other small rodents (white-footed mice, house mice, rats, rabbits) and shrews. Birds (rails, Killdeer, yellowlegs, terns, Horned Larks, woodpeckers, kinglets, American Robins, Red-winged Blackbirds, meadowlarks, grackles, sparrows, juncos, Snow Buntings) form a small portion of their diet. Beetles, grasshoppers, and cutworms are also eaten.

Short-eared Owls wintering in a reclaimed strip-mine area in western Kentucky fed on prairie voles, which formed one-half of their diet. A few other small mice, shrews, and small birds were also eaten.

NESTING AND LIFE CYCLE Courtship of Short-eared Owls takes place in winter, when wing-clapping and other displays occur regularly. Courtship feeding, when the male feeds the female, takes place prior to copulation. The birds remain monogamous during the breeding season.

Five to seven (sometimes four to nine) white eggs are deposited in the nest which is a shallow depression in the ground lined with grass, feathers, and some weeds. Along the Ottertail River near Breckenridge, Minnesota, a Short-eared Owl nested in a denlike burrow in the river's bank.

During years of very high prey density, unusually large clutches (as many as sixteen eggs) are reported. Egg-laying dates vary geographically, but range from early April to early August. The female incubates the eggs for 24 to 29 days. There are reports of nests involving two females incubating the same eggs. Nestlings generally depart their nest when 14 to 18 days old, after which they walk around near their nest but are not able to fly until 24 to 27 days old. Their protective coloration makes the young owls difficult to see. When threatened, juvenile owls sometimes pretend to be injured.

Short-eared Owls, such as this owl perched on a fence post, are partially diurnal. *Photo by Ron Austing.*

The oldest known Short-eared Owl lived for 4 years and 5 months.

BEHAVIOR Short-eared Owls are antagonistic toward Northern Harriers and American Crows, and it is not unusual to see these owls chasing these birds. The owls fly low over the ground using glides and flapping flight. Occasionally they use hovering flight prior to pouncing on prey. It is not uncommon to see Short-eared Owls perched on fence posts, trees, shrubs, and occasionally on the ground—presumably watching for prey.

Short-eared Owls are crepuscular, with the start of their activity taking place at dusk, and continuing into the night, with some activity curtailed after midnight. They also hunt over fields in the dim light of early dawn, and even during the day when conditions are dark and cloudy.

Short-eared Owls in Minnesota are known to hunt in flight and while perched. As many as thirty or more owls sometimes gather in hunting groups. Elsewhere in that state, two Short-eared Owls soared several hundred feet aloft, "barked," dove at, and escorted a Rough-legged Hawk from the owls' feeding area. When a Short-eared Owl captured a vole, it opened its body cavity with its bill, then removed and discarded the stomach and intestines before eating the rest of the prey. It is unknown why these organs were discarded.

During courtship, Short-eared Owls use brief wing-clapping behavior repeated at intervals of five to six per second, audible several hundred yards away. The owls also "bark" to each other during these performances.

In Grimstad Township, Roseau County, Minnesota, a territorial Short-eared Owl engaged in a very vigorous attack—a raspy and hissing alarm call, and repeated dive bombing and striking—on an immature Rough-legged Hawk perched on the ground. The hawk escaped unharmed, even though the owl seemed to use its talons to strike the hawk's back several times.

During the summer of 1997, when vole populations apparently peaked, seven breeding pairs of Short-eared Owls were discovered in western Pennsylvania, especially in reclaimed surface mines with adequate rodent prey bases and grasses needed for nest sites. Three additional pairs were suspected of breeding.

Short-eared Owls tend to be silent birds but are quite vocal when they are on their nesting territory and have nestlings. Vocalizations include a *wak-wak-wak* bark repeated about eight times, and a prolonged *w-a-a-a-k*. A range of other vocalizations as well as bill snapping are also used, the latter also by nestlings.

MIGRATION Short-eared Owls are migratory and sometimes engage in long-distance movements of up to nearly 1,240 miles. Other individuals, however, seem not to move around much or at all. Hence, much remains to be learned about the migratory movements of these birds.

POPULATION In Pennsylvania, the Short-eared Owl is classified as "endangered."

Boreal Owl (*Aegolius funereus*)

Boreal Owls exhibit the most excellent examples of reverse sexual dimorphism (females are larger than males) of any North American owls. They also have a *spotted forehead*—the one absolutely distinctive field mark separating this species from the Northern Saw-whet Owl. However, not all Boreal Owls have yellow bills—some have a light blue or dark bill.

HABITAT The typical breeding habitat of Boreal Owls in eastern North America is boreal (spruce, poplar, aspen, birch, and balsam fir) or mixed forest across Canada that also barely extends into extreme northern Minnesota (and perhaps Wisconsin, Michigan, and Maine).

It is unclear what constitutes prime Boreal Owl habitat in North America. Two important landscape and habitat features, however, are associated with these owls as breeding birds in northern Minnesota: (1) overmature aspen trees approximately 85 to 90 years old, with fungal decay and abandoned woodpecker holes, utilized by nesting Boreal Owls, and (2) black spruce trees forming adjacent lowland stands in which the owls roost.

In Superior National Forest in northern Minnesota, remote and extensive spruce and pine forests, and some mixed northern conifer-deciduous forests, are home to Boreal

A Boreal Owl, seen during one of its periodic irruptions southward from its normal boreal forest habitat. *Photo by Alan Wormington.*

ward in the western Great Lakes region to extreme northern Minnesota. But the owls are absent as breeding birds elsewhere along the Canadian–United States border except perhaps in extreme northern Wisconsin, Michigan, and northwestern Maine. The first nest of a Boreal Owl in the coterminous United States was discovered in 1978 near Grand Marais, Minnesota.

During years when irruptions occur, Boreal Owls might be seen (rarely) as far south as Illinois. There is also one late nineteenth century report for Pennsylvania.

FOOD HABITS The Boreal Owl's diet consists of small mammals (microtine voles, deer mice, jumping mice, shrews, squirrels, and chipmunks, weasels, woodrats, and young snowshoe hares), a few birds (woodpeckers, chickadees, thrushes, kinglets, redpolls, crossbills, and juncos), and some insects (crickets).

NESTING AND LIFE CYCLE Boreal Owls nest in old flicker and Pileated Woodpecker tree cavities and in nest boxes, but if a natural nest tree is selected, it is not used again the next year. Northern Saw-whet Owls occasionally displace Boreal Owls at nest cavities. The saw-whets then use the cavities for their own nesting purposes, as documented in Minnesota.

First clutches are deposited by late March to mid-April in Minnesota. Four to six (sometimes three to seven) white eggs are deposited and incubated by the female for 26 to 32 days. The young owls remain as nestlings for 28 to 36 days, then leave their nest cavity, with the younger nestlings departing first. However, they remain as a loose group close to the nest for about a week while the adults feed them. Finally, 3 to 6 weeks after departing the nest cavity, the juvenile owls disperse considerable distances. Not much is known about this phase of their lives.

Owls. Singing males are widely distributed at low population densities as regular breeders in older, upland-mixed forest as the habitat of choice. Few breeding owls are found where boreal forest does not exist.

Boreal Owls use lowland conifer habitat for roosting and foraging—a juxtaposition of habitats within the landscape in which the owls live. The owls nest in secondary cavities (abandoned woodpecker holes), so their availability doubtless helps to determine the distribution and abundance of these birds in northeastern Minnesota. Occasionally, during winter, a Boreal Owl also appears in an urban environment, such as a bird seen outside the Minneapolis home of one birder in mid-February 1989.

DISTRIBUTION The breeding range of the Boreal Owl extends through the boreal forests of Ontario, Quebec, and Labrador and south-

The maximum lifespan of Boreal Owls in the wild in Europe may be about 3.5 years, but more information is needed, especially for eastern North America.

BEHAVIOR Boreal Owls are mainly solitary and are unfamiliar to most ornithologists and birders. They use flapping flight to maneuver in woodland, and may hover briefly. They also cache food at roosts and in the nest cavity, and thaw frozen prey with their body heat—the latter behavior an adaptation to the cold climate in which they live.

Agonistic behavior includes screeching and flying at intruders coming close to the nest cavity. Fratricide sometimes occurs among nestlings. Away from their nest territory, however, Boreal Owls are unusually "tame" when encountered by people.

The Boreal Owl's voice retains a ventriloquist quality, perhaps an adaptation evolved to confuse predators by making it difficult for them to accurately locate the owl. A variety of vocalizations are made. One is a slow, bell-like tolling *ting-ting-ting-ting* similar to water dropping, or also said to resemble a single-pitched trill lasting for a couple of seconds. Defensive sounds also include bill snapping by adults and young, and hissing.

MIGRATION Boreal Owls are nomadic, especially during years of low prey populations. Some apparently are migratory each year. For example, each spring, at Whitefish Point, Michigan, northward movements of varying magnitudes of migrating Boreal Owls are reported, even an exceptionally high count of 164 owls during 1988.

A pilot study of Boreal Owl migration in Duluth, Minnesota, indicated that the autumn migration of these birds varies greatly from year to year. They appear between October 10 and November 20, with the largest numbers arriving in early November. During irruptive years, several hundred Boreal Owls arrive in northern Minnesota and adjacent northern states, Ontario, and other eastern Canadian provinces. Nevertheless, much remains to be learned about Boreal Owl migrations.

POPULATION Boreal Owl abundance can vary markedly across years, with breeding birds linked with three-to-four year periodicity microtine prey cycles. No comprehensive information is available, however, regarding long-term Boreal Owl population changes.

In a 6-year study of singing male Boreal Owls in northeastern Minnesota, males were detected 234 times along 3,098.8 miles of survey routes.

Northern Saw-whet Owl
(*Aegolius acadicus*)

The Northern Saw-whet Owl is the smallest of the owls found in eastern North America. Its one absolutely distinctive field mark is a *streaked forehead*. Because of its small size, excellent protective coloration, and shy behavior, it is seen infrequently unless intense searches are made to find it. Nevertheless, Northern Saw-whet Owls may be more common than sightings suggest.

A Northern Saw-whet Owl with several albino primary feathers was captured at the Hawk Ridge Nature Reserve, Duluth, Minnesota.

HABITAT Northern Saw-whet Owls live in deciduous and coniferous forests and woodland, mixed conifer-deciduous forests, larger woodlots, pine plantations, honeysuckle thickets, and swamps and marshes. During spring in southern Ontario, roosting Northern Saw-whet Owls selected unusually thick hemlock trees providing especially good overhead concealment. During other seasons, however,

A pair of adult Northern Saw-whet Owls. The larger and heavier female is on the left, the male on the right. *Photo by Ron Austing.*

roosts with other features were used, such as smaller trees providing easier avenues of approach and escape.

Most nesting Northern Saw-whet Owls in Minnesota are found in boreal hardwood forests in the northern part of the state, but some nested in North Oaks (a suburb of St. Paul) and Minneapolis (near the Mississippi River).

In 1968, Northern Saw-whet Owls nested successfully in Wood Duck nest boxes in wetlands at the John F. Kennedy Memorial Wildlife Refuge on Long Island, New York. The first report for Long Island was in 1879.

Northern Saw-whet Owls in the southern Appalachians sometimes are found nesting in conifer (especially spruce-fir) forests with elevations higher than roughly 4,500 feet, but they also occur in mixed conifer-hardwood forests, mostly deciduous hardwoods. Ten wintering Northern Saw-whet Owls in the Big South Fork National River Recreation Area

of Kentucky and Tennessee lived in mixed coniferous-deciduous forest on the tops of ridges adjacent to forested white pine and hemlock slopes.

Old woodpecker cavities in trees are essential components of Northern Saw-whet Owl habitats. Nevertheless, these owls also use Wood Duck nest boxes in marshes and other wetlands.

DISTRIBUTION The breeding range of Northern Saw-whet Owls extends from southern Ontario, Quebec, and most of Atlantic Canada south through the western Great Lakes states, northern portions of Indiana, Illinois, Ohio, Pennsylvania, much of New York including Long Island, and New England. Isolated breeding populations also occur in the mountains of West Virginia, western Maryland, eastern Tennessee, and western North Carolina.

A possible expansion of the breeding range of Northern Saw-whet Owls into northeastern Georgia occurred on April 26, 1995, when one of these owls was heard calling along Old Mud Creek Road (Bald Mountain Road in nearby North Carolina) near Sky Valley, Georgia. The record extends by more than one month the late date for this species in Georgia. Northern Saw-whet Owls may also nest in the mountains of northern Georgia because they breed in nest boxes on Roan Mountain, Tennessee.

Wintering Northern Saw-whet Owls sometimes venture to Florida, southern Georgia, Alabama, Mississippi, and Louisiana, although the southern limits of their wintering range may be changing.

FOOD HABITS Most relatively recent food habit studies of Northern Saw-whet Owls are based on examination of the contents of pellets regurgitated by these birds. The overall results provide a good general picture of their

Two juvenile Northern Saw-whet Owls. Their plumage is strikingly different from the adult plumage. *Photo by Ron Austing.*

diets. They indicate preferences for small mammals (microtine voles, deer mice, some shrews, bats, squirrels, flying squirrels). Rock Doves, swallows, chickadees, kinglets, wood warblers, Northern Cardinals, and sparrows are also prey, and some insects are also captured and eaten.

Autumn food habits of Northern Saw-whet Owls on the Eastern Shore of Virginia consisted of white-footed mice, house mice, short-tailed shrews, a southern flying squirrel, silver-haired bat, and a Vesper Sparrow. Insects consisted of lepidopteron prey. Fifteen road-killed owls fed on a shrew and mouse, and on insects (mostly Lepidoptera).

NESTING AND LIFE CYCLE Depending on location, Northern Saw-whet Owls annually begin nesting between late March and late July, with many between mid-April and mid-May.

During courtship, the male makes a circular flight around the female, who is perched and watching her mate's activities. After cir-

cling the female as many as twenty times, the male lands near her and bobs and shuffles closer until he perches beside her. Sometimes food is brought to the female, who swallows it. After making some tooting calls, the female flies to another tree, followed by the male. She perches about halfway up the tree, and copulation occurs a few times for several nights.

Five to six (sometimes four to seven) white eggs are deposited in old flicker (or less commonly other woodpecker) holes, or occasionally Wood Duck nest boxes, and incubated by the female. Incubation requires about 26 to 28 days, and most nestlings leave their nest when about 34 days old, or perhaps slightly younger. The juvenile owls at that age are able to fly. They are chocolate brown with a white triangular patch (formed by their eyebrows) above the bill and between the eyes—strikingly different in coloration from their parents.

The oldest known Northern Saw-whet Owl lived for 10 years and 4 months.

BEHAVIOR Northern Saw-whet Owls are famous for their remarkable tameness. They often allow a person to approach slowly within a few feet, apparently depending on their protective coloration and small size rather than making moving to another perch necessary. Some owls even allow themselves to be picked up by hand—a most extraordinary experience for everyone who has done so.

These owls prefer to roost low on pine braches or in other suitable vegetation that provides good concealment—commonly a few feet above the ground—although some saw-whets are found as high as 10 feet above the ground amid the branches of hemlock and pine trees. In February 1960, near International Airport in Philadelphia, however, three wintering Northern Saw-whet Owls roosted among dense honeysuckle thickets. The birds were captured by hand, banded, and released into protective cover. Rather than snapping their bills and flying away, two owls opened their mouths and, with great effort, each disgorged a single pellet. The birds attempted to fly to another perch only *after* each owl disgorged a pellet. This behavior was repeated 3 weeks later.

In winter in Minnesota, one Northern Saw-whet Owl was perched on a four-feet-high post near the side of a road rather than being concealed in vegetation. In southern Ontario, however, these owls prefer to roost in thick hemlock trees during their spring migration.

One of the most bizarre episodes involving a Northern Saw-whet Owl's hunting behavior was reported in November 1990, when an owl apparently attempted to capture a house cat. The very upset cat came to the open door of a school with the owl still attached to its back! The school custodian removed the owl, gave it to a former principal (a birder), who carefully examined the bird and released it unharmed.

The vocalizations of Northern Saw-whet Owls sometimes consist of *tang-tang-tang-tang*-ing similar to metal hitting an anvil, a *skreigh-aw skreigh-aw skreigh-aw* in three parts, *hew-hew-hew-hew* whistles, and sounds resembling a saw being filed, for which these owls are named. Other vocalizations are also used.

MIGRATION Northern Saw-whet Owls are migratory in parts of eastern North America. Considerable numbers migrate southward during autumn in the Great Lakes and Atlantic Coast states. Some also migrate in the Appalachians in Pennsylvania into parts of the southeastern states. The magnitude and dynamics of Northern Saw-whet Owl migrations may be linked to prey availability.

Northward spring migrations of Northern Saw-whet Owls occur from early March to late May, depending on location. The farther north a site, the later the migrations occur. Spring migration corridors occur in various locations including western New York and Toronto.

Autumn migrations occur from early September to late November depending on location. Migration corridors during autumn include the western shorelines of the western Great Lakes region, the Ohio River valley, along the Appalachian mountains, and along the Atlantic Coast.

During the spring and autumn of 1993–1994, seventy-two migrating Northern Saw-whet Owls were captured in Wisconsin, and from 1997 to 1999, in central Wisconsin, 833 additional migrating owls were captured. Many winter in Wisconsin.

In 1968, the female of a pair of Northern Saw-whet Owls nesting on Long Island, New York, was found alive (shot with a BB shot in the left eye, she eventually died) in South Portland, Maine—an example of an adult owl moving north from its nesting site.

In 1995, more than 5,900 migrating Northern Saw-whet Owls were banded at Great Lakes and Atlantic Coast banding stations, including 40 percent at five New Jersey, Maryland, and Virginia stations. A large proportion of them were immature females. Although 1995 was an exceptional year, it demonstrated the magnitude of some Northern Saw-whet Owl migrations. Curiously, none of these banded birds were subsequently recovered.

Banding evidence suggests that forests in the southeastern United States are important wintering grounds for Northern Saw-whet Owls, but the southern limits of the wintering range is known imperfectly. Nevertheless, a search of part of Rabun County in northern Georgia revealed three Northern Saw-whet Owls on January 8, 2000, in cove deciduous hardwood forest with few hemlocks and rhododendrons. Subsequent searches in the area, and up to the South Carolina border, produced six or eight more owls. Hence, when large numbers of Northern Saw-whet Owls are migrating southward, some birds include northern Georgia in their winter range.

POPULATION No adequate population data are available for Northern Saw-whet Owls. Moreover, their shy behavior may distort counts that may be considerably larger than records suggest.

During the winter of 2000 (January–March) in the Big South Fork National River Recreation Area of Kentucky and Tennessee—an area of approximately 100,000 acres—a survey of Northern Saw-whet Owls suggested as many as 180 individuals were wintering on the area. The birds reflected a major irruption during the autumn of 1999 in the northeastern United States.

REFERENCES AND FURTHER READING

GENERAL REFERENCES

American Ornithologists' Union

1957 *Check-list of North American Birds.* Fifth Edition. American Ornithologists' Union, Washington, DC.

1998 *Check-list of North American Birds.* Seventh Edition. American Ornithologists' Union, Washington, DC.

2000 Forty-second Supplement to the American Ornithologists' Union *Check-list of North American Birds. Auk,* 117 (3): 847–858.

Barber, D. R., C. R. Fosdick, L. J. Goodrich, and S. Luke

2001 *Hawk Mountain Sanctuary Migration Count Manual.* First Edition. Hawk Mountain Sanctuary Assn., Kempton, PA.

Bent, A. C.

1937 *Life Histories of North American Birds of Prey.* Part 1. Bulletin 167. U.S. National Museum, Washington, DC.

1938 *Life Histories of North American Birds of Prey.* Part 2. Bulletin 170. U.S. National Museum, Washington, DC.

Bildstein, K. L., and K. Meyer

2000 Sharp-shinned Hawk (*Accipiter striatus*). In *The Birds of North America,* No. 482, ed. A. Poole and F. Gill. The Birds of North America, Inc., Philadelphia.

Brashear, C. B., and P. K. Stoddard

2001 *Autumn Raptor Migration through the Florida Keys with Special Focus on the Peregrine Falcon.* Final Report Project NG96–101. Bureau of Wildlife Diversity Conservation, Florida Fish and Wildlife Conservation Commission, Tallahassee.

Brown, L., and D. Amadon

1968 *Eagles, Hawks and Falcons of the World.* Two volumes. McGraw-Hill, New York.

Buehler, D. A.

2000 Bald Eagle (*Haliaeetus leucocephalus*). In *The Birds of North America,* No. 506, ed. A. Poole and F. Gill. The Birds of North America, Inc., Philadelphia.

Bull, E. L., and J. R. Duncan

1993 Great Gray Owl (*Strix nebulosa*). In *The Birds of North America,* No. 41, ed. A. Poole and F. Gill. The Birds of North America, Inc., Philadelphia.

Cade, T. J.

1982 *The Falcons of the World.* Comstock/Cornell University Press, Ithaca, NY.

Chartier, A., and D. Stimac

2002 *Hawks of Holiday Beach.* Second Edition. Holiday Beach Migration Observatory, Holiday Beach Conservation Area, Ontario, Canada.

Clapp, R. B., M. K. Klimkiewicz, and J. H. Kennard

1982 Longevity Records of North American Birds: Gaviidae through Alcidae. *J. Field Ornithology,* 53 (2): 81–124.

Clark, W. S., and B. K. Wheeler

2001 *A Field Guide to Hawks of North America.* Second Edition. Houghton Mifflin, Boston.

Clum, N. J., and T. J. Cade

1994 Gyrfalcon (*Falco rusticolus*). In *The Birds of North America,* No. 114, ed. A. Poole and F. Gill. The Birds of North America, Inc., Philadelphia.

Crocoll, S. T.

1994 Red-shouldered Hawk (*Buteo lineatus*). In *The Birds of North America,* No. 107, ed. A.

Poole and F. Gill. The Birds of North America, Inc., Philadelphia.

Duncan, J. R., and P. A. Duncan

1998   Northern Hawk Owl (*Surnia ulula*). In *The Birds of North America*, No. 356, ed. A. Poole and F. Gill. The Birds of North America, Inc., Philadelphia.

Dunk, J. R.

1995   White-tailed Kite (*Elanus leucurus*). In *The Birds of North America*, No. 178, ed. A. Poole and F. Gill. The Birds of North America, Inc., Philadelphia.

England, A. S., M. J. Bechard, and C. S. Houston

1997   Swainson's Hawk (*Buteo swainsoni*). In *The Birds of North America*, No. 265, ed. A. Poole and F. Gill. The Birds of North America, Inc., Philadelphia.

Ferguson-Lees, J., and D. A. Christie

2001   *Raptors of the World.* Houghton Mifflin, Boston.

Gehlbach, F. R.

1995   Eastern Screech-Owl (*Otus asio*). In *The Birds of North America*, No. 165, ed. A. Poole and F. Gill. The Birds of North America, Inc., Philadelphia.

Gill, F. B. (Editor)

1985   Birds. In *Species of Special Concern in Pennsylvania*, by H. H. Genoways and F. J. Brenner. Special Publication No. 11. Carnegie Museum of Natural History, Pittsburgh, PA.

Goodrich, L. J., S. C. Crocoll, and S. E. Senner

1996   Broad-winged Hawk (*Buteo platypterus*). In *The Birds of North America*, No. 218, ed. A. Poole and F. Gill. The Birds of North America, Inc., Philadelphia.

Haug, E. A., B. A. Millsap, and M. S. Martell

1993   Burrowing Owl (*Speotyto cunicularia*). In *The Birds of North America*, No. 61, ed. A. Poole and F. Gill. The Birds of North America, Inc., Philadelphia.

Hayward, G. D., and P. H. Hayward

1993   Boreal Owl (*Aegolius funereus*). In *The Birds of North America*, No. 63, ed. A. Poole and F. Gill. The Birds of North America, Inc., Philadelphia.

Heintzelman, D. S.

1975   *Autumn Hawk Flights: The Migrations in Eastern North America.* Rutgers University Press, New Brunswick, NJ.

1979   *A Guide to Hawk Watching in North America.* Keystone Books (Pennsylvania State University Press), University Park.

1986   *The Migrations of Hawks.* Indiana University Press, Bloomington.

1992   *Guide to Owl Watching in North America.* Dover Publications, New York.

Houston, C. S., D. G. Smith, and C. Rohner

1998   Great Horned Owl (*Bubo virginianus*). In *The Birds of North America*, No. 372, ed. A. Poole and F. Gill. The Birds of North America, Inc., Philadelphia.

Johnsgard, P. A.

1990   *Hawks, Eagles, and Falcons of North America: Biology and Natural History.* Smithsonian Institution Press, Washington, DC.

Kerlinger, P.

1989   *Flight Strategies of Migrating Hawks.* University of Chicago Press, Chicago.

König, C., F. Weick, and J. Becking

1999   *Owls: A Guide to the Owls of the World.* Yale University Press, New Haven, CT.

Kunkle, D.

2002a   *Bake Oven Knob Autumn Hawk Count Manual.* Wildlife Information Center, Inc., Slatington, PA.

2002b   Updated Records for Bake Oven Knob Autumn Hawk Count, Lehigh County, Pennsylvania. *American Hawkwatcher*, 28: 23–24.

MacWhirter, R. B., and K. L. Bildstein

1996   Northern Harrier (*Circus cyaneus*). In *The Birds of North America*, No. 210, ed. A. Poole and F. Gill. The Birds of North America, Inc., Philadelphia.

Marks, J. S., D. L. Evans, and D. W. Holt

1994   Long-eared Owl (*Asio otus*). In *The Birds of North America*, No. 133, ed. A. Poole and F. Gill. The Birds of North America, Inc., Philadelphia.

Marti, C. D.

1992   Barn Owl (*Tyto alba*). In *The Birds of North America*, No. 1, ed. A. Poole and F. Gill. The Birds of North America, Inc., Philadelphia.

2002   *Enhancing Raptor Populations: A Techniques Manual.* The Peregrine Fund, Boise, ID.

May, J. B.

1935   *The Hawks of North America: Their Field Identification and Feeding Habits.* National Association of Audubon Societies, New York.

Mazur, K. M., and P. C. James

2000 Barred Owl (*Strix varia*). In *The Birds of North America,* No. 508, ed. A. Poole and F. Gill. The Birds of North America, Inc., Philadelphia.

Meyer, K. D.

1995 Swallow-tailed Kite (*Elanoides forficatus*). In *The Birds of North America,* No. 138, ed. A. Poole and F. Gill. The Birds of North America, Inc., Philadelphia.

Morrison, J. L.

1996 Crested Caracara (*Caracara plancus*). In *The Birds of North America,* No. 249, ed. A. Poole and F. Gill. The Birds of North America, Inc., Philadelphia.

Palmer, R. S. (Editor)

1988a *Handbook of North American Birds.* Volume 4. Yale University Press, New Haven, CT.

1988b *Handbook of North American Birds.* Volume 5. Yale University Press, New Haven, CT.

Parker, J. W.

1999 Mississippi Kite (*Ictinia mississippiensis*). In *The Birds of North America,* No. 402, ed. A. Poole and F. Gill. The Birds of North America, Inc., Philadelphia.

Parmelee, D. F.

1992 Snowy Owl (*Nyctea scandiaca*). In *The Birds of North America,* No. 10, ed. A. Poole and F. Gill. The Birds of North America, Inc., Philadelphia.

Patuxent Wildlife Research Center

2002 AOU 2890–3880 Longevity Records. Website: www.pwrc.usgs.gov/BBL/homepage/long2890.htm.

Peterson, R. T., and V. M. Peterson

2002 *A Field Guide to the Birds of Eastern and Central North America.* Fifth Edition. Houghton Mifflin, Boston.

Preston, C. R., and R. D. Beane

1993 Red-tailed Hawk (*Buteo jamaicensis*). In *The Birds of North America,* No. 52, ed. A. Poole and F. Gill. The Birds of North America, Inc., Philadelphia.

Rosenfield, R. N., and J. Bielefeldt

1993 Cooper's Hawk (*Accipiter cooperii*). In *The Birds of North America,* No. 75, ed. A. Poole and F. Gill. The Birds of North America, Inc., Philadelphia.

Smallwood, J. A., and D. M. Bird

2002 American Kestrel (*Falco sparverius*). In *The Birds of North America,* No. 602, ed. A. Poole and F. Gill. The Birds of North America, Inc., Philadelphia.

Smith, D. G., and D. H. Ellis

1989 Snowy Owl. In *Proceedings of the Northeast Raptor Management Symposium and Workshop.* Scientific and Technical Series No. 13. Institute for Wildlife Research. National Wildlife Federation, Washington, DC.

Sodhi, N. S., et al.

1993 Merlin (*Falco columbarius*). In *The Birds of North America,* No. 44, ed. A. Poole and F. Gill. The Birds of North America, Inc., Philadelphia.

Soucy, L.

2000 *New Jersey's Owls.* The Raptor Trust, Millington, NJ.

Sprunt, A., Jr.

1955 *North American Birds of Prey.* Harper and Brothers, New York.

Sykes, P. W., Jr., J. A. Rodgers, Jr., and R. E. Bennets

1995 Snail Kite (*Rostrhamus sociabilis*). In *The Birds of North America,* No. 171, ed. A. Poole and F. Gill. The Birds of North America, Inc., Philadelphia.

Zalles, J. I., and K. L. Bildstein

2000 *Raptor Watch: A Global Directory of Raptor Migration Sites.* BirdLife International, Cambridge, UK, and Hawk Mountain Sanctuary, Kempton, PA.

1 – RAPTOR ECOLOGY

Craighead, J. J., and F. C. Craighead, Jr.

1956 *Hawks, Owls, and Wildlife.* Stackpole Books, Harrisburg, PA.

1966 Raptors. In *Birds in Our Lives,* 200–217. U.S. Department of the Interior, Washington, DC.

Errington, P. L., F. Hamerstrom, and F. N. Hamerstrom, Jr.

1940 *The Great Horned Owl and Its Prey in North-Central United States.* Research Bulletin 277. Agricultural Experiment Station, Iowa State College of Agriculture and Mechanic Arts, Ames.

Heintzelman, D. S.

1970 *The Hawks of New Jersey.* Bulletin 13. New Jersey State Museum, Trenton.

Voous, K. H.

1977   Three Lines of Thought for Consideration and Eventual Action. *Proc. World Conference on Birds of Prey*, 343–347.

Wallace, G. J.

1948   *The Barn Owl in Michigan: Its Distribution, Natural History and Food Habits.* Technical Bulletin 208. Agricultural Experiment Station, Michigan State College, East Lansing.

2 – HAWK MIGRATIONS

Alden, P., and B. Cassie

1999   *National Audubon Society Field Guide to the Mid-Atlantic States.* Alfred A. Knopf, New York.

Alden, P., R. Cech, and G. Nelson

1998   *National Audubon Society Field Guide to Florida.* Alfred A. Knopf, New York.

Allen, P. E., L. J. Goodrich, and K. L. Bildstein

1995   Hawk Mountain's Million-Bird Database. *Birding,* 27 (1): 24–32.

1996   Within- and Among-Year Effects of Cold Fronts on Migrating Raptors at Hawk Mountain, Pennsylvania, 1934–1991. *Auk,* 113 (2): 329–338.

Greer, G.

1994   Large Movement of Ospreys and Other Raptors Seen at Cumberland Island. *Oriole,* 59 (1): 11–12.

Hawk, S., et al.

2002   Ridge Adherence in Bald Eagles Migrating along the Kittatinny Ridge between Bake Oven Knob and Hawk Mountain Sanctuary, Pennsylvania, Autumn 1998–2001. *American Hawkwatcher,* 28: 11–17.

Heintzelman, D. S.

1982   Variations in Utilization of the Kittatinny Ridge in Eastern Pennsylvania in Autumn by Migrating Golden Eagles and Bald Eagles (1968–1981). *American Hawkwatcher,* 3: 1–4.

1990   The 1957–1989 Bake Oven Knob, Pa., Autumn Hawk Migration Field Study: A 30 Year Review and Summary. *American Hawkwatcher,* 17: 1–16.

1993   Spring Hawk Migration Counts at Bake Oven Knob, Lehigh County, Pa. *American Hawkwatcher,* 19: 7–8.

Hoopes, R. E.

2002   The 2002 Bake Oven Knob Migration Season. *American Hawkwatcher,* 28: 5–10.

Kerlinger, P.

1988   Migrating Raptors. *Bird Watcher's Digest,* 11 (2): 58–63.

Klauder, M.

1991   The Year of the Eagles/Militia Hill Hawk Watch Montgomery County. *Pennsylvania Birds,* 5 (4): 189.

McCarty, K. M., et al.

1999   Spring Migration at Hawk Mountain Sanctuary, 1969–1998. *Pennsylvania Birds,* 13 (1): 11–15.

Pittaway, R.

1999   Fall Hawkwatching. *OFO News,* 7 (3): 1–8.

Reese, J. G.

1973   Bald Eagle Migration along the Upper Mississippi River in Minnesota. *Loon,* 45: 22–23.

3 – OWL MIGRATIONS AND INVASIONS

Breckenridge, W. J.

1946   Another Snowy Owl Year. *Flicker,* 18: 10.

Brinker, D. F., et al.

1997   Autumn Migration of Northern Saw-whet Owls (*Aegolius acadicus*) in the Middle Atlantic and Northeastern United States: What Observations from 1995 Suggest. In *Biology and Conservation of Owls of the Northern Hemisphere,* ed. J. R. Duncan, D. H. Johnson, and T. H. Nicholls, 74–89. Second International Symposium, February 5–9, 1997, Winnipeg, Manitoba, Canada. USDA Forest Service General Technical Report NC–190. USDA, Forest Service, North Central Research Station, St. Paul, MN.

Duffy, K. E., and P. E. Matheny

1997   Northern Saw-whet Owls (*Aegolius acadicus*) Captured at Cape May Point, NJ, 1980–1994: Comparison of Two Capture Techniques. In *Biology and Conservation of Owls of the Northern Hemisphere,* ed. J. R. Duncan, D. H. Johnson, and T. H. Nicholls, 131–137. Second International Symposium, February 5–9, 1997, Winnipeg, Manitoba, Canada. USDA Forest Service General Technical Report NC–190. USDA, Forest Service, North Central Research Station, St. Paul, MN.

Eckert, K. R.

1978   Invasion of Great Gray and Boreal Owls, Winter 1977-78. *Loon,* 50: 63–68.

1982 An Invasion of Boreal Owls. *Loon,* 54: 176–177.

1984 A Record Invasion of Great Gray Owls. *Loon,* 56: 143–147.

1989 A Great Gray Owl Influx, Winter 1988–89. *Loon,* 61: 115–117.

1991 An Influx of Northern Raptors, Fall–Winter 1990–1991. *Loon,* 63: 163–167.

1992 A Record Invasion of Northern Owls/Fall-Winter 1991–1992. *Loon,* 64: 189–195.

1996 The 1995–96 Influx of Northern Owls. *Loon,* 68: 221–228.

Erdman, T. C., and D. F. Brinker

1997 Increasing Mist Net Captures of Migrant Northern Saw-whet Owls (*Aegolius acadicus*) with an Audiolure. In *Biology and Conservation of Owls of the Northern Hemisphere,* ed. J. R. Duncan, D. H. Johnson, and T. H. Nicholls, 533–544. Second International Symposium, February 5–9, 1997, Winnipeg, Manitoba, Canada. USDA Forest Service General Technical Report NC–190. USDA, Forest Service, North Central Research Station, St. Paul, MN.

Erdman, T. C., et al.

1997 Autumn Populations and Movements of Migrant Northern Saw-whet Owls (*Aegolius acadicus*) at Little Suamico, Wisconsin. In *Biology and Conservation of Owls of the Northern Hemisphere,* ed. J. R. Duncan, D. H. Johnson, and T. H. Nicholls, 167–172. Second International Symposium, February 5–9, 1997, Winnipeg, Manitoba, Canada. USDA Forest Service General Technical Report NC–190. USDA, Forest Service, North Central Research Station, St. Paul, MN.

Evans, D. L.

1975 Fall Owl Migration at Duluth, Minnesota. *Loon,* 47: 56–58.

1997 The Influence of Broadcast Tape-recorded Calls on Captures of Fall Migrant Northern Saw-whet Owls (*Aegolius acadicus*) and Long-eared Owls (*Asio otus*). In *Biology and Conservation of Owls of the Northern Hemisphere,* ed. J. R. Duncan, D. H. Johnson, and T. H. Nicholls, 173–174. Second International Symposium, February 5–9, 1997, Winnipeg, Manitoba, Canada. USDA Forest Service General Technical Report NC–190. USDA, Forest Service, North Central Research Station, St. Paul, MN.

Evans, D. L., and R. N. Rosenfield

1977 Fall Migration of Boreal Owls. *Loon,* 49: 165–167.

Francis, C. M., and M. S. W. Bradstreet

1997 Monitoring Boreal Forest Owls in Ontario Using Tape Playback Surveys with Volunteers. In *Biology and Conservation of Owls of the Northern Hemisphere,* ed. J. R. Duncan, D. H. Johnson, and T. H. Nicholls, 175–184. Second International Symposium, February 5–9, 1997, Winnipeg, Manitoba, Canada. USDA Forest Service General Technical Report NC–190. USDA, Forest Service, North Central Research Station, St. Paul, MN.

Green, J. C.

1963 Hawk-Owl Invasion, Winter 1962–63. *Flicker,* 35: 77–78.

1966 Influx of Northern Owls, Winter 1965–66. *Loon,* 38: 44–45.

1969 Northern Owl Invasion Winter, 1968–1969. *Loon,* 41: 36–39.

Gross, A. O.

1931 Snowy Owl Migration, 1930–31. *Auk,* 48: 501–511.

1947 Cyclic Invasions of the Snowy Owl and the Migration of 1945–46. *Auk,* 64: 584–601.

Holroyd, G. L., and J. G. Woods

1975 Migration of the Saw-whet Owl in Eastern North America. *Bird-Banding,* 46 (2): 101–105.

Lane, W. H.

1997 Continued Monitoring of Boreal and Other Northern Forest Owls in Northeast Minnesota, 1997 Annual Report. *Loon,* 69 (3): 145–150.

2001 The Status of Boreal Owls in Northeastern Minnesota/2000 Annual Report. *Loon,* 73: 43–48.

Lane, W. H., D. E. Andersen, and T. H. Nicholls

1997 Distribution, Abundance, and Habitat Use of Territorial Male Boreal Owls (*Aegolius funereus*) in Northeast Minnesota. In *Biology and Conservation of Owls of the Northern Hemisphere,* ed. J. R. Duncan, D. H. Johnson, and T. H. Nicholls, 246–247. Second International Symposium, February 5–9, 1997, Winnipeg, Manitoba, Canada. USDA Forest Service General Technical Report NC–190. USDA, Forest Service, North Central Research Station, St. Paul, MN.

Lane, W. H., D. E. Andersen, and T. H. Nicholls

1997 Habitat Use and Movements of Breeding Male Boreal Owls (*Aegolius funereus*) in Northeast Minnesota as Determined by Radio Telemetry. In *Biology and Conserva-*

tion of Owls of the Northern Hemisphere, ed. J. R. Duncan, D. H. Johnson, and T. H. Nicholls, 248–249. Second International Symposium, February 5–9, 1997, Winnipeg, Manitoba, Canada. USDA Forest Service General Technical Report NC–190. USDA, Forest Service, North Central Research Station, St. Paul, MN.

Millard, S.

1997   Minnesota Snowy Owl Notes from 1997. *Loon,* 69 (3): 153–155.

Nicholls, T. H.

1968   Minnesota's 1966–1967 Snowy Owl Invasion. *Loon,* 40: 90–92.

Pittaway, R.

1997   Owls and Snow: Why Northern Forest Owls Invade the South. *OFO News,* 15 (1): 8.

Schladweiler, J. L.

1994   Minnesota Snowy Owl Invasion, 1993–94. *Loon,* 66: 160–165.

Stewart, P. A.

1952   Dispersal, Breeding Behavior, and Longevity of Banded Barn Owls in North America. *Auk,* 69: 227–245.

Svingen, P.

1997   The 1996–97 Influx of Northern Owls into Minnesota. *Loon,* 69 (3): 114–124.

Svingen, P. H., K. V. Haws, and B. A. Lenning

2001   The 2000–2001 Influx of Northern Owls/Record High Numbers of Northern Hawk and Great Gray Owls in Minnesota. *Loon,* 73: 135–143.

Swengel, A. B., and S. R. Swengel

1997   Auditory Surveys for Northern Saw-whet Owls (*Aegolius acadicus*) in Southern Wisconsin 1986–1996. In *Biology and Conservation of Owls of the Northern Hemisphere,* ed. J. R. Duncan, D. H. Johnson, and T. H. Nicholls, 411–420. Second International Symposium, February 5–9, 1997, Winnipeg, Manitoba, Canada. USDA Forest Service General Technical Report NC–190. USDA, Forest Service, North Central Research Station, St. Paul, MN.

Wallace, G. J.

1948   *The Barn Owl in Michigan: Its Distribution, Natural History and Food Habits.* Technical Bulletin 208. Agricultural Experiment Station, Michigan State College, East Lansing.

Wilson, S.

1996   Irruption of Boreal Owls, Winter 1995–1996. *Loon,* 68: 228–231.

1997   Irruption of Boreal Owls, Winter 1996–97. *Loon,* 69 (3): 125–129.

2001   Boreal Owl and Northern Saw-whet Owl Irruptions, Winter 2000–2001. *Loon,* 73: 143–151.

4 – RAPTOR CONSERVATION

Allen, P. E., L. J. Goodrich, and K. L. Bildstein

1992   Million-Bird Database. *Birding.* February, 25–32.

Anderson, B.

1976   Trapping Raptors at Game Farms in Minnesota and Transporting Them Away. *Hawk Chalk,* 15 (3): 40–42.

Anonymous

n. d.   The Raptor Trust. The Raptor Trust, Millington, NJ.

1988   Officials Probe Va. Game Preserve for Possible Hunting Violations. *Washington Post,* March 29, 1988.

1989   The Bounty Law. *Pennsylvania Birds,* 3 (1): 13. Reprinted from *The Cardinal* for 1931.

1993–   *The Kittatinny Raptor Corridor Educational Handbook.* Wildlife Information Center, Inc., Allentown [now Slatington], PA.

1997   Nestboxes for American Kestrels. Hawk Mountain Sanctuary Assn., Kempton, PA.

1998   Introduction. *Talon Tales,* 1 (1): 1.

1999a   1999 Projects. *Talon Tales,* 2 (1): 17.

1999b   Project Track-'em. *Talon Tales,* 2 (3): 15.

2000a   CPF Education Program. *Talon Tales,* 3 (1): 9.

2000b   CPF in Quebec. *Talon Tales,* 3 (3): 9.

2002a   Kittatinny Ridge Conservation Project. *Audubon Pennsylvania,* Spring 2002, 3, 7.

2002b   Acopian Center for Conservation Learning. *Hawk Mountain News,* 97: 10–15.

2002c   Friends of Animals Establishes National Registry and Network of Private Raptor Refuges. *ActionLine,* Fall 2002, 24–26.

2002d   CPF Education Team—The Birds. *Talon Tales,* 5 (1): 2.

Ascani, T. L.

1989   Pennsylvania Wildlife and Its Use: A 1988 Public Opinion Survey. *Wildlife Conservation Report,* No. 9. Wildlife Information Center, Inc., Allentown [now Slatington], PA.

Baker, D. P.

1988   Baronet, Gamekeepers Face a Virginia Jury in Hawk Killing Case. *Washington Post,* May 26, 1988.

1988a   Death Threat Described at Hawk Trial. *Washington Post,* May 27, 1988.

1988b   Gamekeeper Admits Killing Hawks. *Washington Post,* June 1, 1988.

1988c   "I've Not Killed A Single Thing" in Va. *Washington Post,* June 2, 1988.

1988d   Gamekeepers Guilty in Hawk Killing Case. *Washington Post,* June 3, 1988.

Bijleveld, M.

1974   *Birds of Prey in Europe.* Macmillan, London.

Bildstein, K. L.

1998   Long-Term Counts of Migrating Raptors: A Role for Volunteers in Wildlife Research. *J. Wildlife Management,* 62 (2): 435–445.

2001   Raptors as Vermin: A History of Human Attitudes towards Pennsylvania's Birds of Prey. *Endangered Species UPDATE,* 18 (4): 124–127.

Bildstein, K. L., J. Brett, L. Goodrich, and C. Viverette

1993   Shooting Galleries. *American Birds,* 47 (1): 38–43.

Blus, L. J.

1993   Effects of Pesticides on Owls in North America. *J. Raptor Research,* 30 (4): 198–206.

Bortolotti, G. R.

1984   Trap and Poison Mortality of Golden and Bald Eagles. *J. Wildlife Management,* 48 (4): 1173–1179.

Broun, M.

1948   *Hawks Aloft: The Story of Hawk Mountain.* Dodd, Mead, New York.

1956   Pennsylvania's Bloody Ridges. *Nature Magazine,* June–July.

Cade, T., H. Tordoff, and J. Barclay

1999   Re-introduction of Peregrines in the Eastern United States: An Evaluation. *Re-Introduction News,* 19: 19–21.

Caudell, J. N., and K. A. Riddleberger, Jr.

n. d.   *Best Management Practices for Captive Raptors in Georgia: A Technical Guide for the Use of Raptors in Environmental Education Programs.* Georgia Department of Natural Resources, Wildlife Resources Division, Social Circle, GA.

2001   Management of Nonreleasable Raptors for Conservation Education Programs. *J. Raptor Research,* 35 (1): 49–57.

Clark, B.

1988   Pole Trap. *ActionLine,* June–August, 11.

Clark, K.

2000   The Peregrine Falcon in New Jersey Report for 2001. New Jersey Division of Fish and Wildlife, Trenton.

Clark, K. E., L. J. Niles, and W. Stansley

1998   Environmental Contaminants Associated with Reproductive Failure in Bald Eagle (*Haliaeetus leucocephalus*) Eggs in New Jersey. *Bulletin Environmental Contamination and Toxicology,* 61: 247–254.

Clark, K. E., W. Stansley, and L. J. Niles

2001   Changes in Contaminant Levels in New Jersey Osprey Eggs and Prey, 1989 to 1998. *Archives Environmental Contamination and Toxicology,* 40: 277–284.

Connor, J.

1983   The Hawkman of Cape May Point. *Bird Watcher's Digest,* 6 (2): 68–74.

Corser, J. D., M. Amaral, C. J. Martin, and C. C. Rimmer

1999   Recovery of a Cliff-nesting Peregrine Falcon, *Falco peregrinus,* Population in Northern New York and New England, 1984–1996. *Canadian Field-Naturalist,* 113: 472–480.

Davidow, B.

2001   Falcons of the Florida Keys. *Living Bird,* 20 (4): 32–38.

Dickinson, D., and S. Flaherty

2002   Minnesota Men, Pheasant Raising Group Charged with Killing Protected Owls and Hawks. U.S. Fish and Wildlife Service News Release EA 02–34, May 22, 2002.

Driscoll, S.

2000   Is Raptor Rehabilitation a Waste of Time? *Living Bird,* 19 (3): 32–38.

Dunk, J. R.

1991   A Selective Pole Trap for Raptors. *Wildlife Society Bulletin,* 19: 208–210.

Elliott, J. E., and P. A. Martin

1994   Chlorinated Hydrocarbons and Shell Thinning in Eggs of (*Accipiter*) Hawks in Ontario, 1986–1989. *Environmental Pollution,* 86: 189–200.

Elliott, J. E., and L. Shutt

1993   Monitoring Organochlorines in Blood of Sharp-shinned Hawks (*Accipiter striatus*) Migrating through the Great Lakes.

Environmental Toxicology and Chemistry, 12: 241–250.

Fisher, A. K.

1893   *The Hawks and Owls of the United States in Their Relation to Agriculture.* Bulletin 3. Division of Ornithology and Mammalogy, U.S. Department of Agriculture, Washington, DC.

Gallagher, T.

1999   Mission Accomplished. *Living Bird,* 18 (3): 8–16.

Gleason, K. M.

2002   Protecting Raptors from Electrocution. *Birdscapes,* Spring-Summer, 36.

Heintzelman, D. S.

1970   *The Hawks of New Jersey.* Bulletin 13. New Jersey State Museum, Trenton.

1977   A National Inventory of Hawk Migration Lookouts. *Birding,* 9 (2): 57–58.

1985   Remarks for the First National Birds of Prey Conservation Week, 7 October 1984. *Bake Oven Knob Newsletter,* 4: 1–2.

1986   Pennsylvania Wildlife and Its Use: A 1986 Public Opinion Survey. *Wildlife Conservation Report,* No. 1. Wildlife Information Center, Inc., Allentown [now Slatington], PA.

1988   Pole Traps and Raptors: A Protection Crisis. *Wildlife Conservation Report,* 2: 1–10. Wildlife Information Center, Inc., Allentown [now Slatington], PA

1989a Management and Protection of Hawk Watching Lookouts. *Educational Hawkwatcher,* 2: 1–4.

1989b Migrant Raptor Corridor Impacts from Increasing Land Development in the Kittatinny Birds of Prey Migration Area, Pennsylvania. *Wildlife Conservation Report,* 7: 1–4.

1990   The 1957–1989 Bake Oven Knob, Pa., Autumn Hawk Migration Field Study: A 30 Year Review and Summary. *American Hawkwatcher,* 17: 1–16.

1992a Monitoring the Vital Signs of a Mountain: The Kittatinny Raptor Corridor Project. *Wildlife Activist,* 15: 6–8.

1992b The Role of Perches in Limiting American Kestrel Uses on Hilltop Fields within the Kittatinny Raptor Migration Corridor near Bake Oven Knob, Lehigh County, PA. *American Hawkwatcher,* 18: 2–4.

1992c Pioneering Raptor Programs at the Bake Oven Knob Hawk Watch and the Wildlife Information Center, Inc. *American Hawkwatcher,* 18: 8–13.

1993a Kittatinny Raptor Corridor Project. *Wild Earth,* 3 (3): 45–47.

1993b Variations in Counts and Age Ratios of Migrating Sharp-shinned Hawks in Autumn at Bake Oven Knob, Lehigh County, Pa. *American Hawkwatcher,* 19: 4–6.

1994a Autumn Sharp-shinned Hawk Migration Counts and Age Ratio Trends at Bake Oven Knob, Lehigh County, Pa. *American Hawkwatcher,* 20: 4–5.

1994b Further Observations or Raptor Use and Habitat Alteration of Hawk Hill, Heidelberg Township, Lehigh County, Pa. *American Hawkwatcher,* 20: 5.

1999   Proposal for Hawk and Owl Hunting Season Rejected. *Northwestern Press,* Allentown, PA, March 1–7, 1999.

2001   Establishing a North American Network of Private Raptor Sanctuaries. *International Hawkwatcher,* 3: 17–18.

2002   The September 2001 Terrorist Attacks on America: Their Impacts on Raptor Biologists and Research Activities. *International Hawkwatcher,* 5: 15–28.

Hendrickson, R.

1980   Osprey in the Bleachers. *Bird Watcher's Digest,* 2 (5): 60–64.

Henny, C. J.

1998   Toxic Chemicals and Birds of Prey in the mid-1990s: A Personal Perspective. In *Holarctic Birds of Prey,* ed. R. D. Chancellor, G.-U. Meyburg, and J. J. Ferrero. ADENEX-World Working Group on Birds of Prey and Owls, Merida, Spain.

Henny, C. J., P. Mineau, J. E. Elliott, and B. Woodbridge

1999   Raptor Poisoning and Current Insecticide Use: What Do Isolated Kill Reports Mean to Populations? In *Proceedings of the 22nd International Ornithological Congress,* Durban, South Africa. BirdLife South Africa, Johannesburg.

Henny, C. J., W. S. Seegar, and T. L. Maechtle

1996   DDE Decreases in Plasma of Spring Migrant Peregrine Falcons, 1978–96. *J. Wildlife Management,* 60 (2): 342–349.

Hoopes, R. E.

2002   The Lehigh Gap Restoration Project: A Dream Come True. *Wildlife Activist,* 45: 4–7.

Hubley, J.

1999   PGC Commissioner Vernon Shaffer Gets Wings Clipped on Proposal to Shoot Hawks and Owls. *Sunday News Lancaster,* Lancaster, PA, February 28.

Hurt, H.

1988 Slaughter at Albemarle Farms. *Reader's Digest*. November, 82–88.

Kirkham, I.

1989 Kortright Park Refuses to Try Humane Traps for Birds of Prey. *Toronto Star*, January 14, 1989.

Kunkle, D. R.

1999 Letters to the Editor: Reader Questions PA. Game Commission Proposal. *Northwestern Press*, Allentown, PA, March 1–7, 1999.

Manieri, R.

2002 Newtown Square Woman Charged with Killing Federally Protected Birds. August 27, 2002, News Release, United States Attorney's Office, Eastern District, Pennsylvania.

Martell, M., et al.

1991 Survival and Movements of Released Rehabilitated Bald Eagles. *J. Raptor Research*, 25 (3): 72–76.

McInnes, C.

1988a Bird Sanctuary Using Outlawed Trapping Method. *The Globe and Mail*, December 13, 1988, A1.

1988b Ontario Waterfowl Park Alters Illegal Pole Traps. *The Globe and Mail*, December 13, 1988.

1988c No Charges to Be Laid in Park's Use of Traps. *The Globe and Mail*, December 16, 1988, A19.

Meng, H.

1971 The Swedish Goshawk Trap. *J. Wildlife Management*, 35 (4): 832–835.

Millar, J. G.

2002 The Protection of Eagles and the Bald and Golden Eagle Protection Act. *J. Raptor Research*, 36 (1 Suppl.): 29–31.

Miller, G. O.

1999 Just Passing Through. *Living Bird*, 18 (4): 16–20. [Autumn raptor migration at Kiptopeke State Park, VA.]

Millsap, B. A.

2002 Survival of Florida Burrowing Owls along an Urban-Development Gradient. *J. Raptor Research*, 36 (1): 3–10.

Mineau, P., et al.

1999 Poisoning of Raptors with Organophosphorus and Carbamate Pesticides with Emphasis on Canada, U.S., and U.K. *J. Raptor Research*, 33 (1): 1–37.

Moulton, K.

2000 Capturing Raptor Data: From Sky to Database. *Hawk Flights*, August, 1–4.

Moulton, K., and W. Weber

1999 A New Online Era for Hawkwatch Count Data. *HMANA Hawk Migration Studies*, 27 (2): 24–29.

Nash, M.

1999 Director's Message. *Talon Tales*, 2 (1): 2.

Odom, R. R.

1980 Current Status and Reintroduction of the Bald Eagle in Georgia. *Oriole*, 45 (1): 1–14.

The Peregrine Fund

2001 The Peregrine Fund: World Center for Birds of Prey. 2001 Annual Report. The Peregrine Fund, Boise, ID.

Perry, R.

1998 Bald Eagle Killer Fined, Sentenced. *Federal Wildlife Officer*, 10 (10): 5–6.

Peterson, R. T.

1985 Hawk Mountain Celebrates Its Fiftieth Anniversary. *Bird Watcher's Digest*, 7 (3): 83–92.

Pettit, B.

2000 Drafting a Seasonal Hawk Site Field Protocol Manual. *Hawk Flights*, August, 5–7.

Power, J.

1989 Predatory Owls Land Park Official in Trouble. *The Ontario Star*, January 4, 1989, C6.

Roberts, P. M.

2001 The Origins and Early Years of HMANA. *HMANA Hawk Migration Studies*, 26 (2): 16–20.

Soucy, L.

1981 Next Boxes for Raptors. *Bird Watcher's Digest*, 3 (4): 84–89.

1991 Hawk Shooting: The Problem That Hasn't Gone Away. *Bird Watcher's Digest*, 14 (1): 54–55.

Steidl, R. J., C. R. Griffin, L. J. Niles, and K. E. Clark

1991 Reproductive Success and Eggshell Thinning of a Reestablished Peregrine Falcon Population. *J. Wildlife Management*, 55 (2): 294–299.

Steidl, R. J., C. R. Griffin, and L. J. Niles

1991a Differential Reproductive Success of Ospreys in New Jersey. *J. Wildlife Management*, 55 (2): 266–272.

1991b Contaminant Levels of Osprey Eggs and Prey Reflect Regional Differences in Reproductive Success. *J. Wildlife Management*, 55 (4): 601–608.

Strebig, M.

1988 Cruel Practice of Pole-Trapping Must Be Clearly Prohibited. *Seasons*, Spring, 46.

Sullivan, B. L.

1997 Spring Raptor Migration at Derby Hill, New York. *Birding*, 29 (2): 116–126.

Welch, B.

1993 Hawk Rehabilitation. *Bird Watcher's Digest*, 15 (5): 70–71.

Wildlife Information Center, Inc.

1992 National Raptor Flyway Designation Recommended for the Kittatinny Ridge. *Wildlife Activist*, 15: 9–10.

Wood, P. B., C. Viverette, and L. Goodrich

1996 Environmental Contaminant Levels in Sharp-shinned Hawks from the Eastern United States. *J. Raptor Research*, 30 (3): 136–144.

5 – CITIZEN SCIENTISTS

Anonymous

2000 Red-tailed Hawk Migration Study Continues. *American Hawkwatcher*, 26: 20.

2001 Red-tailed Hawk Migration Study Continues. *American Hawkwatcher*, 27: 10.

2002 Red-tailed Hawk Migration Study in Third Year. *American Hawkwatcher*, 28: 10.

Bildstein, K. L.

1998 Long-Term Counts of Migrating Raptors: A Role for Volunteers in Wildlife Research. *J. Wildlife Management*, 62 (2): 435–445.

1999 Racing with the Sun. *Birdscope*, 13 (1): 1–5.

Broley, C. L.

1947 Migration and Nesting of Florida Bald Eagles. *Wilson Bulletin*, 59: 3–20.

Broley, M. J.

1952 *Eagle Man: Charles L. Broley's Field Adventures with American Eagles.* Pellegrini and Cudahy, Publishers, New York.

Byers, D.

1990 Owls of the Pennsylvania CBCs. *Pennsylvania Birds*, 4 (4): 130–133.

Carson, R.

1962 *Silent Spring.* Houghton Mifflin, Boston.

Dean, B.

1989 Short-eared Owls, Mercer County. *Pennsylvania Birds*, 3 (2): 53.

Grove, G.

2000 Winter Raptor Survey in Pennsylvania. *HMANA Migration Studies—Fall 2000*, 27 (1): 17–19.

2001 The 2001 Winter Raptor Survey in Pennsylvania. *Pennsylvania Birds*, 15 (1): 3–5.

Haines, R. L.

1979 Joseph A. Jacobs, 1917–1977. *Cassinia*, 57: 40–41.

Hawk Migration Association of North America

n. d. HawkCount/HMANA Raptors Online. Handout literature at August 2002 Roundtable Meeting at Hawk Mountain Sanctuary, PA.

Heintzelman, D. S.

1966 Distribution and Population Density of Barn Owls in Lehigh and Northampton Counties, Pennsylvania. *Cassinia*, 49: 2–20.

1976 *Endangered or Threatened Birds and Mammals of Lehigh County, Pennsylvania.* Conservation Report No. 1. Lehigh Valley Audubon Society, Emmaus, PA.

1979 *Hawks and Owls of North America: A Complete Guide to North American Birds of Prey.* Universe Books, New York.

Lind, J., and J. Hanowski

2000 Volunteer-based Roadside Raptor Survey Program in Northern Minnesota—A Pilot Study. NRRI/TR–2000/37. Minnesota Department of Natural Resources—Region II, Nongame Wildlife Program, Grand Rapids, MN.

Noss, R.

2001 Citizen Scientist or Amateur Naturalist? *Wild Earth*, 11 (3, 4): 15–17.

Pandolfi, F.

1999 Joining Forces. *Birdscope*, 13 (1): 1–3.

Peterson, R. T.

1988 Broley, The Eagle Man. *Bird Watcher's Digest*, 10 (4): 22, 24, 26–32.

Rohrbaugh, R., and R. Bonney

1999 Citizen Science. *Birdscope*, 13 (4): 1–3.

Stone, W. B., P. E. Nye, and J. C. Okoniewski

2001 Bald Eagles Killed by Trains in New York State. *J. Raptor Research*, 35 (1): 64–65.

Takats, D. L., et al.

2001 Owl Monitoring Protocol Available. *Wingspan*, 9 (2)/10 (1): 3.

6 – RECREATIONAL RAPTOR WATCHING

Anonymous

n. d.   Eagle Watch! in Sullivan County. The Eagle Institute, Barryville, NY.

1993–   *The Kittatinny Raptor Corridor Educational Handbook.* Wildlife Information Center, Inc., Allentown [now Slatington], PA.

Buckley, P. A.

1960   A Record Night. *Linnaean News-Letter,* 14 (1): 1–2.

Coady, G.

2002   Reminiscences of Some Memorable Ontario Owl Adventures. *Toronto Ornithological Club Newsletter,* 128: 2–4.

Dyer, J.

1982   Pennsylvania's Hawk Spots. *Bird Watcher's Digest,* 12 (1): 38–43.

Friederici, P.

1997   Bald Eagles. *Bird Watcher's Digest,* 20 (1): 60–65.

Goodrich, L.

1996   The Place Where Hawk Watching Was Born. *Natural History,* October, 48–49.

Heintzelman, D. S.

1992   Monitoring the Vital Signs of a Mountain: The Kittatinny Raptor Corridor Project. *Wildlife Activist,* 15: 6–8.

1993   Kittatinny Raptor Corridor Project. *Wild Earth,* 3 (3): 45–47.

2001   Maurice Broun: The Father of Hawk-watching. *Northwestern Press,* Allentown, PA, July 30.

2002   *All-Weather Hawk Watcher's Field Journal.* J. L. Darling Corporation, Tacoma, WA.

Ingram, T. N.

1965   *A Field Guide for Locating Bald Eagles at Cassville, Wisconsin.* Southwestern Wisconsin Audubon Club.

McClung, J. M.

1991   Finding Owls. *Bird Watcher's Digest,* 13 (3): 72–76.

Miller, R.

1995   Seeing Hawks in Minnesota. *Bird Watcher's Digest,* 64–66.

Ontario Field Ornithologists

2002   *Ontario Bird Checklist 2002.* Ontario Field Ornithologists, PO Box 455, Station R, Toronto, Ontario M4G 4E1, Canada.

Peterson, R. T.

1991   Ecotourism—The New Buzzword. *Bird Watcher's Digest,* 13 (6): 12–14, 16–18, 20–22.

Pittaway, R.

1998   Owling at Night. *OFO News,* 16 (2): 6–7.

Swicegood, D. R.

1990   A Gift of Eagles. *Bird Watcher's Digest,* 12 (2): 61–64.

Smith, D. G.

1993   Eastern Screech Owls. *Bird Watcher's Digest,* 16 (1): 32–39.

St. Clair, S.

1997   Springbrook Nature Center's Boreal Owl: An Unexpected Adventure. *Loon,* 69 (3): 111–113.

Tainter, F. R.

1990   Boreal Owl Search. *Bird Watcher's Digest,* 12 (3): 62–67.

Torre, J. de la

1991   Swallowtails. *Bird Watcher's Digest,* 13 (4): 61–63.

Turner, J. L.

1998   A River of Eagles. *Bird Watcher's Digest,* 21 (2): 75–81.

Ward, C.

1960   Hawk Flights at Jones Beach. *Linnaean News-Letter,* 14 (2): 1–2.

7 – OSPREYS AND NORTHERN HARRIERS

Bednarz, J. C., D. Klem, Jr., L. J. Goodrich, and S. E. Senner

1988   Migration Counts of Raptors at Hawk Mountain, Pennsylvania, as Indicators of Population Trends, 1934–1986. *Auk,* 107: 96–109.

Berger, D. D., and H. C. Mueller

1969   Ospreys in Northern Wisconsin. In *Peregrine Falcon Populations: Their Biology and Decline,* ed. J. J. Hickey, 340–341. University of Wisconsin Press, Madison.

Bowman, R., et al.

1989   Variation in Reproductive Success between Subpopulations of the Osprey (*Pandion haliaetus*) in South Florida. *Bulletin of Marine Science,* 44 (1): 245–250.

Chubbs, T. E., et al.

2000   First Confirmed Breeding Records and Other Incidental Sightings of Northern Harriers in Labrador. *J. Raptor Research,* 34 (1): 56–57.

Clark, K.

2001   The 2001 Osprey Project in New Jersey. New Jersey Division of Fish and Wildlife, Tuckahoe Field Station, Woodbine, NJ.

Clark, K., and C. D. Jenkins

1994   Status of Ospreys Nesting in New Jersey, 1984 through 1993. *Records of New Jersey Birds*, 19 (4): 74–77.

Dempsey, J. T.

1976   Minnesota's First Winter Osprey. *Loon*, 48: 73–74.

DeReamus, D.

1990   The Early Late Osprey Flight. *Pennsylvania Birds*, 4 (2): 50.

Dittmar, D., and B. Hartgroves

1989   Osprey Restoration. *Bird Watcher's Digest*, 11 (6): 88–93.

Dunstan, T. C.

1968   Breeding Success of Osprey in Minnesota from 1963 to 1968. *Loon*, 40: 109–112.

1973   The Biology of Ospreys in Minnesota. *Loon*, 45: 108–113.

Frey, E. S.

1940   Hawk Notes from Sterrett's Gap, Pennsylvania. *Auk*, 57: 247–250.

Greer, G.

1994   Large Movement of Ospreys and Other Raptors Seen at Cumberland Island. *Oriole*, 59 (1): 11–12.

Hamerstrom, F.

1986   *Harrier: Hawk of the Marshes*. Smithsonian Institution Press, Washington, DC.

Heintzelman, D. S.

1963   Marsh Hawk Attacks a Sparrow Hawk. *Linnaean News-Letter*, 17 (5): 2.

1983   Variations in Numbers of, and Influence of Intersecting Diversion-Lines Upon, Ospreys Migrating along the Kittatinny Ridge in Eastern Pennsylvania in Autumn. *American Hawkwatcher*, 6: 1–4.

2000   Extreme Migration Dates, and Maximum Daily Raptor Counts, during Autumn at Bake Oven Knob, Lehigh County, Pennsylvania USA. *International Hawkwatcher*, 1: 19–21.

Henny, C. J.

1987   Large Osprey Colony Discovered in Oregon in 1899. *Murrelet*, 69: 33–36.

Hoopes, R. E.

2002   The 2002 Bake Oven Knob Migration Season. *American Hawkwatcher*, 28: 5–10.

Ivanovs, M.

1972   Osprey in a Great Blue Heron Nest. *Loon*, 44: 91–92.

Johnson, D. H.

1982   Raptors of Minnesota—Nesting Distribution and Population Status. *Loon*, 54: 73–104.

Kitson, K.

1990   Osprey Surprise. *Pennsylvania Birds*, 4 (4): 144.

Kunkle, D.

2002   A Record-setting Osprey Flight at Bake Oven Knob. *American Hawkwatcher*, 28: 20.

Kuyava, G. C.

1959   Spring Diet of a Marsh Hawk. *Flicker*, 31: 99.

Liston, T. M.

1999   Eagles, Ospreys, and Anthropomorphic Blues. *Bird Watcher's Digest*, 21 (6): 44–49.

Longley, W. H.

1946   Marsh Hawk Captures Sick Yellow-legs. *Flicker*, 18: 107.

Marich, Jr., A. J.

1991   Osprey, *Pandion haliaetus*, Nesting in Southwestern Somerset County. *Pennsylvania Birds*, 5 (2): 62.

Martell, M.

1995   Osprey *Pandion haliaetus* Reintroduction in Minnesota, USA. *Vogelwelt*, 116: 205–206.

Martell, M. S., C. J. Henny, P. E. Nye, and M. J. Solensky

2001   Fall Migration Routes, Timing, and Wintering Sites of North American Ospreys as Determined by Satellite Telemetry. *Condor*, 103: 715–724.

Mathisen, J. E.

1967   Bald Eagle—Osprey Status Report, 1967 Chippewa National Forest, Minnesota. *Loon*, 39: 121–122.

1976   Osprey Feeds at Night. *Loon*, 48: 188.

Link, M.

1974   Interaction between Greater Prairie Chickens and Marsh Hawk. *Loon*, 46: 42.

Odom, R. R., and J. W. Guthrie

1980   Status of the Osprey in Georgia. *Oriole*, 45 (2 and 3): 25–33.

Olson, C. V., and S. A. H. Osborn

2000   First North American Record of a Melanistic Female Northern Harrier. *J. Raptor Research*, 34 (1): 58–59.

Peterson, R. T.

1966   Roger Tory Peterson—Tribute to Maurice and Irma Broun. [Hawk Mountain] *News Letter to Members,* No. 38: 4–11.

1969   Population Trends of Ospreys in the Northeastern United States. In *Peregrine Falcon Populations: Their Biology and Decline,* ed. J. J. Hickey, 333–337. University of Wisconsin Press, Madison.

1988   The Osprey Story. *Bird Watcher's Digest,* 11 (1): 26, 28–41.

Poole, A. F.

1989   *Ospreys: A Natural and Unnatural History.* Cambridge University Press, Cambridge, UK.

Postupalsky, S.

1969   The Status of the Osprey in Michigan in 1965. In *Peregrine Falcon Populations: Their Biology and Decline,* ed. J. J. Hickey, 338–340. University of Wisconsin Press, Madison.

Riddleberger, K. A., Jr.

1986   An Early Nesting Record for the Osprey in Georgia. *Oriole,* 51 (2, 3): 44.

Rodriguez, F., et al.

2001   Osprey Migration through Cuba. In *Hawkwatching in the Americas,* ed. K. L. Bildstein and D. Klem, Jr. Hawk Migration Association of North America, North Wales, PA.

Seabolt, T.

1984   The Aggressive Responses of a Nesting Osprey in a Great Blue Heron Colony. *Loon,* 56: 214–215.

Simmons, R. E.

2000   *Harriers of the World: Their Behaviour and Ecology.* Oxford University Press, New York.

Steidl, R. J., C. R. Griffin, and L. J. Niles

1991a   Differential Reproductive Success of Ospreys in New Jersey. *J. Wildlife Management,* 55 (2): 266–272.

1991b   Contaminant Levels of Osprey Eggs and Prey Reflect Regional Differences in Reproductive Success. *J. Wildlife Management,* 55 (4): 601–608.

Stickel, W. H.

1969   Ospreys in the Chesapeake Bay Area. In *Peregrine Falcon Populations: Their Biology and Decline,* ed. J. J. Hickey, 337. University of Wisconsin Press, Madison.

Stone, W.

1937   *Bird Studies at Old Cape May.* Volume 1. Delaware Valley Ornithological Club, Academy of Natural Sciences of Philadelphia, Philadelphia.

Struthers, D. R.

1955   Great Blue Heron Robs Osprey of Fish. *Flicker,* 27: 129.

Tester, J. R.

1959   Marsh Hawk—Ring-necked Pheasant Encounter. *Flicker,* 31: 104.

8 – KITES

Bolen, E. G., and D. Flores

1993   *The Mississippi Kite: Portrait of a Southern Hawk.* University of Texas Press, Austin.

Brightbill, C.

1991   Mississippi Kite *Ictinia mississippiensis* Franklin/Fulton Counties. *Pennsylvania Birds,* 5 (1): 21–22.

Chandler, C. R., S. A. Lindemann, A. A. Kinsey, and R. Shuford

1997   Late-Summer Congregation of Swallow-tailed Kites in Southeast Georgia. *Oriole,* 62 (3, 4): 29–34.

Cohrs, D.

1983   Swallow-tailed Kites along the Little Satilla. *Oriole,* 48 (4): 64.

Coulson, J. O.

2002   Mississippi Kites Use Swallow-tailed Kite Nests. *J. Raptor Research,* 36 (2): 155–156.

Eckert, K. R.

1994   Proceedings of the Minnesota Ornithological Records Committee. *Loon,* 66: 43–44.

Eisenmann, E.

1971   Range Expansion and Population Increase in North and Middle America of the White-tailed Kite (*Elanus leucurus*). *American Birds,* 25: 529–536.

Heller, J.

1995   Kites and More. *Pennsylvania Birds,* 9 (2): 65.

Hertzel, A.

1995   Adult Mississippi Kite in Roseau County. *Loon,* 67: 119.

Kessen, A. E., and A. X. Hertzel

1999   The Historical Record of the Swallow-tailed Kite in Minnesota. *Loon,* 71: 178–181.

Krienke, C.

1999   A Swallow-tailed Kite in Southern Min-
        nesota. *Loon,* 71: 176–177.

Janssen, R. B.

2000   Minnesota's First White-tailed Kite. *Loon,*
        72: 193–194.

Johnson, D. H.

1982   Raptors of Minnesota—Nesting Distribu-
        tion and Population Status. *Loon,* 54:
        73–104.

McMillian, M. A., and B. Pranty

1997   Recent Nesting of the White-tailed Kite in
        Central Florida. *Florida Field Naturalist,* 25
        (4): 143–145.

Meyer, K. D.

1990   Kites. In *Proceedings Southeast Raptor Man-
        agement Symposium and Workshop,* ed. B. G.
        Pendleton, 38–49. Institute for Wildlife
        Research, National Wildlife Federation,
        Washington, DC.

Nicoletti, F. J.

1996   Three Additional Mississippi Kite Records
        from Hawk Ridge. *Loon,* 68: 215–216.

Parrish, J. W., Jr.

1999   Early Sightings of Mississippi Kites in
        South Georgia. *Oriole,* 64 (3, 4): 53.

Pranty, B., and M. A. McMillian

1997   Status of the White-tailed Kite in Northern
        and Central Florida. *Florida Field Natural-
        ist,* 25 (4): 117–127.

Stevens, A. J., et al.

2002   Temperature Effects on Florida Applesnail
        Activity: Implications for Snail Kite For-
        aging Success and Distribution. *Wildlife
        Society Bulletin,* 30 (1): 75–81.

Stieglitz, W. O., and R. L. Thompson

1967   *Status and Life History of the Everglade Kite
        in the Untied States.* Special Scientific Re-
        port—Wildlife No. 109: 1–21.

Stull, J., and J. Stull

1991   Third Western Pennsylvania Record of
        Mississippi Kite *Ictinia mississippiensis* Erie
        County. *Pennsylvania Birds,* 5 (1): 21.

Sykes, Jr., P. W.

1994   A Closer Look: Snail Kite. *Birding,* 26 (2):
        118–122.

9 – EAGLES

Anonymous

2002   Tough Job: Bald Eagle Recovery Contin-
        ues. *Conserve Wildlife,* Summer, 1.

Bardon, K.

1996   Yellow-billed Loon Killed by Adult Bald
        Eagle. *Loon,* 68: 61.

Barrett, L. L.

1950   Bald Eagle "Stoops" on Old Squaw Duck.
        Flicker, 22: 19–20.

Bechard, M. J., and M. J. McGrady

2002   Preface: Status and Conservation of
        Golden Eagles. *J. Raptor Research,* 36 (1
        Suppl.): 2.

Bednarz, J.

2000   RRF Conservation Activities: Proposed
        Delisting of the Bald Eagle. *Wingspan,* 9
        (1): 6–8.

Bednarz, J. C., D. Klem, Jr., L. J. Goodrich,
and S. E. Senner

1990   Migration Counts of Raptors at Hawk
        Mountain, Pennsylvania, as Indicators of
        Population Trends, 1934–1986. *Auk,* 107:
        96–109.

Bell, M.

2001   Golden Eagle in Bibb County. *Oriole,* 64 (1,
        2): 6–7.

Beohm, M. F.

1999   Golden Eagle Sightings in Upson and
        Monroe Counties. *Oriole,* 64 (1, 2): 7–8.

Brauning, D. W., and B. Peebles

1992   Recent History and Current Status of
        Nesting Bald Eagles, *Haliaeetus leuco-
        cephalus,* in Pennsylvania. *Pennsylvania
        Birds,* 6 (1): 2–5.

Broker, S. P.

2002   The 2001–2002 Connecticut Christmas
        Bird Count. *Connecticut Warbler,* 22 (2):
        43–55.

Buehler, D. A., et al.

1991   Survival Rates and Population Dynamics
        of Bald Eagles on Chesapeake Bay. *J.
        Wildlife Management,* 55 (4): 608–613.

Buehler, D. A., T. J. Mersmann, J. D. Fraser,
and J. K. D. Seegar

1991   Nonbreeding Bald Eagle Communal and
        Solitary Roosting Behavior and Roost
        Habitat on the Northern Chesapeake Bay.
        J. Wildlife Management, 55 (2): 273–281.

Burford, L. S.

1998   Kentucky Midwinter Eagle Survey. *Ken-
        tucky Warbler,* 74 (1): 45–47.

Clark, K. E., L. J. Niles, and W. Stansley

1998   Environmental Contaminants Associated
        with Reproductive Failure in Bald Eagle
        (*Haliaeetus leucocephalus*) Eggs in New Jer-

sey. *Bulletin Environmental Contamination and Toxicology,* 61: 247–254.

Dunstan, T. C.

1969 First Recovery of Bald Eagle Banded in Minnesota. *Loon,* 41: 92.

1971 An Ecosystem Approach to the Study of Minnesota's Bald Eagles. *Loon,* 43: 109–113.

1973 Bald Eagle from Minnesota Recovered in Texas. *Loon,* 45: 132.

Faanes, C. A.

1976 Winter Ecology of Bald Eagles in Southern Minnesota. *Loon,* 48: 61–69.

Frenzel, L. D., and J. Kussman

1973 Bald Eagle–Hawk Interaction. *Loon,* 45: 101.

Fullerton, G. J.

1969a Bald Eagle Captures Duck. *Loon,* 41: 27.

1969b Bald Eagle Captures a Mallard. *Loon,* 41: 57–58.

Garcelon, D. K., et al.

1995 Cooperative Nesting by a Trio of Bald Eagles. *J. Raptor Research,* 29 (3): 210–213.

Gerrard, J. M., and G. R. Bortolotti

1989 *The Bald Eagle.* Smithsonian Institution Press, Washington, DC.

Hale, P. E.

1979 Golden Eagle Sighting in Towns County. *Oriole,* 44 (1): 14.

Hawk, S., et al.

2002 Ridge Adherence in Bald Eagles Migrating along the Kittatinny Ridge between Bake Oven Knob and Hawk Mountain Sanctuary, Pennsylvania, Autumn 1998–2001. *American Hawkwatcher,* 28: 11–17.

Heintzelman, D. S.

1982 Variations in Utilization of the Kittatinny Ridge in Eastern Pennsylvania in Autumn by Migrating Golden Eagles and Bald Eagles (1968–1981). *American Hawkwatcher,* 3: 1–4.

1990 The 1957–1989 Bake Oven Knob, Pa., Autumn Hawk Migration Field Study: A 30 Year Review and Summary. *American Hawkwatcher,* 17: 1–16.

1992 Long Term Monitoring of Migrant Bald Eagle and Golden Eagle Age Ratios and Their Use as Environmental Quality Indicators. *American Hawkwatcher,* 18: 14–18.

1996 A 36-Year Examination of Migrant Bald Eagle and Golden Eagle Age Ratios at Bake Oven Knob, Lehigh County, Pa. *American Hawkwatcher,* 22: 5–6.

2000 Extreme Migration Dates, and Maximum Daily Raptor Counts, during Autumn at Bake Oven Knob, Lehigh County, Pennsylvania, USA. *International Hawkwatcher,* 1: 19–21.

Hines, P., and H. Lipke

1991 Ground-Nesting Bald Eagles in Northwestern Minnesota. *Loon,* 63: 155–157.

Hopkins, D. A.

1990 Non-Breeding Bald Eagles in Northwest Connecticut during Late Spring and Summer. *Connecticut Warbler,* 10 (1): 10–14.

1995 Bald Eagles Successfully Nest in Connecticut in 1992. *Connecticut Warbler,* 12 (4): 121–124.

2001 How Are the Eagles Doing? *Connecticut Warbler,* 21 (1): 23–25.

Hopkins, D. A., G. S. Mersereau, and A. C. Nordell

1999 A Third Adult Again Assists at a Connecticut Bald Eagle Nest. *Connecticut Warbler,* 19 (1): 26–27.

Hopkins, D. A., G. S. Mersereau, and M. J. O'Leary

1993 A Third Adult Bald Eagle Takes an Active Part in Raising Young Eagles in Connecticut. *Connecticut Warbler,* 13 (4): 114–116.

2002 Bald Eagles Build a "Frustration" Nest at Barkhamsted Reservoir. *Connecticut Warbler,* 22 (1): 1–3.

Janssen, R. B.

1972 An Eagle Visits a Feeder. *Loon,* 44: 21–22.

Johnson, D. H.

1982 Raptors of Minnesota—Nesting Distribution and Population Status. *Loon,* 54: 73–104.

Johnson, M. J.

1961 Observation of an attack on a Snow Goose. *Flicker,* 33: 90.

1995 Bald Eagle Predation on Snowy Owl. *Loon,* 67: 107.

Johnson, O. L.

1992 Atypical Food Capture by Bald Eagle. *Loon,* 64: 166.

Keran, D.

1986 Bald Eagle Nest on a Power Pole. *Loon,* 58: 142.

Kochert, M. N., and K. Steenhof

2002 Golden Eagles in the U.S. and Canada: Status, Trends, and Conservation Challenges. *J. Raptor Research,* 36 (1 Suppl.): 32–40.

Kosack, J., and J. Freaser

2002 Pennsylvania's Bald Eagle Population Continues to Grow. News Release 52–02. Pennsylvania Game Commission, Harrisburg.

Lein, C.

1994 Is the Bald Eagle Still Endangered? *Bird Watcher's Digest,* 16 (3): 37–43.

Liston, T. M.

1996 Bald Eagle Attacks Osprey Nestlings. *Loon,* 68: 238–239.

MacKay, B. K.

1989 The Legacy of Jack Miner Means "Sanctuary" Is Selective. *Toronto Star,* January 15, 1989.

Mathisen, J. E.

1967 Bald Eagle—Osprey Status Report, 1967 Chippewa National Forest, Minnesota. *Loon,* 39: 121–122.

1970 A Note on Eagle Nest Adornment. *Loon,* 42: 37.

McCarty, K., and K. L. Bildstein

2000 Autumn Raptor Migration Summary 2000. *Pennsylvania Birds,* 14 (4): 210–216.

2001 Spring Raptor Migration Summary 2001. *Pennsylvania Birds,* 15 (2): 53–56.

Millar, J. G.

2002 The Protection of Eagles and the Bald and Golden Eagle Protection Act. *J. Raptor Research,* 36 (1 Suppl.): 29–31.

Miller, M.

1990 Minnesota's Bald Eagles: A Success Story. *Loon,* 62: 52–55.

Miller, M., and L. Pfannmuller

1991 Bald Eagle Population in Minnesota. *Loon,* 63: 268–271.

Mogenweck, R.

1973 Bald Eagle—Hawk Interaction. *Loon,* 45: 101.

Nelson, E.

1994 Bald Eagle Migration. *Loon,* 66: 105–106.

Nicoletti, F. J.

1995 A Tale of "Tales": New Records At Hawk Ridge. *Loon,* 67: 9–12.

Odom, R. R.

1980 Current Status and Reintroduction of the Bald Eagle in Georgia. *Oriole,* 45 (1): 1–14.

Pennaz, T., and C. Pennaz

1996 Bald Eagle Predation on a Common Loon. *Loon,* 68: 69–70.

Siesennop, G. D.

1999 Bald Eagle Preys on Herring Gull. *Loon,* 71: 49.

Snodgrass, R.

2000 Unusual Bald Eagle and Wild Turkey Interaction. *Loon,* 72: 181.

Smith, L., K. E. Clark, and L. J. Niles

2001 New Jersey Bald Eagle Management Project 2001. New Jersey Division of Fish and Wildlife, Trenton.

Stamm, A. L., and J. Durell

1980 The 1980 Bald Eagle Count in Kentucky. *Kentucky Warbler,* 56 (3): 55–58.

Stanley, J.

2002 An Example of Cooperative Hunting in Bald Eagles. *International Hawkwatcher,* 6: 14–16.

Stolen, E. D.

1996 Black and Turkey Vulture Interactions with Bald Eagles in Florida. *Florida Field Naturalist,* 24 (2): 43–45.

Warnke, E. K., et al.

2002 Provisioning Rates and Time Budgets of Adult and Nestling Bald Eagles at Inland Wisconsin Sites. *J. Raptor Research,* 36 (2): 121–127.

Whitledge, J.

1994 Wild Goose Chase. *Bird Watcher's Digest,* 16 (3): 42–43.

10 – ACCIPITERS

Apfelbaum, S., and A. Haney

1984 Note on Foraging and Nesting Habits of Goshawks. *Loon,* 56: 132–133.

Backstrom, P.

1991 Northern Goshawk Predation on Sharp-tailed Grouse. *Loon,* 63: 74.

Bednarz, J. C., D. Klem, Jr., L. J. Goodrich, and S. E. Senner

1990 Migration Counts of Raptors at Hawk Mountain, Pennsylvania, as Indicators of Population Trends, 1934–1986. *Auk,* 107: 96–109.

Block, W. M., M. L. Morrison, and M. H. Reiser, Editors

1994 *The Northern Goshawk: Ecology and Management.* Studies in Avian Biology No. 16. Cooper Ornithological Society, Lawrence, KS.

Blust, B.

1994 A Sharp-shinned Duck Hawk? *Pennsylvania Birds,* 8 (2): 96.

Bolgiano, N. C.

1997   Pennsylvania CBC Counts of Sharp-shinned and Cooper's Hawks. *Pennsylvania Birds,* 11 (3): 134–137.

Bosakowski, T.

1999   *The Northern Goshawk: Ecology, Behavior, and Management in North America.* Hancock House, Blaine, WA.

Bosakowski, T., and R. Speiser

1994   Macrohabitat Selection by Nesting Northern Goshawks: Implications for Managing Eastern Forests. In *The Northern Goshawk: Ecology and Management,* ed. W. M. Block, M. L. Morrison, and M. H. Reiser. Studies in Avian Biology No. 16. Cooper Ornithological Society, Lawrence, KS.

Brasher, C. G., and P. K. Stoddard

2001   Autumn Raptor Migration through the Florida Keys with Special Focus on the Peregrine Falcon. Final Report. Bureau of Wildlife Diversity Conservation, Florida Fish and Wildlife Conservation Commission, Tallahassee.

Breckenridge, W. J.

1988   Cooper's Hawk at Bird Bath. *Loon,* 60: 127–128.

Chartier, A.

1994a Sharp-shinned Hawk Declines: An Inland Perspective. *Ontario Birds,* 12 (1): 7–10.

1994b Sharp-shinned Hawk Declines: An Inland Perspective. *Winging It,* 6 (6): 8–9.

Cohrs, D.

1984   A Northern Goshawk at Athens. *Oriole,* 49 (1): 11–12.

Elliott, J. E., and P. A. Martin

1994   Chlorinated Hydrocarbons and Shell Thinning in Eggs of (*Accipiter*) Hawks in Ontario, 1986–1989. *Environmental Pollution,* 86: 189–200.

Elliott, J. E., and L. Shutt

1993   Monitoring Organochlorines in Blood of Sharp-shinned Hawks (*Accipiter striatus*) Migrating through the Great Lakes. *Environmental Toxicology and Chemistry,* 12: 241–250.

Evans, D. L.

1978   Partial Albinism: Saw-whet Owl and Goshawk. *Loon,* 50: 52–53.

Fisher, A. K.

1893   *The Hawks and Owls of the United States in Their Relation to Agriculture.* Bulletin 3. Division of Ornithology and Mammalogy, U.S. Department of Agriculture, Washington, DC.

Frock, R.

2000   Cooper's Hawk, Banded in PA, Recovered in New Brunswick. *Pennsylvania Birds,* 14 (1): 10.

Fulton, J. T.

1983   A Northern Goshawk in Georgia. *Oriole,* 48 (1): 5.

Gobris, N. M.

1994   Sharp-shinned Hawk Breeds in Lower Piedmont. *Oriole,* 59 (2, 3): 64–65.

Goodrich, L.

1994   Flying the Not-So-Friendly Skies. *Appalachian Trailway News,* 55 (4): 12–14.

Gullion, G. W.

1965   Raptor Predation Upon Raptors. *Loon,* 37: 108.

1981   The Impact of Goshawk Predation upon Ruffed Grouse. *Loon,* 53: 82–84.

Heintzelman, D. S.

1993   Variations in Counts and Age Ratios of Migrating Sharp-shinned Hawks in Autumn at Bake Oven Knob, Lehigh County, Pa. *American Hawkwatcher,* 19: 4–6.

1994   Autumn Sharp-shinned Hawk Migration Counts and Age Ratio Trends at Bake Oven Knob, Lehigh County, Pa. *American Hawkwatcher,* 20: 4–5.

1997   A Dramatic Sharp-shinned Hawk and Red-tailed Hawk Interaction during Autumn Migration. *American Hawkwatcher,* 23: 10.

2000a Extreme Migration Dates, and Maximum Daily Raptor Counts, during Autumn at Bake Oven Knob, Lehigh County, Pennsylvania USA. *International Hawkwatcher,* 1: 19–21.

2000b Northern Goshawk (*Accipiter gentilis*) Observed in Allentown, Lehigh County, Pennsylvania USA. *International Hawkwatcher,* 2: 39–40.

Hohenleitner, F.

1993   The Return of the Cooper's Hawk. *Pennsylvania Birds,* 7 (2): 52.

Hopkins, D. A., G. S. Mersereau, and L. Fischer

1988   Nesting Sharp-shinned Hawks in Connecticut. *Connecticut Warbler,* 7 (2): 18–19.

Jacobs, E. A.

2002   Sharp-shinned Hawk *Accipiter striatus.* In *Wisconsin Breeding Bird Atlas,* in press.

Johnson, D. H.

1982   Raptors of Minnesota—Nesting Distribution and Population Status. *Loon,* 54: 73–104.

Keith, L. B.

1963   *Wildlife's Ten-Year Cycle.* University of Wisconsin Press, Madison.

Kopischke, E. D.

1973   Sharp-shinned Hawk Kills Robin. *Loon,* 45: 65.

Kunkle, D. R.

2002   The 2002 Autumn Hawk Count at Bake Oven Knob, Lehigh County, Pa. *American Hawkwatcher,* 28: 2–5.

Longley, W. H.

1952   Some Notes on Hawks, Owls, and Their Prey. *Flicker,* 24: 127–129.

1965   Goshawk Feeds on a Barred Owl. *Loon,* 37: 110.

May, J. B.

1935   *The Hawks of North America.* National Association of Audubon Societies, New York.

Meng, H. K.

1951   Cooper's Hawk, *Accipiter cooperii* (Bonaparte). Unpublished Ph. D. dissertation, Cornell University, Ithaca, NY.

Miles, J.

2002   Cooper's Hawk Cannibalism. *OFO News,* 20 (1): 4.

Nicoletti, F. J.

1995   An Unusual Plumage in Sharp-shinned Hawks. *Loon,* 67: 66.

Rosenfield, R. N., and D. L. Evans

1980   Migration Incidence and Sequence of Age and Sex Classes of the Sharp-shinned Hawk. *Loon,* 52: 66–69.

Schwalbe, P., and G. Schwalbe

1995   Cooper's Hawk Utilizing Carrion. *Pennsylvania Birds,* 8 (4): 215.

Siebenheller, B., and N. Siebenheller

1990   The Waiting Game. *Bird Watcher's Digest,* 13 (1): 42–43.

Sparling, D. W., Jr.

1975   Prairie Chicken Killed by Goshawk. *Loon,* 47: 191–192.

Svedarsky, W. D.

1981   Goshawk Kills Prairie Chicken on Booming Ground in Northwest Minnesota. *Loon,* 53: 112–113.

Trexel, D. R., R. N. Rosenfield, J. Bielefeldt, and E. A. Jacobs

1999   Comparative Nest Site Habitats in Sharp-shinned and Cooper's Hawks in Wisconsin. *Wilson Bulletin,* 111 (1): 7–14.

Viverette, C., L. Goodrich, and M. Pokras

1994   Levels of DDE in Eastern Flyway Populations of Migrating Sharp-shinned Hawks and the Question of Recent Declines in Numbers Sighted. *HMANA Migration Studies,* September, 5–7.

Viverette, C. B., S. Struve, L. J. Goodrich, and K. L. Bildstein

1996   Decreases in Migrating Sharp-shinned Hawks (*Accipiter striatus*) at Traditional Raptor-Migration Watch Sites in Eastern North America. *Auk,* 113 (1): 32–40.

Weidensaul, S.

1991   Food Hoarding in Raptors. *Bird Watcher's Digest,* 14 (2): 65–71.

Wood, P. B., et al.

1996   Environmental Contaminant Levels in Sharp-shinned Hawks from the Eastern United States. *J. Raptor Research,* 30 (3): 136–144.

11 – SOARING HAWKS

Austing, G. R.

1964   *The World of the Red-tailed Hawk.* J. B. Lippincott, Philadelphia.

Beck, H.

2001   Red-tails, Raven, and Turkey Vulture Interaction. *American Hawkwatcher,* 27: 17–18.

Bednarz, J. C., D. Klem, Jr., L. J. Goodrich, and S. E. Senner

1990   Migration Counts of Raptors at Hawk Mountain, Pennsylvania, as Indicators of Population Trends, 1934–1986. *Auk,* 107: 96–109.

Bickley, D.

1991   Feeding a Red-shouldered Hawk. *Bird Watcher's Digest,* 13 (3): 64–65.

Bildstein, K. L.

1999   Racing with the Sun. *Birdscope,* 13 (1): 1–5.

Blust, B.

1990   A Hawk at Play. *Pennsylvania Birds,* 4 (3): 96.

Bohm, R. T.

1985   Use of Artificial Nests by Great Gray Owls, Great Horned Owls, and Red-tailed Hawks in Northeastern Minnesota. *Loon,* 57: 150–152.

Eckert, K. R.

1982   Proceedings of the Minnesota Ornithological Records Committee. *Loon,* 54: 147–150.

Fingerhood, E.

1993   Record Broad-Winged Hawk Flight Philadelphia. *Pennsylvania Birds*, 7 (3): 93.

Fisher, S.

2001   Dark Morph Broad-winged Hawk. *American Hawkwatcher*, 27: 19.

Floyd, T.

1992   Dark-Morph "Western" Red-tailed Hawk *Buteo jamaicensis calurus* Centre County. *Pennsylvania Birds*, 6 (1): 6.

Goodrich, L. J., and S. E. Senner

1988   Recent Trends of Wintering Great Horned Owls (*Bubo virginianus*), Red-tailed Hawks (*Buteo jamaicensis*) and Two of Their Avian Prey in Pennsylvania. *J. Pennsylvania Academy of Science*, 62 (3): 131–137.

Heintzelman, D. S.

1962   Winter Grouping of American Rough-legged Hawks. *Linnaean News-Letter*, 15 (9): 2.

1965   Cannibalism at a Broad-winged Hawk Nest. *Auk*, 83: 307.

1990   The 1957–1989 Bake Oven Knob, Pa., Autumn Hawk Migration Field Study: A 30 Year Review and Summary. *American Hawkwatcher*, 17: 1–16.

1995   Peak Broad-winged Hawk September Migration Dates at Bake Oven Knob, Lehigh County, Pa. *American Hawkwatcher*, 21: 5–6.

2000a A 39-Year Analysis of Major Autumn Broad-winged Hawk (*Buteo platypterus*) Flights at Bake Oven Knob, Pennsylvania USA. *International Hawkwatcher*, 1: 16–19.

2000b Red-tailed Hawk Carrying Stick at Bake Oven Knob, Pennsylvania USA. *International Hawkwatcher*, 1: 19.

2000c Extreme Migration Dates, and Maximum Daily Raptor Counts, during Autumn at Bake Oven Knob, Lehigh County, Pennsylvania USA. *International Hawkwatcher*, 1: 19–21.

2002   Another Red-tailed Hawk Attacks Twigs. *International Hawkwatcher*, 7: 21.

Heintzelman, D. S., and D. Kunkle

1989   A Mid-November Swainson's Hawk Record at Bake Oven Knob, Lehigh County, Pa. *American Hawkwatcher*, 16: 1–2.

Hopkins, J.

2001   Broad-winged Hawk "Playing" with a Leaf. *American Hawkwatcher*, 27: 17.

Iron, J.

1995   Red-shouldered Hawk Update. *OFO News*, 13 (2): 8.

Jacobs, J. P., and E. A. Jacobs

1999   The Red-shouldered Hawk in Wisconsin. *Passenger Pigeon*, 61 (3): 291–293.

Johnson, D. H.

1982   Raptors of Minnesota—Nesting Distribution and Population Status. *Loon*, 54: 73–104.

Kunkle, D. R.

1989   Broad-winged Hawks Flying in Rain at Bake Oven Knob, Lehigh County, Pa. *American Hawkwatcher*, 14: 1–2.

1997   Unusual Red-tailed Hawk Flight Behavior at Bake Oven Knob, Lehigh County, Pa. *American Hawkwatcher*, 23: 9.

1998   Long Term Trends in Rough-legged Hawk Migrations at Bake Oven Knob, Pa. *American Hawkwatcher*, 24: 11–13.

2000   Raven and Red-tailed Hawk Engage in Aerial Duel. *American Hawkwatcher*, 26: 22.

Le Duc, P.

1970   The Nesting Ecology of Some Hawks and Owls in Southeastern Minnesota. *Loon*, 42: 48–62.

Longley, W. H.

1952   Some Notes on Hawks, Owls, and Their Prey. *Flicker*, 24: 127–129.

MacClay, B.

1990   Notes from PA Rt. 183 Hawk Watch Schuylkill/Berks Counties. *Pennsylvania Birds*, 4 (4): 176.

Maransky, B. P., and K. L. Bildstein

2001   Follow Your Elders: Age-related Differences in the Migration Behavior of Broad-winged Hawks at Hawk Mountain Sanctuary, Pennsylvania. *Wilson Bulletin*, 113 (3): 350–353.

Martell, M., S. Willey, and J. Schladweiler

1998   Nesting and Migration of Swainson's Hawks in Minnesota. *Loon*, 70: 72–81.

Marti, C. D., and M. N. Kochert

1995   Are Red-tailed Hawks and Great Horned Owls Diurnal-Nocturnal Dietary Counterparts? *Wilson Bulletin*, 107 (4): 615–628.

Maxson, S. J., and A. M. Herr

1990   Rough-legged Hawk Preys on Short-eared Owl. *Loon*, 62: 108.

McClintock, E.

1990   Rough-legged Hawk Seen in Sumter County. *Oriole*, 56 (4): 80.

Millard, S.

1987   A Kettle of Swainson's Hawks. *Loon*, 59: 158.

Moore, T. S.
1981 Swainson's Hawk Sightings in Georgia. *Oriole,* 46 (1, 2): 14.

Nicoletti, F. J.
1995 A Tale of "Tales": New Records at Hawk Ridge. *Loon,* 67: 9–12.

Nicoletti, F. J., S. Millard, and B. Yokel
1998 First Description of Albinism in a Dark-Morph Red-tailed Hawk in North America. *Loon,* 70: 117–118.

Perkins, D. W., D. M. Phillips, and D. K. Garcelon
1996 Predation on a Bald Eagle Nestling by a Red-tailed Hawk. *J. Raptor Research,* 30 (4): 249.

Pittaway, R.
1993 Recognizable Forms: Subspecies and Morphs of the Red-tailed Hawk. *Ontario Birds,* 11 (1): 23–29.

Pogacnik, J.
2001 A Leucistic Rough-legged Hawk in Ohio. *Ohio Cardinal,* 25 (1): 40–41.

Post, W., and D. B. McNair
1990 Winter Specimens of the Broad-winged Hawk in Georgia and South Carolina: Some Corrections. *Oriole,* 55 (1): 21.

Pranty, B.
2002 Red-shouldered Hawk Feeds on Carrion. *J. Raptor Research,* 36 (2): 152–153.

Preston, C. R.
2000 *Wild Bird Guides: Red-tailed Hawk.* Stackpole Books, Mechanicsburg, PA

Rogers, B.
1991 A Hawk at the Feeder. *Bird Watcher's Digest,* 13 (3): 60–67.

Wiltraut, R.
1991 Dark-morph Red-tailed Hawk *Buteo jamaicensis* Northampton County. *Pennsylvania Birds,* 5 (1): 22.

12 – CARACARAS AND FALCONS

Amadon, D.
1965 Sparrow Hawk Takes Bat on the Wing. *Linnaean News-Letter,* 19 (4): 5.

Anderson, S. H., and J. R. Squires
1997 *The Prairie Falcon.* University of Texas Press, Austin.

Anonymous
1997 *Nestboxes for American Kestrels.* Hawk Mountain Sanctuary Assn., Kempton, PA.

2002 Storied A. C. Peregrine Dies: State's Oldest Nesting Falcon Was N. J. Native. *Conserve Wildlife,* Winter–Spring, 1.

Ardia, D. R.
2001 Winter Roosting Behavior of American Kestrels. *J. Raptor Research,* 35 (1): 58–61.

Ardia, D. R., and K. L. Bildstein
2001 Sex-related Differences in Habitat Use in Wintering American Kestrels. *Auk,* 118 (3): 746–750.

Baetsen, R.
1993 Kestrel Boxes. *Bird Watcher's Digest,* 15 (4): 38–42.

Baumgartner, C.
1992 The Peregrine Patrol. *Bird Watcher's Digest,* 14 (4): 70–71.

Bednarz, J. C., D. Klem, Jr., L. J. Goodrich, and S. E. Senner
1990 Migration Counts of Raptors at Hawk Mountain, Pennsylvania, as Indicators of Population Trends, 1934–1986. *Auk,* 107: 96–109.

Berger, D. D., C. R. Sindelar, Jr., and K. E. Gamble
1969 The Status of Breeding Peregrines in the Eastern United States. In *Peregrine Falcon Populations: Their Biology and Decline,* ed. J. J. Hickey, 165–173. University of Wisconsin Press, Madison.

Bowman, R.
1987 Size Dimorphism in Mated Pairs of American Kestrels. *Wilson Bulletin,* 99 (3): 465–467.

Bowman, R., and D. M. Bird
1985 Reproductive Performance of American Kestrels Laying Replacement Clutches. *Canadian J. Zoology,* 63: 2590–2593.

1986 Ecological Correlates of Mate Replacement in the American Kestrel. *Condor,* 88: 440–445.

1987 Behavioral Strategies of American Kestrels during Mate Replacement. *Behavioral Ecology and Sociobiology,* 20: 129–135.

Brauning, D., and C. Dooley
1991 Recent History and Current Status of Nesting Peregrine Falcons, *Falco peregrinus,* in Pennsylvania. *Pennsylvania Birds,* 5 (2): 59–61.

Breen, T. F., J. W. Parrish, K. Boyd, and B. Winn
1995 Southeastern American Kestrel Nests in Bulloch, Evans and Columbia Counties, Georgia. *Oriole,* 60 (2, 3): 33–36.

Cade, T. J.

1953   Behavior of a Young Gyrfalcon. *Wilson Bulletin,* 65 (1): 26–31.

1982   *The Falcons of the World.* Comstock/Cornell University Press, Ithaca, NY.

Cade, T. J., J. H. Enderson, L. F. Kiff, and C. M. White

1997   Are There Enough Good Data to Justify De-listing the American Peregrine Falcon? *Wildlife Society Bulletin,* 25 (3): 730–738.

Cade, T. J., J. H. Enderson, C. G. Thelander, and C. M. White

1988   *Peregrine Falcon Populations: Their Management and Recovery.* The Peregrine Fund, Inc., Boise, ID.

Choate, E. A.

1972   Spectacular Hawk Flight at Cape May Point, New Jersey on 16 October 1970. *Wilson Bulletin,* 84: 340–341.

Clark, K.

2001   The Peregrine Falcon in New Jersey Report for 2001. New Jersey Division of Fish and Wildlife, Trenton.

Corser, J. D., M. Amaral, C. J. Martin, and C. C. Rimmer

1999   Recovery of a Cliff-nesting Peregrine Falcon, *Falco peregrinus,* Population in Northern New York and New England, 1984–1996. *Canadian Field-Naturalist,* 113: 472–480.

Craighead, J., and F. Craighead

1940   Nesting Pigeon Hawks. *Wilson Bulletin,* 52 (4): 241–248.

Davidow, B.

2001   Falcons of the Florida Keys. *Living Bird,* 20 (4): 32–38.

EEckert, K. R.

1991   An Influx of Northern Raptors, Fall–Winter 1990–1991. *Loon,* 63: 163–167.

1995   Proceedings of the Minnesota Ornithological Records Committee [Crested Caracara record]. *Loon,* 67: 45.

Egli, W.

1995   Peregrine Falcon Reintroduction in Williamsport. *Pennsylvania Birds,* 9 (4): 199.

Enderson, J. H., W. Heinrich, L. Kiff, and C. M. White

1995   Population Changes in North American Peregrines. *Trans. 60th North American Wildlife and Natural Resources Conference,* 142–161.

Fingerhood, E. D.

1984a   The Lancaster County Gyrfalcon Incursion of 1981–1983. *Cassinia,* 60: 34–40.

1984b   Gyrfalcon Records in Pennsylvania: Part Two. *Cassinia,* 60: 41–46.

Fingerhood, E. D., and S. Lipschutz

1982   Gyrfalcon (*Falco rusticolus*) Records in Pennsylvania. *Cassinia,* 59: 68–76.

Frank, S.

1994   *City Peregrines: A Ten-year Saga of New York City Falcons.* Hancock House Publishers, Blaine, WA.

Fuller, M. R., W. S. Seegar, and L. S. Schueck

1998   Routes and Travel Rates of Migrating Peregrine Falcons *Falco peregrinus* and Swainson's Hawks *Buteo swainsoni* in the Western Hemisphere. *J. Avian Biology,* 29: 433–440.

Hartley, J.

1998   Merlin Takes Songbird in Flight While Migrating Past Bake Oven Knob. *American Hawkwatcher,* 24: 17.

Heintzelman, D. S.

1964   Spring and Summer Sparrow Hawk Food Habits. *Wilson Bulletin,* 76 (4): 323–330.

1966   Observations and Comments on the Aerial Capture of Prey by the Sparrow Hawk. *Linnaean News-Letter,* 20 (6, 7): 1–4.

1976   Bird Survey on Aves Island. *Explorers Journal,* 54 (2): 65.

1989   A Record Count of Merlins at Bake Oven Knob, Lehigh County, Pa. *American Hawkwatcher,* 15: 1–2.

1992   The Role of Perches in Limiting American Kestrel Uses on Hilltop Fields within the Kittatinny Raptor Migration Corridor Near Bake Oven Knob, Lehigh County, Pa. *American Hawkwatcher,* 18: 2–4.

1994   Further Observations of Raptor Use and Habitat Alteration of Hawk Hill, Heidelberg Township, Lehigh County, Pa. *American Hawkwatcher,* 20: 5.

1997   Peregrine Falcon Stoops at Turkey Vulture during Autumn Migration. *American Hawkwatcher,* 23: 10.

2000   Extreme Migration Dates, and Maximum Daily Raptor Counts, during Autumn at Bake Oven Knob, Lehigh County, Pennsylvania USA. *International Hawkwatcher,* 1: 19–21.

Hess, P.

1998   A Winter Roost of Merlins in Urban Pittsburgh, Pa. *American Hawkwatcher,* 24: 13–16.

Hickey, J. J., Editor

1969 *Peregrine Falcon Populations: Their Biology and Decline.* University of Wisconsin Press, Madison.

Highhouse, W.

1989 American Kestrel Nesting Box Project in Warren County. *Pennsylvania Birds,* 3 (4): 132.

Jacobs, E. A.

1995 American Kestrel Reproduction and Dispersal in Central Wisconsin. *J. Raptor Research,* 29 (2): 135–137.

Johnson, D. H.

1982 Raptors of Minnesota—Nesting Distribution and Population Status. *Loon,* 54: 73–104.

Klucsarits, J. R., B. Robertson, and S. Robertson

1997 Breeding Success of American Kestrels Nesting in Boxes in Eastern Pennsylvania, 1987–1994. *Pennsylvania Birds,* 11 (3): 138–140.

Knight, R. L., and R. M. Hatcher

1997 Recovery Efforts Result in Returned Nesting of Peregrine Falcons in Tennessee. *Migrant,* 68 (2): 33–39.

Krammes, D.

2001 American Kestrel Captures Tree Swallow. *American Hawkwatcher,* 27: 19.

Longley, W. H.

1955 A Feeding Procedure of a Short-eared Owl and a Sparrow Hawk. *Flicker,* 27: 134.

Martell, M. S., J. L. McNicoll, and P. T. Redig

2000 Probable Effect of Delisting of the Peregrine Falcon on Availability of Urban Nest Sites. *J. Raptor Research,* 34 (2): 126–132.

Maxson, G.

1993 Immature Peregrine Falcon Preys on Sharp-shinned Hawk. *Loon,* 65: 213–214.

Menze, C.

1994 Gyrfalcon in Duluth. *Loon,* 66: 104.

Miller, K. E., and J. A. Smallwood

1997 Natal Dispersal and Philopatry of Southeastern American Kestrels in Florida. *Wilson Bulletin,* 109 (2): 226–232.

Moore, T. S.

1981 Prairie Falcon Sightings in Georgia. *Oriole,* 46 (1, 2): 13.

Morrison, J. L.

1998 Effects of Double Brooding on Productivity of Crested Caracaras. *Auk,* 115 (4): 979–987.

1999 Breeding Biology and Productivity of Florida's Crested Caracaras. *Condor,* 101: 505–517.

Morrison, J. L., and S. R. Humphrey

2001 Conservation Value of Private Lands for Crested Caracaras in Florida. *Conservation Biology,* 15 (3): 675–684.

Morrison, J. L., M. A. McMillian, S. M. McGehee, and L. D. Todd

1994 First Record of Crested Caracara Nesting in a Cypress. *Florida Field Naturalist,* 25 (2): 51–53.

Nicoletti, F. J.

1995 Eye to Eye with a Gyrfalcon. *Loon,* 67: 118–119.

1996 American Kestrel and Merlin Migration Correlated with Green Darner Movements at Hawk Ridge. *Loon,* 68: 216–221.

Parrish, J. W., Jr.

2000 Possible Prevention of European Starling Nesting by Southeastern American Kestrels at a Power Substation in Southern Georgia. *J. Raptor Research,* 34 (2): 152.

Pittaway, R.

1994 Recognizable Forms / Merlin. *Ontario Birds,* 12 (2): 74–80.

Richard, A.

1986 "Street" Hawks. *Bird Watcher's Digest,* 9 (1): 24–25.

Sewell, J.

1996 A Merlin during the Month of June in Clayton County. *Oriole,* 61 (1): 8–9.

Shanahan, D.

1996 Gyrfalcon Harassing a Snowy Owl. *Ontario Birds,* 12 (2): 80–81.

Solensky, M. J.

2000 Merlins Nesting in Minneapolis. *Loon,* 72: 72–75.

Steidl, R. J., et al.

1997 Prey of Peregrine Falcons from the New Jersey Coast and Associated Contaminant Levels. *Northeast Wildlife,* 52: 11–19.

Steidl, R. J., C. R. Griffin, L. J. Niles, and K. E. Clark

1991 Reproductive Success and Eggshell Thinning of a Reestablished Peregrine Falcon Population. *J. Wildlife Management,* 55 (2): 294–299.

Stolen, E. D.

1996 Black and Turkey Vulture Interactions with Bald Eagles in Florida. *Florida Field Naturalist,* 24 (2): 43–45.

Stotz, N. G., and L. J. Goodrich

1989 Sexual Differences in Timing of American Kestrel Migration at Hawk Mountain Sanctuary, PA. *J. Raptor Research,* 23 (4): 167–171.

Svingen, P. H.

2000 First Minnesota Breeding Record of the Richardson's Merlin. *Loon,* 72: 66–72.

Svingen, P. H., K. V. Haws, and B. A. Lenning

2001 The 2000–2001 Influx of Northern Owls/Record High Numbers of Northern Hawk and Great Gray Owls in Minnesota. *Loon,* 73: 135–143.

Swengel, A.

1992a Peregrine Comeback. *Bird Watcher's Digest,* 14 (4): 64–74, 76, 78.

1992b Peregrine Projects. *Bird Watcher's Digest,* 14 (4): 66–67.

Tordoff, H. B., J. S. Castrale, M. S. Martell, and P. T. Redig

1998 Effect of Fledge Site on Choice of Nest Site by Midwestern Peregrine Falcons. *Loon,* 70: 127–129.

2000 Brood Size and Survival to Breeding in Midwestern Peregrine Falcons. *J. Field Ornithology,* 71 (4): 691–693.

Upton, R.

2002 *Arab Falconry: History of a Way of Life.* Hancock House Publishers, Blaine, WA.

Valdez, U., S. Robertson, R. Robertson, and K. L. Bildstein

2000 Nestbox Use by American Kestrels (*Falco sparverius*) and European Starlings (*Sturnus vulgaris*) in Eastern Pennsylvania. *Pennsylvania Birds,* 14 (3): 150–153.

Wasilewski, R. L., and R. Koval

1998 Notes on the Physical Characteristics and Behavior of Peregrine Falcons (*Falco peregrinus*) in the Wyoming Valley, Luzerne County, Pennsylvania. *Pennsylvania Birds,* 12 (4): 179–181.

1999 Successful Nesting by Wyoming Valley Peregrine Falcons. *Pennsylvania Birds,* 13 (4): 169–171.

Weidensaul, S.

1991 Food Hoarding in Raptors. *Bird Watcher's Digest,* 14 (2): 65–71.

13 – BARN OWLS

Boyd, E. M., and J. Shriner

1954 Nesting and Food of the Barn Owl (*Tyto alba*) in Hampshire County, Massachusetts. *Auk,* 71: 199–201.

Bunn, D. S., A. B. Warburton, and R. D. S. Wilson

1982 *The Barn Owl.* Buteo Books, Vermillion, SD.

Colvin, B. A.

2002 Annual Report on the New Jersey Study Area 2001. Barn Owl Research Foundation, San Antonio, TX.

Crawford, R. L.

1979 Analysis of Barn Owl Pellets from Worth County, Georgia. *Oriole,* 44 (2, 3): 52.

Ferguson, R. F.

1987 The Saga of the Lake Vermilion Common Barn-Owls. *Loon,* 59: 72–76.

Heintzelman, D. S.

1966 Distribution and Population Density of Barn Owls in Lehigh and Northampton Counties, Pennsylvania. *Cassinia,* 49: 2–20.

Johnson, D. H.

1982 Raptors of Minnesota—Nesting Distribution and Population Status. *Loon,* 54: 73–104.

König, C., F. Weick, and J. Becking

1999 *Owls: A Guide to the Owls of the World.* Yale University Press, New Haven, CT.

Miller, K. E.

1994 Prey Selection of the Common Barn-Owl in a Northern Florida Wetland. *Florida Field Naturalist,* 22 (1): 11–13.

Roulin, A.

2002 Offspring Desertion by Double-Brooded Female Barn Owls (*Tyto alba*). *Auk,* 119 (2): 515–519.

Speirs, J. M.

1985 *Birds of Ontario.* Volume 2. Natural Heritage/Natural History, Inc., Toronto, Ontario, Canada.

Trapp, D.

1989 The (Not So) Common Barn Owl. *Bird Watcher's Digest,* 12 (1): 32–37.

Wilson, K. A.

1938 Owl Studies at Ann Arbor, Michigan. *Auk,* 55 (2): 187–197.

14 – OTHER OWLS

Atkins, A.

1983 Brooding Eastern Screech-Owl Not Fooled by Blind. *Oriole,* 51 (2, 3): 46–47.

Ascani, T. L.

1989 Pennsylvania Wildlife and Its Use: A 1988 Public Opinion Survey. *Wildlife Conservation Report* No. 9. Wildlife Information Center, Inc., Allentown [now Slatington], PA.

Austing, G. R., and J. B. Holt, Jr.

1966 *The World of the Great Horned Owl*. J. B. Lippincott Company, Philadelphia.

Axelrod, M.

1980 Diet of a Minnesota Hawk Owl. *Loon,* 52: 117–118.

Barrett, L. L.

1950 Some Snowy Owl Observations for the Winter of 1949–1950. *Flicker,* 22: 111–112.

Barringer, J. N.

1980 Unusual Plumaged Short-eared Owl. *Loon,* 52: 92.

Bateman, H.

2001 Habitat Preferences of Boreal Owls Nesting in Artificial Boxes. *Birding,* 33 (5): 413.

Beaton, G.

1999 Northern Saw-whet Owls in Rabun County. *Oriole,* 66 (3, 4): 56–57.

Blakemore, L. A.

1940 Barred Owl Food Habits in Glenwood Park, Minneapolis, Minnesota. *Flicker,* 12: 21–23.

Bohm, R. T.

1985 Use of Artificial Nests by Great Gray Owls, Great Horned Owls, and Red-tailed Hawks in Northeastern Minnesota. *Loon,* 57: 150–152.

1988 Use of Nestboxes by Great Gray Owls in Northern Minnesota. *Loon,* 60: 121–123.

Breckenridge, W. J.

1945 Great Horned Owl and Giant Water Beetle. *Flicker,* 17: 18.

Brinker, D. F., et al.

1997 Autumn Migration of Northern Saw-whet Owls (*Aegolius acadicus*) in the Middle Atlantic and Northeastern United States: What Observations from 1995 Suggest. In *Biology and Conservation of Owls of the Northern Hemisphere*, ed. J. R. Duncan, D. H. Johnson, and T. H. Nicholls. Second International Symposium, February 5–9, 1997, Winnipeg, Manitoba. USDA Forest Service, General Technical Report NC–190. North Central Research Station, St. Paul, MN.

Brunton, D. F., and R. Pittaway, Jr.

1971 Observations of the Great Gray Owl on Winter Range. *Canadian Field Naturalist,* 85: 315–322.

Carlson, S., and T. Carlson

1989 Boreal Owl in Minneapolis. *Loon,* 61: 85–87.

Chaffin, D. C.

1995 Northern Saw-whet Owl Heard in NE Georgia. *Oriole,* 60 (2, 3): 51–52.

Christenson, G., and M. R. Fuller

1975 Food Habits of Two Long-eared Owl Families in East-Central Minnesota. *Loon,* 47: 58–61.

Coyle, M., M. Martell, and D. Newbauer

1995 Prey Items of Long-eared Owls Wintering in Minnesota. *Loon,* 67: 238–240.

Cunningham, R.

1990 Owls and Moths. *Loon,* 62: 72–75.

Duncan, J. R., D. H. Johnson, and T. H. Nicholls

1997 Biology and Conservation of Owls of the Northern Hemisphere. Second International Symposium, February 5–9, 1997, Winnipeg, Manitoba, Canada. USDA Forest Service, General Technical Report NC–190. North Central Research Station, St. Paul, MN.

Dunstan, T. C., and S. D. Sample

1972 Biology of Barred Owls in Minnesota. *Loon,* 44: 111–115.

Eckert, K.

1978 Unusual Diurnal Hunting Behavior of a Long-eared Owl. *Loon,* 50: 122.

1979a First Boreal Owl Nesting Record South of Canada: A Diary. *Loon,* 51: 20–27.

1979b Duluth—Superior Snowy Owl Study. *Loon,* 51: 218–219.

Erdman, T. C., T. O. Meyer, J. H. Smith, and D. M. Erdman

1997 Autumn Populations and Movements of Migrant Northern Saw-whet Owls (*Aegolius acadicus*) at Little Suamico, Wisconsin. In *Biology and Conservation of Owls of the Northern Hemisphere*, ed. J. R. Duncan, D. H. Johnson, and T. H. Nicholls. Second International Symposium, February 5–9, 1997, Winnipeg, Manitoba. USDA Forest Service, General Technical Report NC–190. North Central Research Station, St. Paul, MN.

Errington, P. L., F. Hamerstrom, and F. N. Hamerstrom, Jr.

1940 The Great Horned Owl and Its Prey in North-Central United States. Research

Bulletin 277. Agricultural Experiment Station, Iowa State College and Agriculture and Mechanic Arts, Ames.

Evans, D. L.

1978 Partial Albinism: Saw-whet Owl and Goshawk. *Loon*, 50: 52–53.

2000 Interactions between Snowy Owls and Large Falcons at Duluth. *Loon*, 72: 37–39.

Evans, D. L., and R. N. Rosenfield

1977 Fall Migration of Boreal Owls. *Loon*, 49: 165–167.

Fedak, J. G., and D. Brauning

1998 Short-eared Owls Breed in Pennsylvania in 1997. *Pennsylvania Birds*, 12 (2): 47–48.

French, R.

1990 Saw-whet Owl Attacks Feline. *Pennsylvania Birds*, 4 (4): 144.

Gibbs, E. L.

1988 A Unique Nesting Site of a Barred Owl. *Oriole*, 53 (1): 11.

Glassel, R.

1996 Unusual Numbers of Wintering Long-eared Owls, Winter 1994–95. *Loon*, 68: 73.

Godfrey, W. E.

1967 Some Winter Aspects of the Great Gray Owl. *Canadian Field-Naturalist*, 81 (2): 99–101.

Goodrich, L. J., and S. E. Senner

1988 Recent Trends of Wintering Great Horned Owls (*Bubo virginianus*), Red-tailed Hawks (*Buteo jamaicensis*) and Two of Their Avian Prey in Pennsylvania. *J. Pennsylvania Academy of Science*, 62 (3): 131–137.

Grisez, T.

1992 First Live Record of Great Gray Owl in the 20th Century in Pennsylvania Warren County. *Pennsylvania Birds*, 6 (1): 10–11.

Haas, F. C.

1991 First Documented Northern Hawk Owl, *Surnia ulula*, in Pennsylvania in the Twentieth Century. *Pennsylvania Birds*, 5 (1): 16–18.

Heintzelman, D. S.

1960 Behavior Pattern of Wintering Saw-whet Owls. *Linnaean News-Letter*, 14 (6): 5.

1986 Pennsylvania Wildlife and Its Use: A 1986 Public Opinion Survey. *Wildlife Conservation Report* No. 1. Wildlife Information Center, Inc., Allentown [now Slatington], PA.

Hertzel, A. X.

1999 Northern Saw-whet Owls Nesting in Washington County. *Loon*, 71: 220–222.

2002 Barred Owl Takes Cooper's Hawk? *Loon*, in press.

Hertzel, P., and A. X. Hertzel

2000 Locating Wintering Long-eared Owls in Minnesota. *Loon*, 72: 4–9.

Holkestad, K.

1976 Snowy Owl Behavior. *Loon*, 48: 76.

Huber, R. L.

1960 Owl Pellett [*sic*] Studies from Three Areas in Hennepin and Scott Counties. *Loon*, 32: 13–14.

Johnsgard, P. A.

1988 *North American Owls: Biology and Natural History*. Smithsonian Institution Press, Washington, DC.

Johnson, D. H.

1980 Barred Owls Use Nest Boxes. *Loon*, 52: 193–194.

1982 Raptors of Minnesota—Nesting Distribution and Population Status. *Loon*, 54: 73–104.

1987 Barred Owls and Nest Boxes—Results of a Five-Year Study in Minnesota. In *Biology and Conservation of Northern Forest Owls: Symposium Proceedings*, ed. R. W. Nero, et al., February 3–7, 1987, Winnipeg, Manitoba. General Technical Report RM–142. U.S. Department of Agriculture, Forest Service, Rocky Mountain Forest and Range Experiment Station, Fort Collins, CO.

Johnson, O. L.

1976 Winter Vocalization of Snowy Owl. *Loon*, 48: 76.

Jones, T.

2000 Record of Ground-Nesting of Long-eared Owls in Aitkin County. *Loon*, 72: 244–245.

Kehoe, M.

1982 Nesting Hawk Owls in Lake of the Woods Country. *Loon*, 54: 182–185.

Lane, B.

1991 Physical Interaction between a Male Boreal Owl and Male Northern Saw-whet Owl. *Loon*, 63: 74–75.

Lane, P. A., and J. R. Duncan

1987 Observations of Northern Hawk-Owls Nesting in Roseau County. *Loon*, 59: 165–174.

Lane, W. H.

1988   1988 Boreal Owl Survey in Cook County. *Loon*, 60: 99–104.

Lane, W. H., D. E. Andersen, and T. H. Nicholls

2001   Distribution, Abundance, and Habitat Use of Singing Male Boreal Owls in Northeast Minnesota. *J. Raptor Research*, 35 (2): 130–140.

Leck, C. F.

1984   *The Status and Distribution of New Jersey's Birds*. Rutgers University Press, New Brunswick, NJ.

Le Duc, P.

1970   The Nesting Ecology of Some Hawks and Owls in Southeastern Minnesota. *Loon*, 42: 48–62.

Lint, G.

1974   Saw-whet Owl Observation. *Loon*, 46: 88–89.

Liston, T. M.

1995   Seeking the Boreal Owl. *Bird Watcher's Digest*, 17 (3): 51–55.

Longley, W. H.

1952   Some Notes on Hawks, Owls, and Their Prey. *Flicker*, 24: 127–129.

1955   A Feeding Procedure of a Short-eared Owl and a Sparrow Hawk. *Flicker*, 27: 134.

Machniak, A., and C. Elliott

1997   Comparison of Long-eared and Short-eared Owl Winter Food Habitats on a Reclaimed Stripmine in Western Kentucky. *Kentucky Warbler*, 73 (3): 58–65.

Martell, M. S., J. Schladweiler, and F. Cuthbert

2001   Status and Attempted Reintroduction of Burrowing Owls in Minnesota, U.S.A. *J. Raptor Research*, 35 (4): 331–336.

Martinson, T.

1982   Possible Cannibalism in Boreal Owls. *Loon*, 54: 246.

Mescavage, B., and R. Wiltraut

1994   Winter of the Long-eared Owls. *Pennsylvania Birds*, 8 (1): 13–15.

Millard, S.

1987   Wintering Short-eared Owls. *Loon*, 59: 157–158.

Millsap, B. A.

2002   Survival of Florida Burrowing Owls along an Urban-Development Gradient. *J. Raptor Research*, 36 (1): 3–10.

Nero, R. W., R. J. Clark, R. J. Knapton, and R. H. Hamre, Editors

1987   *Biology and Conservation of Northern Forest Owls: Symposium Proceedings*, February 3–7, 1987, Winnipeg, Manitoba. General Technical Report RM–142. U.S. Department of Agriculture, Forest Service, Rocky Mountain Forest and Range Experiment Station, Fort Collins, CO.

Nero, R. W., S. G. Sealy, and H. W. R. Copland

1974   Great Gray Owls Occupy Artificial Nest. *Loon*, 46: 161–165.

Newman, J. R.

1987   Some Boreal and Northern Saw-whet Owl Comparisons. *Loon*, 59: 151–153.

Nicoletti, F. J.

2001   Boreal Owl Migration in Duluth: A Pilot Study in November 2000. *Loon*, 73: 165–168.

Nero, R. W.

1980   *The Great Gray Owl: Phantom of the Northern Forest*. Smithsonian Institution Press, Washington, DC.

Orr, D. J.

1979   Mallards Nesting in Great Blue Heron Nests and Near an Active Great Horned Owl Nest. *Loon*, 51: 100–101.

Otnes, F., and M. Otnes

1981   Unusual Nest Site, Short-eared Owl. *Loon*, 53: 230–231.

Paget, J.

1988   A Burrowing Owl in the Georgia Piedmont. *Oriole*, 53 (2, 3): 31.

Pittaway, R.

1993   Recognizable Forms: Subspecies of the Great Horned Owl. *Ontario Birds*, 11 (2): 64–69.

1995   Recognizable Forms: Morphs of the Eastern Screech-Owl. *Ontario Birds*, 13 (2): 66–71.

Poole, E. L.

1964   *Pennsylvania Birds: An Annotated List*. Delaware Valley Ornithological Club/Livingston Publishing Company, Narberth, PA.

Schaeffer, F.

1969   A Saw-Whet Owl Recovery. *Linnaean News-Letter*, 23 (2, 3): 3–4.

Schmalz, G.

2001   Long-eared Owl in Fernbank Forest. *Oriole*, 66 (1, 2): 16–17.

Schmid, W.

1959   Note on Food Habits of the Burrowing Owl in Minnesota. *Flicker*, 31: 103.

Schwalbe, G., and P. Schwalbe

1993   Breeding Season Record of a Short-eared Owl Clearfield County. *Pennsylvania Birds*, 7 (2): 53.

Smith, D. G.

1993   Eastern Screech Owls. *Bird Watcher's Digest*, 16 (1): 32–39.

Smith, D., and B. Smith

1993   Northern Hawk Owl Breeding Behavior Observed. *Loon*, 65: 102–103.

Stedman, S. J.

2001   Northern Saw-whet Owl Surveys in the Big South Fork National River and Recreation Area, Kentucky and Tennessee. *Kentucky Warbler*, 77 (4): 68–75).

Struthers, D. R.

1941   Horned Owl Preys on Brown Rat. *Flicker*, 13: 21.

Sundquist, K.

1982   Unusual Barred Owl Behavior. *Loon*, 54: 65–66.

Svingen, P.

1996   Short-eared Owl Interaction with a Rough-legged Hawk in Roseau County. *Loon*, 68: 179.

Svingen, P. H., K. V. Haws, and B. A. Lenning

2001   The 2000–2001 Influx of Northern Owls: Record High Numbers of Northern Hawk and Great Gray Owls in Minnesota. *Loon*, 73: 135–143.

Taft, S. J., E. A. Jacobs, and R. N. Rosenfield

1997   Hematozoa of Spring- and Fall-Migrating Northern Saw-whet Owls (*Aegolius acadicus*) in Wisconsin. *J. Helminthology Society of Washington*, 64 (2): 296–298.

Taft, S. J., C. D. Kerstner, and E. A. Jacobs

2000   Ectoparasitic Insects from Migrating Saw-whet Owls (*Aegolius acadicus*) in Central Wisconsin. *Proceedings Entomological Society of Washington*, 102 (3): 755–756.

Tague, C.

1997   Nesting Short-eared Owls at Imperial. *Pennsylvania Birds*, 11 (4): 216.

Todd, W. E. C.

1940   Birds of Western Pennsylvania. University of Pittsburgh Press, Pittsburgh, PA.

VanCamp, L. F., and C. J. Henny

1975   The Screech Owl: Its Life History and Population Ecology in Northern Ohio. *North American Fauna* No. 71. U.S. Fish and Wildlife Service, Washington, DC.

Weidensaul, S.

1991   Food Hoarding in Raptors. *Bird Watcher's Digest*, 14 (2): 65–71.

2001   Tracking the Tooting Legions. *PSO Newsletter*, 12 (4): 6–8.

Whalen, D. M., B. D. Watts, and D. W. Johnston

2000   Diet of Autumn Migrating Northern Saw-whet Owls on the Eastern Shore of Virginia. *J. Raptor Research*, 34 (1): 42–44.

Wink, J., S. E. Senner, and L. J. Goodrich

1987   Food Habits of Great Horned Owls in Pennsylvania. *Proceedings Pennsylvania Academy of Sciences*, 61: 133–137.

Wilson, K. A.

1938   Owl Studies at Ann Arbor, Michigan. *Auk*, 55 (2): 187–197.

Wolter, P. T., and W. H. Lane

2001   A Look at Boreal Owl Nesting Habitat in Minnesota Using Landsat Thematic Mapper Data. *Loon*, 73: 192–199.

Woolsey, R.

1930   Unusual Nesting Site of the Great Horned Owl. *Flicker*, 2: 19.

INDEX

Page numbers in **boldface** type indicate photographs, drawings, and maps.

bluegill (*Lepomis macrochirus*), 60

Blue Ridge Parkway, 42

bobcat (*Lynx rufus*), 26

Bobolink (*Dolichonyx oryzivorus*), 65, 146

Bobwhite, Northern (*Colinus virginianus*), 6, 92, 102, 108, 138

Bolivia, 106

Bowling Green State University, 134

Braddock Bay Raptor Research, 45

Brazil, 63, 70

Breeding Bird Surveys (BBS), 102, 140

Broley, Charles L. (?–1959), 48

Broun, Maurice, 46

Bubo virginianus, 137

Bunting, Indigo (*Passerina cyanea*), 116

Bunting, Snow (*Plectrophenax nivalis*), 123, 157

Buteo albonotatus, 107

Buteo brachyurus, 102

Buteo jamaicensis, 107

Buteo lagopus, 112

Buteo lineatus, 96

Buteo platypterus, 99

Buteo regalis, 112

Buteo swansoni, 104

cadmium, 30

California, 57, 83, 108

Canada, 13, 19, 26, 32, 38, 39, 42, 46, 49, 51, 57, 63, 64, 67, 81, 84, 86, 87, 89, 90, 91, 92, 95, 98, 104, 112, 120, 123, 124, 125, 126, 128, 129, 130, 131, 138, 140, 141, 144, 145, 147, 149, 150, 151, 152, 156, 158, 159, 160, 161, 163; Alberta, 140; Amherst Island, Ontario, 124; Arctic, 126; Arctic islands, 123, 124; Atlantic Coast, 59, 65, 78, 80, 99, 101, 108, 149, 152, 156, 161; Baie-Comeau, Quebec, 57; Bay of Fundy, 67; Canada–United States border, 159; Churchill Falls, Labrador, 65; Essex Region Conservation Authority, Ontario, 42; Hawk Cliff, Ontario, 31, 55; Holiday Beach Conservation Area, Ontario, 42; Hudson Bay, 65, 78, 112, 118, 125, 129, 144, 149, 152; Kortright Waterfowl Park, Ontario, 28, 29; Labrador, 39, 59, 60, 65, 82, 123, 125, 144, 159; Maritime provinces, 39; New Brunswick, 77, 87, 91, 117; Newfoundland, 21, 65, 78, 121, 124, 144; Nova Scotia, 21, 68, 74, 77, 104, 106, 107, 117, 121; Ontario, 18, 21, 29, 31, 46, 55, 57, 58, 59, 65, 68, 74, 78, 82, 84, 88, 89, 90, 91, 96, 99, 100, 101, 104, 106, 108, 111, 112, 114, 119, 120, 121, 122, 124, 125, 129, 131, 135, 141, 149, 152, 159, 160, 161, 163; Ottawa, Ontario, 149; Point Pelee,

Ontario, 55; Quebec, 21, 39, 50, 57, 59, 65, 78, 82, 96, 99, 104, 106, 108, 120, 123, 125, 135, 144, 149, 150, 151, 152, 159, 161; St. John, New Brunswick, 91; St. Lawrence River, Quebec, 57; Selkirk Provincial Park, Ontario, 90; Toronto, Ontario, 58, 95, 163; Windsor, Ontario, 101; Yukon Territory, 140

Canadian Peregrine Fund, 46

cannibalism, 90, 109

Cape May Bird Observatory, 45

captive breeding, of raptors, 46

Caracara cheriway, 115–117

Caracara, Crested (*Caracara cheriway*), 34, 37, **115**, 115–117; age, 116; behavior, 116–117; distribution, 115; food habits, 115–116; habitat, 115; migration, 117; nesting and life cycle, 116; population, 117

carbamate pesticides, 32

carbofuran, 32

Cardinal, Northern (*Cardinalis cardinalis*), 65, 154, 162

Caribbean, 64, 70, 129

carrying capacity, 1

carrion (raptor food), 74, 78, 82, 90, 93, 96, 108, 113, 115, 118, 123, 126, 138

Carson, Rachel, 49

cat, house (*Felis domesticus*), 108, 112, 138, 163

Central America, 13, 59, 63, 65, 76, 87, 101; raptor watch sites, 106

chemical contaminants, 30–33

Chesapeake Bay area, 39, 61, 63, 77, 78, 112; indiscriminate logging in, 39; undeveloped forested shorelines of, 39

Chickadee, Black-capped (*Poecile atricapilla*), 154

chipmunk, eastern (*Tamias striatus*), 90

chlorinated hydrocarbons, 31

Christmas Bird Counts (CBC), 51, 91, 111, 140

Chrysler, Walter P., 25

cicadas, periodical (*Magicicada septendecim*), 5–6

Circus cyaneus, 64

citizen scientists, 48–52

Code of Federal Regulations, 28

College of Veterinary Medicine, University of Minnesota, 46

Colombia, 63

conferences (raptor), 45

Connecticut, 31, 42, 53, 54, 67, 74, 77, 79, 99, 141; Barkhamsted Reservoir, 79; Essex, 53; Greenwich, 42; Hartland, 31; New Haven, 54; Lighthouse Point Park, 54; Tunxis State Forest, 31

Connecticut Audubon Society, 53

Connecticut River, 39, 53, 77

turtle, box (*Terrapene* sp.), 75
Tuscarora Summit hawk-watching site, 76
Tyto alba, 131

United Kingdom, 24
U.S. Attorney's Office, 24–25
U.S. Congress, 25
U.S. District Court, 32
U.S. Fish and Wildlife Service, 28, 29, 95
U.S. Forest Service, 51; Citizen Science
 Coordinator, 51
U.S. National Park Service, 42
University of Minnesota, 46
Utah, 83

Venezuela, 63
vermin, 24
Vermont, 67, 68, 93, 99, 131, 135, 152
veterinary care (of raptors), 38
Virginia, 15, 16, 18, 24, 42, 63, 70, 74, 77, 88,
 104, 106, 112, 162, 164; Chincoteague
 National Wildlife Refuge, 15; Eastern shore,
 162; Kiptopeke, 88; Kiptopeke State Park, 16,
 42; Virginia Coast Reserve, 16, 42
vole, meadow (*Microtus pennsylvanicus*), 3, 5, 70,
 108, 119, 126, 131, 133, 144, 146, 148, 150,
 152, 153, 157
vole, prairie (*Microtus ochrogaster*), 153, 157
vole, red-backed (*Clethrionomys gapperi*), 144,
 150, 153
volunteers in raptor conservation, 51–52
Vulture, Black (*Coragyps atratus*), 11, 32, 62, 79,
 80
Vulture, Turkey (*Cathartes aura*), 11, 71, 73, 80,
 105, 115, 129

Warbler, Yellow-rumped (*Dendroica coronata*),
 131
Washington, 58, 108; Tacoma, 58
weather conditions, 14–15; extreme, 26
web of life, 1
West Indies, 54, 59, 63
West Nile virus, 27
West Virginia, 18, 92, 161
wetland quality indicators, 33
wetland *refugia,* 33
Whitefish Point Bird Observatory, 11, 47, 88
Wildlife Information Center, Inc., 25, 28, 30, 42,
 43, 44, 45, 50
wind generators, 33
winter Bald Eagle watching, 53–54
wintering areas, for raptors, 43
Wisconsin, 6, 21, 36, 43, 53, 54, 66, 67, 68, 70,
 74, 79, 81, 86, 89, 90, 92, 97, 98, 99, 110, 111,
 112, 113, 131, 134, 156, 158, 159, 163; Buena
 Vista Wildlife Refuge, 66; Cassville, 53; Ferry
 Bluff Eagle Council Overlook, 54; Prairie du
 Sac, 54; St. Croix National Scenic Riverway,
 54; Sauk City, 54; Stillwater, 54; Taylor's Falls,
 54
Wisconsin River, 54, 77, 109
wolverine (*Gulo luscus*), 26
woodchuck (*Marmota monax*), 82, 138
Woodcock, American (*Scolopax minor*), 121
Woodpecker, Pileated (*Dryocopus pileatus*), 99,
 121, 159
World Center for Birds of Prey, 37, 46
World War II, 30
written raptor records, 57–58

zinc, 30

ABOUT THE AUTHOR

DONALD S. HEINTZELMAN has served as Associate Curator of Natural Science at the William Penn Memorial Museum (The State Museum of Pennsylvania) and Curator of Ornithology at the New Jersey State Museum. Later, he was ornithologist on board the ecotourism ship M. S. *Lindblad Explorer* on expeditions to Amazonia, the Antarctic, and the Galapagos Islands. He cofounded the Wildlife Information Center, Inc., and until recently was its president. A wildlife consultant, author, and photographer, Heintzelman has traveled widely in eastern North America, the West Indies, South America, the Falkland and Galapagos Islands, East Africa, and the Antarctic photographing and studying wildlife. He has published eighteen books, including *A Guide to Hawk Watching in North America, The Migrations of Hawks,* and recently *The Complete Backyard Birdwatcher's Home Companion.* Heintzelman's scientific articles have appeared in leading ornithology magazines, and his nontechnical articles and photographs have been published in *ActionLine, Audubon, Defenders, National Wildlife, Organic Gardening,* and *Ranger Rick's Nature Magazine.* Until recently, he wrote a nature column for several Pennsylvania newspapers.

598.944   Heintzelman, Donald
H   S.

           Hawks and owls of
           eastern North
           America.

DATE			

29.95   02-03-04